Joyce and Ibsen

Joyce and Ibsen

A STUDY IN
LITERARY INFLUENCE

by

B. J. TYSDAHL

NORWEGIAN UNIVERSITIES PRESS
OSLO

HUMANITIES PRESS
NEW YORK

NORWEGIAN UNIVERSITIES PRESS

Distribution offices:

NORWAY
Blindern, Oslo 3

UNITED KINGDOM
16 Pall Mall
London S.W. 1

Published in Oslo, Norway
by Norwegian Universities Press (Universitetsforlaget)

Published in the United States of America
by Humanities Press Inc., New York

(Library of Congress Catalogue Card Number 68-21914)

PREFACE

The work on this book was begun when I was a research fellow in the University of Oslo from 1961 to 1964. My research has been simplified by the unstinted assistance of the staffs of the British Institute in the University of Oslo and of the British Museum. The MS was finished too early for me to make extensive use of Volumes II and III of the *Letters of James Joyce*. I find that these letters corroborate a number of points that I have made; and there is a certain amount of reassurance to be found in the fact that they seem to refute nothing that I say.

For their assistance at various stages of this work I want to thank J. S. Atherton, Edvard Beyer, Peter Bilton, Adaline Glasheen, Ragnhild Nessheim, Diderik Roll-Hansen, Orm Øverland, and my wife Bjørg. I owe a special debt of gratitude to Professor Kristian Smidt and my colleague Keith Brown. Professor Smidt first aroused my interest in Joyce studies; and the whole manuscript has, at one stage or another, been discussed with him. Mr Brown has helped me by his detailed and constructive criticism of important parts of Chapters I, II, and VIII.

I am indebted to the editors of *Orbis Litterarum* and *A Wake Newslitter* for permission to reprint material which first appeared in their journals, and to Clive Hart, the co-author of the appendix on 'Norwegian Words in "The Norwegian Captain"', for permission to use it here.

Oslo, January 1968   *Bjørn J. Tysdahl*

CONTENTS

NOTE ON REFERENCES

References to Joyce's own works are included in the text (and identified by page number only) wherever feasible; in footnotes, and most often in the text, a short title is used. The editions referred to are the following:

Chamber Music. London: Jonathan Cape, 1927.

The Critical Writings of James Joyce, ed. E. Mason and R. Ellmann. London: Faber and Faber, 1959.

Dubliners. London: Jonathan Cape, 1950.

Epiphanies, ed. O. A. Silverman. Buffalo: Lockwood Memorial Library, 1956.

Exiles. London: Jonathan Cape, 1952.

Finnegans Wake. London: Faber and Faber, 1950.

Letters of James Joyce, ed. Stuart Gilbert. London: Faber and Faber, 1957.

Pomes Penyeach. Paris: Shakespeare and Company, 1927.

A Portrait of the Artist as a Young Man. New York: The Viking Press, 1964.

Stephen Hero, ed. Theodore Spencer. New York: New Directions, 1955.

Ulysses. New York: The Modern Library (Random House), 1934.

I

INTRODUCTION

It may perhaps be convenient to specify at the outset some of the things which this study will, and will not, attempt. I shall not, for instance, examine every single point of *similarity* between Henrik Ibsen and James Joyce. Admittedly, a complete series of such comparisons might enable us to see certain aspects of their works more clearly; but it would also result in distorted pictures of them both unless one attempted to establish, at every point, the particular degree of similarity (or dissimilarity) involved. And this would require a comprehensive criticism of the whole of the works of both writers – a task too great for any one book. My primary aim in this study is more limited. I am concerned simply to investigate the nature and extent of Ibsen's *influence* on Joyce's work. I discuss the background to Joyce's literary achievement only on two occasions: Chapter II gives an account of his early enthusiasm for Ibsen; and in Chapter IV I consider the question whether those attitudes and actions from Joyce's early life which found their way into his portrait of Stephen can be regarded as influenced by Ibsen. However, the focus of interest is the indebtedness to Ibsen that can be seen in Joyce's work, not in his personal development; and Chapters III–VIII contain analyses of his novels and his one play. A study in literary influence invites questions about the relationship between indebtedness and originality in works of art, and in my final chapter I attempt to relate the influence from Ibsen to the great and undoubted originality of Joyce's work.

In 1900 Ibsen read one article and in the next year a letter by Joyce.[1] But this was after the publication of his last play;

---

[1] The article was Joyce's long review of *When We Dead Awaken*. Ibsen mentioned the review in a letter to William Archer: 'I have also read – or spelt my way through – a review by Mr James Joyce in the "Fortnightly Review", which is very favourable and for which I should indeed have liked to thank the author if I only knew the language.' (My transl.. Br. M. Add.

obviously, therefore, Ibsen's own work was not at all influenced by that of the younger writer, sixty years his junior. Nevertheless, a twentieth-century interpretation of Ibsen can be influenced by an acquaintance with Joyce's work; in this special sense there is a reciprocal influence at work between Ibsen and Joyce. They provide a particular instance of the relationship between artists that T. S. Eliot outlines in 'Tradition and the Individual Talent':

> No poet, no artist of any art, has his complete meaning alone. His significance, his appreciation is the appreciation of his relation to the dead poets and artists. You cannot value him alone; you must set him, for contrast and comparison, among the dead.[2]

Though an analysis of literary influence in this sense is not my main aim, it is obvious that a study of the influence of Ibsen on Joyce would lack an important perspective if the two authorships involved were not shown to explain each other as co-existent and simultaneous entities. In my last chapter I mention a couple of ways in which Ibsen and Joyce thus interpret each other, and my reading of the two authors in the other parts of this study also implies such a mutual interpretation.

The second half of the present chapter is an attempt to give a similar perspective to the backgrounds of Ibsen and Joyce. An examination of the backgrounds of the two is relevant to a study of influence for two reasons. Influence is, I think, like a plant that will only strike root in soil similar to that from which it comes. If Joyce's circumstances had not in some ways been analogous to those of Ibsen, influence from the one to the other would seem inconceivable. Moreover, a discussion of these analogies will also clear the ground for an examination of Joyce's literary debts to Ibsen as distinct from mere analogies between the two authors.

My long chapter on *Finnegans Wake* needs an explanatory comment as it goes beyond a study of influence in its discussion

MS 45292, p. 258.) Archer sent the greeting on to Joyce, who thanked Ibsen in a long letter written in March 1901 (Richard Ellmann, *James Joyce* (New York: Oxford Univ. Press, 1959), gives the English version, pp. 89–91).

[2] *Selected Essays* (London: Faber and Faber, 1934), p. 15.

of Ibsen allusions. It is not self-evident that a lengthy analysis
of allusions in such a controversial work is a rewarding exercise: but a consideration of the special state of *FW* studies
may justify it. Past and present criticism of the book, including
my own, reveals that as yet the book is not fully understood;
and it follows that until it is, or until more extensive research
has shown with some conclusiveness that it is incomprehensible,
it cannot be properly appreciated. (It is also, of course, possible
to envisage another outcome, namely, that *FW* studies might
die out from lack of interest before any final conclusions are
reached – which would in itself constitute a judgement, however ruthless. But so far there are no signs of flagging interest
in *FW;* and the very fact that the book is attacked may justify
the critical and scholarly labours bestowed on it. For worthless
writing very rarely provokes serious critical argument a quarter
of a century after publication.) While the critical – and sometimes uncritical – battle over *FW* is still being fought, a discussion of the nature of the whole work, which an analysis of
influence always begs for, must be aided by the spadework that
an *explication de texte* involves. Moreover, a thorough analysis
of the passages in *FW* where Ibsen occurs can improve our
understanding of Joyce's earlier works. Since *FW* may be read
as an inventory of Joyce's mind, the presence of Ibsen in this
work provides a useful background for a study of Ibsen's influence on any of Joyce's earlier works.

For obvious reasons conclusions about the nature of *FW*
must be tentative. So, too, must the conclusions drawn about
literary influence in the other chapters of this study. To claim
accuracy or finality in answers to questions about literary indebtedness seems to me a denial of the complexity of art, history, and human psychology – a complexity without which
artistic achievement would be inconceivable. The best I can
hope for my conclusions is that they approach the degree of
certainty and precision that the material at our disposal war-
rants. The word 'influence', here and in the following chapters
simply used in contrast to similarities that are not due to 'influence', begs further definition; and in my final chapter,

'Indebtedness and Originality', I discuss it further and propose a use of the word which the analyses in the previous chapters suggest. The usage that I propose indicates a way in which a study of influence can make sense within the framework that the modern emphasis on the autonomy of each work of art provides, and not only in a historical study of literature.

The task I have set myself in this book is somewhat different from that of earlier studies of the relationship between Ibsen and Joyce, first and primarily in that I attempt to survey the whole of Joyce's work. Vivienne Kock Macleod in her article 'The Influence of Ibsen on Joyce'[3] and James T. Farrell in 'Exiles and Ibsen'[4] both analyse Stephen's character and its counterparts in Joyce's personality in the light of Ibsen's life and plays. I disagree with Mrs Macleod on the question of Ibsen's influence on Joyce's behaviour, and with Mr Farrell on a number of points concerning the debts to Ibsen in *Exiles;* but my study differs from these two articles mainly because the examination of Ibsen's presence in all Joyce's books gives a new perspective to his portrait of Stephen or Richard Rowan. My account of *FW* is different from Marvin Carlson's article 'Henrik Ibsen and *Finnegans Wake*'[5] for similar reasons: a study of Ibsen elements in Joyce's earlier books can explain (and may itself be illuminated by) allusions to the Norwegian playwright in *FW*.[6] One result of the study of this interaction between earlier and later works may be seen in the fact that the list of Ibsen allusions in Chapter VII runs to a considerably greater number of items than do Mr Atherton's and Mr Carlson's lists together.

James R. Baker's article 'Ibsen, Joyce and the Living-Dead: A Study of Dubliners'[7] analyses an important symbolic pattern in *Dubliners* and relates it very neatly to Joyce's reading of

[3] *PMLA*, Vol. 60, No. 3 (September 1945), pp. 879–898.
[4] Published in *James Joyce: Two Decades of Criticism*, ed. Seon Givens (New York: The Vanguard Press, 1963), pp. 95–131.
[5] *Comparative Literature*, Vol. 12, No. 2 (Spring 1960), pp. 133–141.
[6] Other works on *FW* are discussed on pp. 123–124.
[7] Published in *A James Joyce Miscellany, Third Series*, ed M. Magalaner (Carbondale: Southern Illinois University Press, 1962), pp. 19–32.

Ibsen. Far more provocative – and more closely argued than most of the articles mentioned above – is Hugh Kenner's 'Joyce and Ibsen's Naturalism'.[8] Mr Kenner holds that Joyce does not write in a naturalistic vein and quotes from the 'Ithaca' episode of *Ulysses* to show that Joyce parodies 'the methods of naturalism proper'. From this starting-point Mr Kenner goes on to examine other ways in which Joyce may be indebted to Ibsen, and finds the indebtedness mainly in the cruder aspects of Stephen's attitude to his home, his church, and his country, much as did Mrs Macleod and Mr Farrell. It seems to me that Kenner's first point can be met by the observation that Joyce often parodies what he makes important use of. Parody, in Joyce, very rarely amounts to an abnegation of the thing parodied. However, this is not to imply that Kenner's article does not say a great many stimulating, though not always convincing, things about Ibsen and Joyce.

Together these articles make up what is virtually an indispensable platform for further studies of the relationship between Ibsen and Joyce. I am indebted to them because they indicate where some of the most interesting problems can be found, and also because of the answers they suggest to some of these problems – answers that, in my view, quite often need modification, but which are nevertheless useful starting-points for further discussion. However, the picture of Ibsen that emerges from Kenner's, Farrell's and Vivienne K. Macleod's articles is disturbingly simple: his provincial background, his individualism, the arrogance of Peer Gynt and Brand, the vindication of an artist's way of life, the realism, and (in Kenner's study) the poetry – these aspects of Ibsen's life and work are stated and related to Joyce's early work in a way which tends to present Ibsen as a writer whose work is lacking in subtlety, sophistication, and ambiguity. A natural result of this presentation is the fact that sometimes in these essays Ibsen does not provide a very illuminating commentary on the finer

[8] *Sewanee Review*, Vol. 59, No. 1 (Winter 1951), pp. 75–96. Most of the material in the article is incorporated in Kenner, *Dublin's Joyce* (London: Chatto and Windus, 1955).

aspects of Joyce's art. It is tempting, though perhaps not fair to these critics, to assume that a reading of Ibsen in translation, without an awareness of the ways in which most Ibsen translations distort the original, is responsible for portraits of the dramatist in such rather broad strokes.

It it not surprising – nor is it an indirect criticism of these articles – that a study of Joyce that only casts an occasional glance in the direction of Ibsen, S. L. Goldberg's *The Classical Temper*, can give a finely shaded account of *Ulysses* which, by implication, can serve as a highly rewarding study of the relationship between Joyce and Ibsen. For Ibsen's plays, as Joyce knew them and as he used them, do not give us an explanation of the mysteries of literary art in general and Joyce's novels in particular. It is for the critic to say as succinctly and fully as he can what he thinks is the essence of a work of art. But Ibsen was no critic in this sense. His plays enrich a reading of Joyce's books, but they do not define Joyce's art in the language of the critic: and they should not be put in a Procrustean bed to perform this task. A philosopher, for instance Kierkegaard, may offer a comprehensive and explicit formulation of a view of life that can be made to explain and organize contrasting attitudes in Joyce criticism.[9] But Ibsen sums up neither Joyce's work nor critical attitudes to it. His relevance to Joyce studies is found in the influence he exerted on Joyce and in the humane commentary that his plays provide, but in no formula but one which is almost a truism: the author must 'express his fable in terms of his characters' and these characters must be taken from 'life – real life'.[10]

*

An examination of the influence of Ibsen on Joyce asks for as clear a distinction as possible between impulses from Ibsen on the one hand and influence that more naturally can be assigned to the *Zeitgeist* on the other, and also between *influence* from Ibsen and *analogies* to Ibsen. The first of these

---

[9] See A. Goldman's attempt in *The Joyce Paradox: Form and Freedom in His Fiction* (London: Routledge and Kegan Paul, 1966).

[10] Joyce's own words in two articles on Ibsen. See *Critical Writings*, pp. 44, 100.

problems of demarcation will be attacked in the course of the following chapters; the second will be simplified by an awareness at this stage of where the analogies can be found. An example will illustrate this: Joyce's parents resemble the father and mother in *Peer Gynt*, and there is a corresponding portrait of a family in *A Portrait of the Artist as a Young Man*. In this case a realization of the fact that Joyce had a model for this family in his own home will save us from erroneously arguing for an exclusively literary indebtedness, as Mrs Macleod seems to do.[11] The following survey of the families and the countries of the two authors reveals a number of such striking similarities.

Joyce once said about the Viking invaders in Ireland that they 'did not leave the country, but were gradually assimilated into the community, a fact that we must keep in mind if we want to understand the curious character of the modern Irishman.'[12] For Joyce this assimilation was an important link between Norway and Ireland, as we can see in *Finnegans Wake*, in which HCE, the Irish innkeeper, is also a Scandinavian invader. The racial link probably also served as an explanation for Joyce of the many similarities in the history of the two countries.

Ireland and Norway are small countries on the outskirts of Europe; in 1900 Ireland had a population of about 4,500,000, Norway one of 2,250,000. Both countries have as their neighbours greater and richer powers, and perhaps mainly for this reason the history of Ireland and that of Norway offer surprisingly close parallels. Like Ireland, Norway can boast of a period of considerable cultural achievements in the Middle Ages. Sagas and scaldic poetry were composed (in Norway and by Norwegian settlers in Iceland), churches and monasteries built, manuscripts written and illuminated, and poetry and history recited at the King's table. When her political stability foundered, Norway was left a province under her most powerful neighbour, Denmark, for more than four centuries. At the conclusion of the Napoleonic Wars Norway gained

---

[11] See V. K. Macleod, *op. cit.*, p. 879, and Chapter IV below.
[12] *Critical Writings*, p. 160.

self-government in internal affairs in the alliance with Sweden; and enthusiasts spread the idea of a national renaissance to literature, music, and art. Joyce had this development in mind when he wrote to his brother Stanislaus in 1905, the year when Norway became fully independent again: 'Is it not possible for a few persons of character and culture to make Dublin a capital such as Christiania has become?'[13]

In both countries the re-emergence to independence in politics and art was accompanied by great pride in the noble past and by an underlying feeling of inferiority. The Irish never forgot their suppression by the mighty neighbour to the east; and Norwegians viewed with envy the superior wealth and the unbroken political and cultural traditions of Denmark and Sweden. This naturally resulted in a stubborn insistence on the intrinsic worth of everything native (of which the Troll King in *Peer Gynt* is such an eloquent advocate). In the lives of both Ibsen and Joyce there is a period of participation in the national literary movements. When Ibsen came to Christiania in 1850 the marriage between romanticism and patriotic enthusiasm was firmly established in Norwegian literature, and Ibsen felt sufficiently comfortable in this movement to work as adviser and playwright for the national theatres in Bergen and Christiania from 1851 to 1862. The corresponding period in Joyce's life was much shorter – from 1900, when the *Fortnightly Review* published his article on *When We Dead Awaken,* to 1904, when he left Ireland; but Joyce encountered a similar blend of nationalism and romanticism in the leaders of the Irish literary renaissance. Neither Ibsen nor Joyce accepted these ideas and ideals for long. Ibsen felt Scandinavia rather than Norway to be his home country; Joyce saw Ireland as the 'old sow that eats her farrow'[14] at a time when most authors hailed her as the good, old, and much-injured mother. Still, both authors cared for the countries they left: Stephen wants 'to forge in the smithy of my soul the uncreated conscience of my race';[15] and

---

[13] See Ellmann, p. 216.
[14] *A Portrait,* p. 203.
[15] *Ibid.,* p. 253.

as an exile on the Continent Ibsen confesses in 'Burnt Ships' that his thoughts go north every night.

The political renaissance in Ireland and Norway was accompanied by attempts to re-establish a national language. The Norwegian counterpart to the attempted revival of Gaelic was less radical in that the Norwegian language that had been spoken and written in Norway before the centuries of Danish domination was similar to Danish; indeed, Swedish, Danish, and Norwegian of the Middle Ages, as well as of today, can be spoken of as three dialects of Scandinavian. Still, when the general reaction against things Danish set in, a movement in favour of a language more Norse and less Danish naturally sprang up. The movement soon split into two factions, one that wanted to use the language of the principal towns of Norway, a form of the language that was – and is – close to Danish in spelling and grammar, as the basis for a norm, and one that would base the new spelling and grammar on the regional dialects that had preserved Old Norse forms to a greater extent. This finally resulted in two official forms of Norwegian, first called *riksmål* and *landsmål*. Joyce's interest in this linguistic situation is reflected in *Finnegans Wake,* where a mutation of the word *landsmål* on one occasion (p. 292) appears in a discussion of the development of languages and nations.

An interesting effect of these efforts to establish a new language can be found in both Ireland and Norway. The movements resulted in a general interest in language, and helped to inspire a keen awareness of words and shades of meaning in people with an ear for languages. Joyce had the feeling that in a way the language he used was not quite his own;[16] and this may have increased his interest in Ibsen's language – so close to Danish and yet different – as a possible model for his own use of English.[17] Both Ibsen and Joyce reacted against the attempts at linguistic puritanism that factions of the national movements in Ireland and Norway favoured. Joyce gave up

---

[16] Cf. *A Portrait*, pp. 188–189, 251.
[17] The extent of Joyce's fascination with Norwegian is best illustrated in *Finnegans Wake*. See Appendix.

Irish lessons partly because the teacher 'found it necessary to exalt Irish by denigrating English'.[18] Ibsen was willing enough, in 1865, to comply with his publisher's wish to moderate his Norwegian spelling; and in the next year he replaced a number of typically Norwegian forms by Danish in a revision of *Love's Comedy* without any incitation from his Copenhagen publishing-house.[19]

There are a number of equally striking similarities between the two families in which Henrik Ibsen and James Joyce were brought up. Knud Ibsen, Henrik's father, came from a middle-class family and was for a time a prosperous, though extravagant, merchant. When Henrik was six years old Knud Ibsen lost most of his fortune through unlucky transactions and just avoided being declared bankrupt. From this time to his death in 1877 he tried hopelessly, almost pathetically, to pass as a well-to-do man and a wit. Henrik Ibsen's daughter-in-law, Bergliot, has given a description of him which, apart from some of the physical features, might have been a Dubliner's impression of John Joyce:

> Knud Ibsen was fair, of small stature, and slight, though well proportioned. He had very pronounced features, a hooked nose and a pair of arrestingly sparkling eyes, at the same time almost cunning in expression. He always wore a cap rather like a beret, and had a good flair for dress. He was witty and quick at repartee, amusing and ironical and loved telling stories. In his younger days he must have had great charm and yet, because of his sharp tongue, he was considered a dangerous enemy.[20]

John Joyce came from a corresponding layer of society in Ireland and lived comfortably enough on his salary as a Collector of Rates in Dublin until, in 1892, when his son James was ten, he was pensioned. From this year and until his death John Joyce lived beyond his means. Being just as prodigal and irresponsible in money matters as Knud Ibsen had been, and

---

[18] Ellmann, p. 62.

[19] Halvdan Koht, *Henrik Ibsen, eit diktarliv*, Vol. I (Oslo: Aschehoug, 1928), p. 340, and Vol. II (1929), pp. 20–21.

[20] Bergliot Ibsen, *The Three Ibsens* (London: Hutchinson & Co., 1951), p. 10.

having a larger family to support, John Joyce, in Richard Ellmann's words, 'filled his house with children and with debts' in
the course of a few years.[21] He, too, tried to keep up a reputation as a witty man and a story-teller, and was more successful
in this respect than the father of the Norwegian dramatist.

Henrik Ibsen's mother was, in contrast to her husband, a
quiet and conscientious woman who devoted her life to her
children and was remembered as a good and loving parent. In
later years she was much given to religious speculation. Mrs
John Joyce was also a dutiful homemaker who managed to
keep the family together in spite of the inveterate improvidence
of her husband. She was a pious Roman Catholic and viewed
with dismay the radical ideas adopted by her eldest sons James
and Stanislaus. Both Henrik and James were second sons, but
the first to grow up. The first child in the Ibsen family died
when Henrik was only a few weeks old; James's elder brother
had died in 1881. This, naturally, bound Mrs Joyce and fru
Ibsen closely to their second children, who must have been a
solace to them in their bereavement. In their turn, both writers
alienated themselves from their mothers and were on better
terms with other members of their families.[22]

Joyce and Ibsen had their education impeded by the finan-
cial troubles of their families. After he had left the good Jesuit
boarding school at Clongowes, Joyce was a pupil for two years
at a Christian Brothers' school where he learnt little and felt
very out of place. Ibsen had only two years of formal education
before his confirmation in 1843, and was then apprenticed to
an apothecary in the small coastal town of Grimstad in the
south of Norway. Joyce later became a pupil at a Jesuit day
school in Dublin, and proceeded to University College, from
which he got his degree. Ibsen read for the entrance examination of the University, first with a tutor in Grimstad, later at a
private school in Christiania. But he failed the first time he
presented himself and never tried again. The education Joyce
received, however, was more thorough than Ibsen's. He attend-

[21] Ellmann, p. 20.
[22] See Koht, *op. cit.*, Vol. I, pp. 30–34.

ed Clongowes and later Belvedere College, which were among the best schools in the country, and his scholarly standing was high both in these places and at University College.

In their late teens – the one an undergraduate, the other an apprentice – Joyce and Ibsen dedicated themselves to literature. Ibsen rose above his pills and vials by his wide reading, by assimilating the radical thoughts that swept Europe in 1848, and then, tentatively, by his writing. And in the freedom and vastness of literary art Joyce glimpsed a way out of the insularity of his surroundings. Before they were twenty-one both had written poetry and a drama: *Catilina* was completed in the early months of 1849; Joyce's 'A Brilliant Career' was written in the summer of 1900.

The estrangement from the literary and national movements of Norway and Ireland was completed when Ibsen went abroad in 1864 and Joyce left Ireland in 1904. Ibsen's exile was never as unbroken as was Joyce's; he visited Norway from time to time and finally settled in Christiania in 1891, whereas after his visit to Ireland in 1912 Joyce shunned his mother country. But in their bastions on the Continent, both writers were keenly interested in their home countries, which they regarded with a curious mixture of love and hatred.

It should be remembered, at this stage in our account of the analogies, that Joyce's reaction against the literary circles of Dublin, as well as his subsequent exile, occurred after he had read Ibsen; we have, in other words, moved from mere parallels in the lives of the two to similarities that can be due to influence. Though striking, the similarities outlined in the preceding paragraphs should not, of course, be taken to indicate that the backgrounds of Joyce and Ibsen are identical. There are great differences – for instance in religion, in the richer impulses from theatrical productions and music that were available to Joyce, and in the languages that were the mother tongues of the two. Hugh Kenner is right, I think, when he contends that Ireland, more 'European' than Norway, the most rugged of the Scandinavian countries, provided Joyce with a 'civilized heritage of sensibility' that was not available to Ibsen in Skien,

Grimstad, or Christiania.[23] Still, the parallels between the two milieus were close enough for Joyce to discover them and be struck by them; and they enabled him to identify himself with Ibsen. The feeling of identification made it natural for Joyce to study Ibsen's approach to the problems they had in common, and, what is equally important, it opened his mind also to those aspects of Ibsen's life and art to which there were no parallels in his own early life.

This is a background against which the many parallels in the works of the two authors must be seen. Similar characters, incidents, and settings can be found in both Joyce and Ibsen, and in both there are the same disregard for conventions, the same praise of the individual who is not intimidated by his surroundings, and the same preoccupation with the problem of exile and later also with the values that the common man represents. And Ibsen's art and craft is reflected in Joyce's early work as well as in *Ulysses* and *Finnegans Wake*.

[23] Kenner, *op. cit.*, p. 89.

II
YOUTHFUL ENTHUSIASM

> ... at this time Stephen suffered
> the most enduring influence of
> his life.
>
> *Stephen Hero*

Reading Ibsen

When James Joyce entered his sixteenth year on February 2, 1897, he was a very pious boy. Two months earlier he had taken part in a retreat. It left him in a state of 'eager spirituality' that lasted well into the new year.[1] Then, as the zest of the spiritual exercises waned, he gradually gave up his faith in what his family and his schools had taught him and began an unflinching search for new values and new points of orientation. He read widely and came across Ibsen. Immediately he was stirred and amazed his family by his enthusiasm. Writing in the nineteen-fifties, Stanislaus Joyce still remembered the day when an Ibsen play arrived:

> One afternoon comes back to me distinctly, the afternoon when Ibsen's *Master Builder* arrived from Heinemann's in William Archer's translation with his excellent preface, a slim volume in yellow paper covers with a vignette of Hilde Wangel, alpenstock in hand, on the outside. It was an event; and my brother stayed up that night to read the play. In the morning I must have been the first to come down for I found the large armchair pulled near to the extinguished hearth and the table to the armchair. The lamp had been pulled to the edge of the table so that the table-cover drooped on the floor. The whole room bore witness that he had read late into the night. My brother had been keeping vigil to hear the message from Norway of the younger generation that sooner or later comes knocking at the door.[2]

---

[1] According to Ellmann, p. 50. Stanislaus Joyce says: 'I cannot be certain how long my brother's conversion lasted, rather more than a year I should say, ...' *My Brother's Keeper* (London: Faber and Faber, 1958), p. 98.
[2] Stanislaus Joyce, *op. cit.*, pp. 98–99.

Ellmann assumes that this adulation of Ibsen began while Joyce was still at school, i.e. before the summer of 1898.[3] But in *Stephen Hero* Joyce implies that he first read Ibsen as an undergraduate,[4] and his writings from these years seem to support this. There are no references, direct or oblique, to Ibsen in those of Joyce's essays that are extant and printed in *Critical Writings*, until 'Ecce Homo', written in September 1899. In the earlier essays on 'Force' and 'The Study of Languages' there are contexts that seem to invite to a mention of the Norwegian dramatist, but Ibsen was apparently not in Joyce's mind when he wrote them.[5]

That Joyce's enthusiasm should fall on a dramatist is no wonder. He was a theatre-goer in a Dublin where the National Literary Society had been established in 1892 and where W. B. Yeats and Lady Gregory worked to found the Irish National Theatre, whose first plays were staged in 1899. Those who were interested in literature could scarcely avoid the contagious zest of the founders of the new theatre. And Joyce's essays reveal that by advocating Ibsen he thought of himself as taking up an *avant-garde* position, which pleased him immensely. He preferred to overlook the fact that Ibsen had champions in Ireland earlier than himself. George Moore and Edward Martyn, both Joyce's seniors by more than twenty years, were known to be admirers of Ibsen; and the actor and producer Frank Fay encouraged the study of the Norwegian dramatist among the younger generation of Irish playwrights.[6] Yeats was critical of Ibsen, but not blind to the virtues of his plays. Indeed, all the better-known figures in Irish literature at the turn of the century were so frequently in London that they could scarcely avoid discussions of Ibsen's plays.

In his second year as an undergraduate Joyce felt assured enough in his judgement of Ibsen to pronounce his views in

[3] Ellmann, p. 42.
[4] See *Stephen Hero*, pp. 39–40.
[5] See also my discussion, pp. 37–40.
[6] Cf. Padraic Colum, 'Ibsen in Irish Writing', *Irish Writing*, No. 7 (Feb. 1949), p. 66, and Gerard Fay, *The Abbey Theatre: Cradle of Genius* (London: Hollis and Carter, 1958).

public: on January 20, 1900, he read a paper entitled 'Drama and Life' to the Literary and Historical Society of University College. That winter Joyce also wrote a review of *When We Dead Awaken* (in a French translation) which he sent to the *Fortnightly Review*. The editor accepted the contribution from the eighteen-year-old Dublin undergraduate, and Joyce had the pleasure of seeing it in the April issue under the title of 'Ibsen's New Drama'. It is, like 'Drama and Life', an unqualified tribute to the old Norwegian playwright. A review by Joyce of a French translation of *Catilina* was published in the *Speaker* on March 21, 1903.

Ibsen, whose English was poor, came across Joyce's article on *When We Dead Awaken*, liked it, and wrote to William Archer in April 1900: 'Jeg har også læst – eller stavet mig igennem en anmeldelse af Mr. James Joyce i "Fortnightly Review", som er meget velvillig og som jeg ret skulde have lyst til at takke forfatteren for dersom jeg blot var sproget mægtig.'[7] This was the finest initiation Joyce could wish for; and he wrote to William Archer, who had relayed Ibsen's words to him: 'I am a young Irishman, eighteen years old, and the words of Ibsen I shall keep in my heart all my life.'[8]

With Ibsen's towering example before him Joyce tried his hand at playwriting himself. After the winter of 1900 when he had earned some fame and money through his interest in the Norwegian dramatist he accompanied his father to Mullingar, where Joyce senior had obtained employment for the summer. Here he found time to write a play, which he called 'A Brilliant Career'. Joyce destroyed the manuscript in 1902, and, apart from four lines of a song, the only sources of information we have are William Archer's letter of criticism and Stanislaus Joyce's account of the play. In his sympathetic letter Archer points to some obvious defects and says bluntly enough that the play is impossible for the stage. But parts of it impressed him,

[7] Br. Museum Add. MS 45292, p. 258. 'I have also read – or spelt my way through a review by Mr James Joyce in "Fortnightly Review", which is very favourable and for which I should indeed have liked to thank the author if I only knew the language.'

[8] Quoted from Ellmann, p. 77.

and he found one scene 'curiously strong and telling'.[9] The following is what Stanislaus remembers of it:

> I have little recollection of the plot, but as much as I recall of it was a rehash of ingredients borrowed, unconsciously I am sure, from *When We Dead Awaken, A Doll's House* and *The League of Youth*.[10]

There is no reason to doubt that Stanislaus's main impression is correct, though Joyce may have borrowed as much from other Ibsen plays. The rough outline of the play that can be reconstructed from Archer's letter also leads us to Ibsen: Paul, the main person, leaves the girl he loves to marry a rich woman, and finds in the end that he was wrong – just as Rubek in *When We Dead Awaken* sees his fatal mistake when he meets Irene again. A young opportunist wanting to marry into the best circles is also the target of Ibsen's satire in *The League of Youth*. Further, Paul is a doctor who by chance becomes responsible for the welfare of a town, just like Dr Stockmann in *An Enemy of the People*.

At this time translations were available of nearly all of Ibsen's plays, as well as of some of his poetry. But in spite of this Joyce was sufficiently interested in Ibsen to study Norwegian so that he might read the works of the master in the original. In March 1901 he wrote a long letter to Ibsen in Norwegian. The English draft is still extant. Though he felt confident enough to write the final copy in Norwegian, he apologized for his mistakes in the language: 'My own knowledge of your language is not, as you see, great but I trust you will be able to decipher my meaning.'[11] About the same time Joyce recited Ibsen's 'Med en vandlilje' in Norwegian to his friends.[12]

---

[9] See Ellmann, pp. 82–83, where the letter is given in full.
[10] Stanislaus Joyce, *op. cit.*, p. 126.
[11] Quoted from Ellmann, p. 90. The letter will be discussed below.
[12] Padraic Colum, who is the source of this information, rightly questions his mastery of the language: 'His pronunciation of the words of the poem could not have been, I now realize, any better than that of a German with a few English lessons speaking a lyric of Shakespeare in the original.' Mary and Padraic Colum, *Our Friend James Joyce* (London: Victor Gollancz, 1959), pp. 47–48.

When he gave an address on Mangan to the Literary and Historical Society in February 1902, he had sufficient knowledge
of the language to show off a bit and quoted from *When We
Dead Awaken* in Norwegian. This quotation, which is given
without any reference to Ibsen or his play and thus gave no clue
to Joyce's fellow-students, becomes an intimate, youthfully
extravagant greeting from the Irishman to the Norwegian.

Thus, when Joyce was twenty-one he had read almost all
Ibsen's plays – as well as Shaw's *The Quintessence of Ibsenism*.[13] He had taught himself Norwegian and he had declared
his partisanship to his fellow-students and teachers. He had –
and this is even more surprising – excited the curiosity of his
father to the extent that John Joyce, who never cared for books,
sat down to read *The League of Youth*, though 'after reading
through two acts of provincial intrigue, [he] abandoned the
enterprise as tedious'.[14] His mother was more sympathetic and
read some of Ibsen's plays. Joyce makes her say in *Stephen
Hero:* 'He must be a great writer from what you say of him'
(p. 84).

This is indeed what all Joyce's sayings and writings about
Ibsen from this time amount to: Ibsen is great, Ibsen is the
Master. Without hesitation Joyce dismisses earlier dramatists:

> It may be a vulgarism, but it is literal truth to say that Greek
> drama is played out. For good or for bad it has done its work,
> which, if wrought in gold, was not upon lasting pillars. Its revival
> is not of dramatic but of pedagogic significance. ... [Shake-
> speare's work] was far from mere drama, it was literature in dia-
> logue. Here I must draw a line of demarcation between literature
> and drama. (*Critical Writings,* p. 39)

while Ibsen is placed on a pedestal:

> If sanity rules the mind of the dramatic world there will be ac-
> cepted what is now the faith of the few, there will be past dispute

[13] Cf. *Critical Writings,* p. 48. The following plays are mentioned in the
essays: *Catilina, Peer Gynt, Brand, Pillars of Society, A Doll's House,
Ghosts, An Enemy of the People, The Wild Duck. Rosmersholm, Hedda
Gabler, The Masterbuilder, John Gabriel Borkman* and *When We Dead
Awaken.* Joyce had also read *Love's Comedy* (Ellmann, p. 79).
[14] *Stephen Hero,* p. 88.

written up the respective grades of Macbeth and The Master Builder. (*Critical Writings*, p. 42)

From time to time Joyce completely prostrates himself before the Master:

> It is hardly possible to criticize The Wild Duck, for instance; one can only brood upon it as upon a personal woe. Indeed in the case of all Ibsen's later work dramatic criticism, properly so called, verges on impertinence. (*Critical Writings*, p. 42)

He strikes the same note in 'Ibsen's New Drama' where he contends that the Norwegian dramatist 'is one of the world's great men before whom criticism can make but feeble show. Appreciation, hearkening is the only true criticism'.[15]

This prostration limits the usefulness of Joyce's dramatic criticism as such, but it does not affect its relevance to our understanding of Joyce. The dramatic craft of *Exiles* can be seen as an application of the theories Joyce expounds in his early essays; and, more importantly, these writings reveal Joyce's ideas about literature at the time when he was young and malleable and at the height of his enthusiasm for Ibsen. The wide range of topics covered in these essays gives them added interest, as does the fact that at this time drama was not simply one of three main genres for Joyce, it was *the* genre. His ideas about drama were his ideas about the highest form of literary achievement; and as Joyce's own plans never tended in the direction of *Kleinkunst*, drama was synonymous, though vaguely, with his own aspirations.

A review is normally the application of a critic's established standards of value to a particular work of art, and Mr M. Magalaner seems to imply that this is the case in Joyce's essays on Ibsen:

> There is no question, however, that even at eighteen Joyce knew what he *wanted* to do in literature. Writing admiringly of Ibsen's *When We Dead Awaken* in 1900, he revealed his own artistic ambitions as he evaluated the elder writer's accomplishment.[16]

---

[15] *Critical Writings*, pp. 66–67.
[16] *Time of Apprenticeship: The Fiction of Young James Joyce* (London: Abelard-Schuman, 1959), p. 16.

It seems to me, however, that this interpretation leaves out of consideration the very special situation in which Joyce wrote these essays. He was still in his teens, he had just discovered Ibsen, adopted him as his great ideal, and opened himself to the dramatic world of the Norwegian. When Joyce praises things in Ibsen's plays, he often does so in sheer wonder and admiration: Ibsen is judged as a dramatist according to standards that he himself inspires. Joyce must not, of course, be thought of as an empty vessel which it was for Ibsen to fill; but his ideas about drama were necessarily vague before he read Ibsen. And thus, the more 'technical' the thing Joyce praises in Ibsen, the greater the likelihood that he does not judge it against a preconceived idea. As we shall see later, the *Weltanschauung* of the essays was probably established in outline before Joyce's reading of Ibsen.

There is so much of the iconoclast in the young Joyce that a great deal of space in his early writings is devoted to proclamations of what drama should not be. In 'Drama and Life' he draws a sharp line of demarcation between literature and drama:

> Human society is the embodiment of changeless laws which the whimsicalities and circumstances of men and women involve and overwrap. The realm of literature is the realm of these accidental manners and humours – a spacious realm; and the true literary artist concerns himself mainly with them. Drama has to do with the underlying laws first, in all their nakedness and divine severity, and only secondarily with the motley agents who bear them out. When so much is recognized an advance has been made to a more rational and true appreciation of dramatic art. Unless some such distinction be made the result is chaos. Lyricism parades as poetic drama, psychological conversation as literary drama, and traditional farce moves over the boards with the label of comedy affixed to it.[17]

There is definite contempt in the words Joyce uses to outline the realm of literature: 'the whimsicalities and circumstances

[17] *Critical Writings*, p. 40. As the editors of *Critical Writings* remind us, the contempt for 'literature' was something Joyce had found in Verlaine.

of men and women', 'accidental manners and humours', and 'motley agents'.

There were more things that had to be fenced off: Joyce finds, in 'Drama and Life', that drama depends on myth, but if the mythical element becomes communal worship, 'the possibilities of its drama have lessened considerably.' The idea that art should teach a moral lesson, 'should instruct, elevate, and amuse . . . is eating itself fast, like the tiger of story, tail first.' There is no room for mystery plays or moralities in Joyce's theories. 'Art for art's sake' is also summarily dismissed. Drama cannot be restricted to a presentation of what is beautiful, it must stick to the true rather than to the lovely. The dramatist must be unmoved by all demands from religion and aestheticism as Ibsen had been in his 'absolute indifference to public canons of art, friends and shibboleths'.[18]

The proper subject-matter for drama is the 'underlying laws' of life: 'Human society is the embodiment of changeless laws'.[19] What these 'changeless laws' are, is left largely unexplained. They are not divine, though they are said to be divinely severe; and Joyce comes nearest a definition, quite inadvertently, I think, when he stresses the human aspect of this severe and changeless subject for the dramatist: according to 'Drama and Life' 'the deathless passions, the human verities which so found expression then [i.e., in earlier writers], are indeed deathless...' (p. 45). In 'Ecce Homo' Joyce had said, drama 'concerns itself with the everlasting hopes, desires and hates of humanity, or deals with a symbolic presentment of our widely related nature' (p. 32). What is essentially and for ever human is the proper subject for the playwright. Commonplace though it is, this view served Joyce the rest of his life.

Another idea concerning the subject-matter rises out of Joyce's preoccupation with passion as essential to drama, and is couched in more precise language: 'drama is strife, evolution, movement in whatever way unfolded.' That the eighteen-year-

[18] Joyce's letter to Ibsen, quoted in Ellmann, p. 90.
[19] *Critical Writings*, p. 40. The following references to Joyce's essays are all from *Critical Writings*.

old Joyce, full of alert response to the scientific, philosophical, and literary ideas of his day, should find evolution, and evolution coupled with strife, a basic truth in life is no wonder. Forty years had elapsed since Darwin's *On the Origin of Species,* but the philosophy whose textbook it became still invited people to take sides, as Joyce does in 'Drama and Life' with some emphasis. But how far Joyce is from any naturalist approach to the idea of evolution, is seen from another passage in the essay, the style of which Joyce rightly calls 'fantastic':

> It might be said fantastically that as soon as men and women began life in the world there was above and about them, a spirit, of which they were dimly conscious, which they would have had sojourn in their midst in deeper intimacy and for whose truth they became seekers in after times, longing to lay hands upon it. For this spirit is as the roaming air, little susceptible of change, and never left their vision, shall never leave it, till the firmament is as a scroll rolled away. (P. 41)

By stating that 'drama is strife, evolution, movement in whatever way unfolded' Joyce comes near the ideas on the essence of drama which Professor Francis Fergusson has developed in *The Idea of a Theater.* Ferguson finds the basic shape of a play in a 'tragic rhythm of action' which underlies and gives life and significance to plots and characters.[20] In his review of *When We Dead Awaken* Joyce says:

> Ibsen's plays do not depend for their interest on the action,[21] or on the incidents. Even the characters, faultlessly drawn though they be, are not the first thing in his plays. But the naked drama – either the perception of a great truth, or the opening up of a great question, or a great conflict which is almost independent of the conflicting actors, and has been and is of far-reaching importance – this is what primarily rivets our attention. (P. 63)

However, in his next review of an Ibsen play Joyce praises the dramatist for what is almost the opposite virtue: Ibsen expresses

---

[20] F. Fergusson, *The Idea of a Theater* (Garden City, New York: Doubleday Anchor Books, 1953), p. 31.

[21] 'Action' is here used as a near-synonym for 'incidents' and differently from Fergusson's use of the word.

'his fable in terms of his characters' (p. 100). And this principle is one that Joyce adheres to through his whole career.[22]

Drama, as Joyce sees it in these early writings, is a communal art: 'Drama is essentially a communal art and of widespread domain. The drama – its fittest vehicle almost presupposes an audience, drawn from all classes' (p. 42). But this idea remains a loose end; and when Joyce wrote *Exiles* he put so much personal material directly into it that it has very little of the 'communal' about it. Nor is the idea related to a discussion of drama as a social renovator – a literary ideal clearly illustrated by some of Ibsen's plays. This is surprising as Joyce had read *The Quintessence of Ibsenism* and might also have read Brandes's works by that time, but it is probably due to the highly individual approach to the Norwegian which Joyce adopted. From the first meeting between the two minds, Joyce saw and made use of his own Ibsen – a playwright somewhat different from the one William Archer or Bernard Shaw admired. And as Joyce got to know Ibsen in his works (and in the original) more than in the Ibsen-literature that was available in English, he could afford to ignore the things in the plays that did not impress him directly.

Joyce is most emphatic on another point: given the proper subject-matter, the proper dramatic setting must be a realistic one. He asks, 'Shall we put life – real life – on the stage?' and his answer is an unqualified yes. Life may be dull, but 'Still I think out of the dreary sameness of existence, a measure of dramatic life may be drawn. Even the most commonplace, the deadest among the living, may play a part in a great drama.' (P. 45) Joyce criticizes *Catilina* for its romanticism, 'The romantic temper, imperfect and impatient as it is, cannot express itself adequately unless it employs the monstrous or heroic' (p. 100), and praises *The Masterbuilder* for the absence of 'spiritual glamour':

At the close of *The Master Builder,* the greatest touch of all was the horrifying exclamation of one without, 'O! the head is all

[22] Cf. pp. 117–121.

crushed in.' A lesser artist would have cast a spiritual glamour
over the tragedy of Bygmester Solness. (P. 62)

The same ideal of realism lies behind his appreciation of
When We Dead Awaken. Curiously blind to some of the symbolic sides of the play, Joyce praises it for its realism:

> Ibsen has chosen the average lives in their uncompromising truth
> for the groundwork of all his later plays. He has abandoned the
> verse form, and has never sought to embellish his work after the
> conventional fashion. Even when his dramatic theme reached its
> zenith he has not sought to trick it out in gawds or tawdriness.
> (P. 63)

No critic today would, I think, choose the phrase 'average lives'
to sum up Rubek, Irene, Ulfheim, and Maja. The gospel Joyce
found in Ibsen – defiant realism – was too overwhelming to
give room for an appreciation of the elaborate symbolism and
interest in the specific problems of the artist which other
readers find in *When We Dead Awaken*. Joyce calls the Sister
of Mercy 'a voiceless shadow with her own symbolic majesty'
(p. 64); but he leaves it at that, unable, it seems, to comprehend
or express the function of the symbolism in the play. The *al
fresco* scenes in the play are given an equally inconclusive
comment: 'And this feature, which is so prominent, does not
seem to me altogether without its significance' (p. 66).

Later in his career Joyce was anything but blind to the symbolic possibilities of Ibsen's plays; and when he wrote *Finnegans Wake* he made a number of Ibsen-characters important
symbols in it. But in these early essays Ibsen is the great realist
– and he is the other thing Joyce needed in him: a valiant
fighter for freedom against conventions. Joyce ends 'Drama
and Life' on Lona Hessel's proclamation in *Pillars of Society*
that she is going to let in fresh air. In his essay on Mangan he
turns to Ibsen, to Irene's nostalgic tribute to life in *When We
Dead Awaken*, to express his own vision of a free and happy
existence:

> When the sterile and treacherous order is broken up, a voice or a
> host of voices is heard singing, a little faintly at first, of a serene

spirit which enters woods and cities and the hearts of men, and of the life on earth – det dejlige vidunderlige jordliv det gaadefulde jordliv – beautiful, alluring, mysterious. (P. 83)

Joyce's more extravagant dreams about the future are clothed in lines and ideas from Ibsen, but he was also aware of more prosaic qualities in the Norwegian. Joyce makes a point of Ibsen's energy and perseverance: in 'Ibsen's New Drama' he praises 'the sustained energy' and 'the gradual, irresistible advance of this extraordinary man' (pp. 48–49) and he quotes Ulfheim's speech on his and Rubek's work:

> ... We both work in a hard material, madam – both your husband and I. He struggles with his marble blocks, I daresay; and I struggle with tense and quivering bear-sinews. (P. 52)

Further, he felt himself capable of being a dauntless and independent writer; and this vision was mirrored in Ibsen's career, too: 'Very few recognize the astonishing courage of such a work' (p. 101).

The independence that Joyce cherished so highly is hardly in itself a trait in the Irishman that Ibsen can be made responsible for; but that independence and aloofness could serve the purposes of the writer was clearly illustrated in the Norwegian, whose social dramas are praised, not only for their skill, but also for their 'intellectual self-possession'. Ibsen becomes the prototype of the artist who stands above 'cries of hysteria' and 'the voices of war and statecraft and religion' (p. 101). Joyce found that this aloofness was also present in Ibsen's attitude to the world of his plays:

> Ibsen treats ... all things ... with large insight, artistic restraint, and sympathy. He sees it steadily and whole, as from a great height, with perfect vision and angelic dispassionateness, with the sight of one who may look on the sun with open eyes. (P. 65)

This idea was later developed, probably (as the editors of *Critical Writings* say in a footnote) 'with some assistance from Flaubert' into the famous passage in *A Portrait* where Stephen discourses upon the artist who should remain 'within or behind or beyond or above his handiwork, invisible, refined out of existence, indifferent, paring his fingernails.'[23] Joyce's first attempts to relate this theory to other *genres* are seen in his Paris notebook from 1904.[24] This was to become not only Stephen's theory, but an important part of Joyce's practice in his later works; and as Ibsen provided an initial impulse towards it we shall trace its development in the following chapters.

En passant in these essays Joyce shows awareness of other aspects of Ibsen's dramatic art. He makes a point of the way in which Professor Rubek's life is presented to us by retrospection,[25] but does not enlarge on his observation. As we shall see in our discussion of *Exiles,* Joyce had grasped only a fraction of what this technique means in Ibsen. Further, Joyce noticed how suggestive Ibsen's dialogue can be: 'with apparently easy dialogue, he presents his men and women passing through different soul-crises'; and Joyce praises the significance that Ibsen extracts from the commonplace: 'The leaven of prospective drama is gradually discerned working amid the *fin-de-siècle* scene' (p. 50). This was an approach which Joyce made more felicitous use of in *Exiles,* in which some of the apparently trivial dialogue attains rich overtones. And the presentation of crises, common to all drama, becomes the main structural principle behind Joyce's revision of *Stephen Hero.*

The ideas about drama and the writing of plays which Joyce propounds in these early writings are those of a very young man. He does not yet see the realm of drama as Ibsen saw his characters, 'with large insight . . . steadily and whole, as from a great height.' There is something helpless about the review of *When We Dead Awaken.* After a survey of Ibsen's career up to the last play, Joyce devotes fourteen pages to a re-hash of the story of the play interspersed with critical comments some of which are only too obvious; others are excessively laudatory, while only a very few testify to Joyce's originality. Four pages at the end are devoted to a more general analysis of the play,

---

[23] *A Portrait,* p. 215.
[24] *Critical Writings,* pp. 143–145.
[25] *Ibid.,* p. 50.

but most of it does not reach beyond a description of the characters. With his usual brashness (it must have been this quality
which appealed to the editor of the *Fortnightly Review*) Joyce
hides his lack of familiarity with dramatic craftsmanship behind an attitude that is sincere enough – that of a reverent and
awestruck disciple.

Three years later, in 1903, Joyce wrote the review of *Catilina;* and this is a piece of criticism which reveals a new and
more mature grasp of Ibsen's work. Ibsen is still the great
master, but now Joyce sees his career as a development – not
free from flaws – from the romantic to the classical. The blame
for the failure of *Catilina* is put on its romantic properties, but
Joyce's understanding is so perspicacious by now that he can
praise *Peer Gynt* for the same qualities: 'This manner [the
romantic] continues . . . as far as *Peer Gynt,* in which, recog-
nizing its own limitations and pushing lawlessness to its extreme limit, it achieves a masterpiece' (p. 101). The crowning
glory of the development is of course the 'classical temper' of
Ibsen's plays after *Peer Gynt;* and on this 'second manner'
Joyce has a comment which shows him in possession of greater
insight into a playwright's workshop: this second phase unites
'construction and speech and action more and more closely in a
supple rhythm' (p. 101). Though not particularly precise or
subtle, this observation is superior to any summing up of Ibsen's
art in the earlier essays.

There is one thing that is remarkable, if not always admir-
able, in these essays on drama: Joyce's own style. It ranges from
the fairly matter-of-fact to the highly wrought, and testifies to
an acute ear for prose rhythms and a lively literary imagination. The metaphors are sometimes elaborate,

> Ghosts, the action of which passes in a common parlour, is of uni-
> versal import – a deepset branch on the tree, Igdrasil, whose roots
> are struck in earth, but through whose higher leafage the stars of
> heaven are glowing and astir. (P. 45)

and the allusions may be recondite; Joyce was seldom above
showing off what quaint odds and ends he had stored in his
memory:

The forms of things, as the earth's crust, are changed. The timbers
of the ships of Tarshish are falling asunder or eaten by the wanton
sea; time has broken into the fastnesses of the mighty; the gardens
of Armida are become as treeless wilds. (P. 45)

In this prose lie hidden a number of seeds that were to grow
into major stylistic components of Joyce's later works: the conscious importance attached to rhythm, the 'difficult' allusions,
and the will and ability in the author to stretch his verbal
imagination very nearly to its limits are essential parts of
Ulysses and *Finnegans Wake*. I do not want to make a case for
any influence from Ibsen upon these aspects of Joyce's art.
Ibsen was the subject of some of the early writings where we
find them in embryo, but the style cannot easily be derived
from Ibsen's dialogue. Here, as elsewhere in the present study,
the most likely conclusion is that Ibsen's role was that of a con-
firmer; in him Joyce found a justification of his attempts to
write in his own way without concern for conventions, literary
or otherwise.

Joyce's dramatic and literary interests at this time were of
course not restricted to his avid study of Ibsen. He felt himself
to be the champion of the Irish poet James Clarence Mangan;
and there are tributes to other playwrights in his essays:
'Earnest dramatists of the second rank, Sudermann, Bjørnson,
and Giacosa, can write very much better plays than the Irish
Literary Theatre has staged' (p. 70). Six other writers of plays
– Maeterlinck, Haddon Chambers, Echegaray, Strindberg,
Tolstoy, and Wagner – are summoned *en passant* as representatives of the new drama. Bernard Shaw is not mentioned as
one; but *The Quintessence of Ibsenism* is quoted in 'Ibsen's New
Drama',[26] and a review of the novels of A. E. W. Mason in-
cludes another reference to him.[27]

Above these Joyce placed Gerhard Hauptmann, who is hailed as Ibsen's successor at the end of 'The Day of the Rabble-

[26] Joyce quotes Shaw as if *he* had said that Ibsen was 'a muck-ferreting
dog' (*Critical Writings*, p. 48) while Shaw in *The Quintessence of Ibsenism*
(London: Walter Scott, 1891), p. 92, quotes the phrase from the catalogue of
abuse on Ibsen's followers which William Archer had collected.
[27] See *Critical Writings*, p. 131.

ment'. He translated two of Hauptmann's plays, *Vor Sonnen-aufgang* and *Michael Kramer*, into English at this time. To my knowledge, the question of Hauptmann's influence on Joyce has not been examined. There is little doubt that an investigation of it would enrich our understanding of Joyce's work, as would a study that discussed and compared the importance to Joyce's development of all the dramatists and novelists that he read as a young man. However, judging from Joyce's own statements and from the biographical information at present available, none of these writers occupied Joyce to the extent that Ibsen did. They were found, with the exception of Hauptmann, to be 'of the second rank'. There was, however, a third writer that Joyce placed in a group with Ibsen and Hauptmann. 'The Day of the Rabblement' ends on this prophecy:

> Elsewhere there are men who are worthy to carry on the tradition of the old master who is dying in Christiania. He has already found his successor in the writer of *Michael Kramer*, and the third minister will not be wanting when his hour comes. Even now that hour may be standing by the door. (P. 72)

The third minister is, of course, the young critic himself.

The most enduring influence?

The material that I have presented in the previous pages indicates very clearly that Ibsen is the most important figure in the literary and dramatic landscape which the young Joyce explores. All other writers seem to be of a smaller stature, and none is so dear to Joyce as Ibsen. We have already seen what Joyce admired in Ibsen, but the very special and exalted position of the dramatist in Joyce's mind suggests that one may find not only admiration, but also a significant indebtedness in this relationship. In the following pages I shall discuss what the first stages in Joyce's development as a writer may owe to his enthusiasm for Ibsen. We shall consider the most basic question first: was it because of his reading of Ibsen that Joyce turned to literary art? Then certain aspects of Ibsen's art that

Joyce singles out for praise will be examined in an attempt to determine in what ways Joyce may have been influenced in his early career by Ibsen.

The *annus mirabilis* of Joyce's youth – a suitable starting-point for a discussion of Ibsen's importance to Joyce the creative writer – was 1897, in which 'his faith in Catholicism tottered, ... his faith in art ... grew great.'[28] This development is described in Chapters IV and V of *A Portrait of the Artist as a Young Man* as a process in which books played little or no part. Naturally, *A Portrait* is no psychological case history; Stephen Dedalus is not James Joyce in all respects. Joyce alters facts to focus on the main theme, the growth of the young artist; and he may well have omitted literary influences to make the hero appear the more original and independent. Still, it can be demonstrated that on this point his autobiographical novel is basically true to what actually happened. There were impulses other than literature in Joyce's life at the time strong enough to alter its course. His early and significant choice of art as his vocation sprang from a composite psychological situation, which presents us with more than a simple story of an intellectually alert and receptive young mind which fully and freely opens itself to a couple of decisive literary influences.

James Joyce was the outstanding boy in his class at Belvedere – a promising scholar who won exhibitions in 1894, 1895, and 1897, and a prize for English composition in 1898. He was captain of his house in his last year at school; and before that, in September 1896, he had been chosen prefect of the school's Sodality of the Blessed Virgin Mary. The other boys looked up to him, and sometimes envied him his knowledge, independence, and precociously mature judgement. This was in itself enough to give James the idea that he was unlike the other boys and that he might pursue a career of another sort than theirs. This sense of his own unique position among his fellow pupils was also strengthened when the director of studies suggested to him that he might consider becoming a Jesuit. He felt, when he

[28] Ellmann, p. 50.

contemplated the solemn position of priesthood, that he was destined for a station of similarly lofty significance.[29] When in the course of 1897 his Catholic faith dwindled, Joyce was not left in a spiritual vacuum. His sense of holy dedication was intact and demanded another object which he immediately found in art. In an analysis of a central episode in *A Portrait* – Stephen's vision of the young woman wading on the shore – Professor Kristian Smidt has shown how forceful and elaborate was Joyce's view of art as a religion at the time when he wrote his autobiographical novel. The new faith is marked by its conspicuous debts to Roman Catholicism: there is a woman-figure like the Virgin Mary, as well as a setting that suggests the baptism of Christ; and the acolyte, Stephen, is there to adore the deity.[30] I think *A Portrait of the Artist as a Young Man* gives an essentially true picture of what happened to the young Joyce: it was not only a vocation but a religion he sought and found in art; and the earnestness and zeal of his earlier faith survived and helped him to *believe* in it.

Another aspect of Joyce's situation in 1897 also led him towards the artist's part in life. He felt oppressed – by his bullying father, by his actively Catholic mother, by the poverty of his home, the sedate atmosphere of Belvedere and the rigid orthodoxy of his Jesuit teachers. Whatever his future life was to be, it had to give him more scope than his home, school, and religion could afford him. So he looked to art for freedom from conventions and commonly accepted ideas that he thought unbearably stolid.

Art, to Joyce, meant literature. He had an unusual linguistic awareness, probably derived from his father, who was known as a fine story-teller; and in *Stephen Hero* and *A Portrait* he makes much of the love of and feeling for words which he had even as a child. For the schoolboy the nearest entrance to the realm of art was through writing: English composition was the subject in which he excelled at school; and in 1897 he had not

[29] Cf. Ellmann, p. 56 and *A Portrait,* pp. 153–162.
[30] Cf. Kristian Smidt, *James Joyce and the Cultic Use of Fiction* (Oslo: Oslo University Press, 1959), pp. 38–42.

yet discovered how fine his voice was. He had no specific literary projects in store; but the prospects, vague and dazzling
products of his imagination, needed no foundation in metre or
dialogue or narrative at this stage.

   This is not, of course, meant as a full explanation of why and
how Joyce became a writer. But it does indicate that Joyce first
established his ideal world of art without Ibsen's help. *Stephen
Hero*, written in 1904–1906, gives further corroboration of this
point: Stephen says that he 'suffered the most enduring influence of his life', that of Ibsen, after he had left school, *i.e.*, after
the summer of 1898 (p. 40).

   In Ibsen Joyce found a *confirmation* of his new-won ideas.
Ibsen's dramas were a shock, but in the main a shock of recognition rather than of revelation. The Norwegian dramatist gave
him, in a play like *Love's Comedy*, a conflict that resembled his
own: a young artist brushing against a placid society of tea-
drinking match-makers. No wonder that he liked to surprise his
friends by praising this little-known play.[31] *Hedda Gabler*,
another play about which we know he was enthusiastic,[32] presents an example of a superbly egotistical character in humdrum surroundings – again a situation Joyce found similar to
his own. Thus, when he remembers and makes prominent use of
Lona Hessel's words from *Pillars of Society* about letting in
'fresh air' in his 'Drama and Life', it is not, I think, because
Ibsen was the liberator who opened his eyes to the pleasures of
a freer life, but because Joyce recognized in Ibsen longings he
had nursed but not yet been able to *express* with similar vivid-
ness. A great many of Ibsen's plays extol the person who lets in
fresh air; and Ibsen's heroes, often at war with a narrow and
authoritarian society, gave Joyce a pattern for and a confirmation of his wish to break out and realize his own nonconforming
self. Rather naïvely, the Stephen of *Stephen Hero* associates
art with anti-conventionalism: 'Stephen had begun to regard
himself seriously as a literary artist: he professed scorn for the
rabblement and contempt for authority' (pp. 122–123).

   [31] Ellmann, p. 79.
   [32] M. and P. Colum, *Our Friend James Joyce* (London: V. Gollancz,
1959), p. 47.

A similar somewhat simplified conception of the artist's part in life can be discerned in a letter Ibsen wrote to Brandes. It is quoted in Archer's introduction to *An Enemy of the People* (1901), which Joyce probably read:

> They really do not need poetry at home; they get along so well with the *Parliamentary News* and the *Lutheran Weekly*. . . . I have not the gifts that go to make a good citizen, nor yet the gift of orthodoxy; and what I possess no gift for, I keep out of. Liberty is the first and highest condition for me. At home they do not trouble much about liberty, . . .

Ibsen in his plays, and Joyce in his mature understanding of Ibsen, show an awareness of freedom as something much more complex. But as a young man Joyce needed a simple, strong example, and Ibsen is associated with the open air in *A Portrait*, too: 'he foreknew that . . . as he went by Baird's stonecutting works in Talbot Place the spirit of Ibsen would blow through him like a keen wind, a spirit of wayward boyish beauty' (p.176). The other authors mentioned in the same passage are remembered for their style or for some special feature in their works: 'the girls and women in the plays of Gerhard Hauptmann', 'the cloistral silverveined prose of Newman', 'the dark humour of Guido Cavalcanti', and a song by Ben Jonson. But it was Ibsen's message and his personality, more than any one play or any one aspect of his dramatic art, which first caught Joyce's attention.

Ibsen's anti-conventionalism as well as the tenacity implied in his artistic career is praised in the letter Joyce wrote to him in 1901:

> But we always keep the dearest things to ourselves. . . . I did not say how what I could discern dimly of your life was my pride to see, how your battles inspired me – not the obvious material battles but those that were fought and won behind your forehead – how your wilful resolution to wrest the secret from life gave me heart, and how in your absolute indifference to public canons of art, friends and shibboleths you walked in the light of your inward heroism.[33]

[33] Quoted from Ellmann, p. 90.

There is little or nothing in this letter to indicate that Joyce found Ibsen 'first and foremost, a remarkable prototype of the successful provincial artist'.[34] Being himself a writer from the outskirts of Europe, Joyce was not unconscious of Ibsen's provincial background; indeed, the similarities in the backgrounds of the two make up a highly important reason why Joyce could identify himself with Ibsen. But in his writings Joyce never paid much attention to it. He saw the Norwegian, not as a townsman of Skien or Christiania, but as the denizen of a central domain in the land of art. The public canons of art which, according to his Irish admirer, Ibsen had so successfully risen above, were not seen as the representatives of any *provincial* bourgeoisie.

The letter ends on a note of buoyant assurance. Joyce knows himself to be Ibsen's successor:

> You have only opened the way – though you have gone as far as you could – . . . But I am sure that higher and holier enlightenment lies – onward.
>
> As one of the young generation for whom you have spoken I give you greeting – not humbly, because I am obscure and you in the glare, not sadly because you are an old man and I a young man, not presumptuously, nor sentimentally – but joyfully, with hope and with love, I give you greeting.[35]

It was Ibsen, who received these highflown words by Joyce on Joyce, who had helped the Irishman to this new mood of joy, hope, and love by suggesting a way from dreams about a writer's career to writing itself. Joyce's own account, in *Stephen Hero*, of his early Ibsen-enthusiasm implies this. In one way Ibsen became more than a confirming oracle:

> It must be said simply and at once that at this time Stephen suffered the most enduring influence of his life. The spectacle of the world which his intelligence presented to him with every sordid

---

[34] Hugh Kenner, 'Joyce and Ibsen's Naturalism,' *Sewanee Review*, Vol. 59, No. 1 (Winter 1951), p. 77.
[35] Quoted from Ellmann, pp. 90–91.

and deceptive detail set side by side with the spectacle of the world which the monster in him, now grown to a reasonably heroic stage, presented also had often filled him with such sudden despair as could be assuaged only by melancholy versing. He had all but decided to consider the two worlds as aliens one to another – however disguised or expressed the most utter of pessimisms – when he encountered through the medium of hardly procured translations the spirit of Henrik Ibsen. He understood that spirit instantaneously. . . . Ibsen had no need of apologist or critic: the minds of the old Norse poet and of the perturbed young Celt met in a moment of radiant simultaneity. Stephen was captivated first by the evident excellence of the art: he was not long before he began to affirm, out of a sufficiently scanty knowledge of the tract, of course, that Ibsen was the first among the dramatists of the world . . . But it was not only this excellence which captivated him: it was not that which he greeted gladly with an entire joyful spiritual salutation. It was the very spirit of Ibsen himself that was discerned moving behind the impersonal manner of the artist: . . . a mind of sincere and boylike bravery, of disillusioned pride, of minute and wilful energy. (Pp. 40–41)

The praise of Ibsen as 'the first among the dramatists of the world' and as a courageous and independent personality – 'a mind of sincere and boylike bravery, of disillusioned pride, of minute and wilful energy' – is here, as it was in the essays; but the emphasis is on a more concrete point: Ibsen helped him to establish a fruitful relationship between 'the spectacle of the world which his intelligence presented to him with every sordid and deceptive detail' and his vision of the world of literary art. His only attempt at writing up to this time, his 'melancholy versing', had not bridged that gap. Joyce was in an impasse, from which Ibsen suggested a way out.

Joyce does not, in *Stephen Hero*, go into particulars about the literary ideal he found in Ibsen, but from his other writings we can infer what he learnt. The dichotomy between sordid, everyday life and art is the same as in 'Drama and Life', and there the answer is given: 'Still I think out of the dreary sameness of existence, a measure of dramatic life may be drawn' (p. 45). This is the lesson from Ibsen: ordinary life can be, and should be, used as subject-matter. It is the realistic-naturalistic side of Ibsen's art that appeals to Joyce. Talking of Joyce's 'early attitudes toward life and art', Harry Levin maintains that 'they stem naïvely out of the naturalistic movement.'[36] There is, no doubt, a certain naïveté in Joyce's early relationship to Ibsen, and to other writers of the realistic school, a naïveté he became aware of and subdued in *A Portrait of the Artist as a Young Man*. Still, from the beginning he imbibed something more than a crude naturalism from his reading of Ibsen's plays. The 'real life' he praises as dramatic subject-matter is of a special sort; it is life when it reveals its 'underlying laws first, in all their nakedness and divine severity, and only secondarily ... the motley agents who bear them out.'[37] This is, for all the grandiloquence, little more than what any naturalist could claim that he wrote about; but the use Joyce made of this principle in *Dubliners, A Portrait,* and *Ulysses* implies a highly selective use of real life which goes beyond the practices of mere naturalism.

Joyce was aware that realism in itself was insufficient as a programme. The attitude of the writer towards his material had to be taken into account, too; and in the review of *Catilina* it is Ibsen's approach, his 'classical temper', which is praised. Ibsen has 'intellectual self-possession' and 'a method so calm, so ironical' (pp. 100–101). That this praise goes beyond the adulation of the dramatist as untroubled by 'the voices of war and statecraft and religion', can be seen from the chapter in *Stephen Hero* where Joyce continues his discussion of the 'classical temper'.[38] It is well summed up, with as much clarity and precision as Joyce allows, by S. L. Goldberg:

> ... the classical temper is essentially dramatic. It accepts the ordinary world of humanity as the primary object of its attention, and endeavours to see it and present it steadily and whole. In order to do so, it seeks patiently for maturity, detachment, impersonality of judgement and an artistic method, that, while it begins with the

---

[36] *James Joyce: A Critical Introduction* (London: Faber and Faber, 1944), p. 23.
[37] *Critical Writings*, p. 40.
[38] *Stephen Hero*, p. 78.

local and concrete as its foundation, enables it to penetrate beyond them. The classical temper thus involves a moral as well as an artistic ideal, an ideal of spiritual completeness and impersonal order.[39]

The similarity between this artistic programme and what Joyce saw in Ibsen is obvious from his dramatic criticism. Indeed, in summing up Joyce's view it is difficult to avoid the very words he used about Ibsen, who saw his dramatic world 'steadily and whole, as from a great height.'[40] The art of the theatre has no room for direct comments by the author; and Joyce's admiration of Ibsen's aloofness is partly, I think, a tribute to the distancing that all drama creates, simply by being drama. But this does not diminish Ibsen's importance; his plays allowed this effect of the theatre its full force. It is a long way from seeing and admiring such a presentation of life on the stage to writing novels, where, in a narrative medium, there is a similar effect. That Joyce did achieve this stands as a testimony to the endurance of Ibsen's influence as well as to his own intrepidity and perseverance as a writer.

The naïveté in Joyce's enthusiasm for the 'real life' he found in Ibsen becomes less noticeable when we consider how his attitude marks a preference for what was not fashionable. The *Fortnightly Review*, for example, was not inimical to the school of realists and naturalists, but it was silently taken for granted that it was something essentially Continental and foreign to the English tradition. Ibsen was tolerated: two months before Joyce's article George Moore had declared himself an Ibsenite in 'A preface to "The Bending of the Bough"', and in doing so had placed Yeats and Martyn firmly at his side.[41] Yeats was there, however, by a sleight of Moore's hand rather than by his own will; and the prevailing attitude towards realism in the *Fortnightly*, like that of English critics in general, was far from enthusiastic. Thus, realism without moral ideals is dismissed

[39] *The Classical Temper: A Study of James Joyce's* Ulysses (London: Chatto and Windus, 1961), p. 32.
[40] *Critical Writings*, p. 65.
[41] *The Fortnightly Review*, Vol. 67, pp. 317–324.

by Hannah Lynch in an article in which Tolstoy is praised at
the expense of Flaubert;[42] later in the year d'Annunzio is welcomed in the *Fortnightly* as a Romantic.[43] Other impulses from
London, e.g. the late flowering of Romanticism in *The Yellow
Book*, made realism seem a paltry thing. The work that Gosse,
Archer, Shaw, and others had done to make Ibsen acceptable
had not resulted in any great changes in the literary climate.
The trend was the same in Joyce's immediate surroundings in
Dublin: the weird world of *The Countess Cathleen* or the
mysticism of A. E. was not likely to imbue anyone with a taste
for stuffy parlours, middle-class people, and their seemingly
trivial problems. It took Yeats thirty years of writing to realise
that his best material was found in the 'rag-and-bone shop of
the heart'. Joyce learnt this from Ibsen at the outset of his
literary career.

[42] *Ibid.*, pp. 69–78.
[43] Vol. 68 (September 1, 1900), p. 392.

III
EARLY REALISM

The human mind is never entirely consistent; and Joyce continued to write melancholy verses even after the moment when he met 'the spirit of Ibsen'. Some of the poems intended for a collection he intended to call 'Shine and Dark' are dated 1899 and 1900[1]; and *Chamber Music* shows that he did not abandon this genre with his departure from Ireland. He was on the highway of realism, but allowed himself to play occasionally in the blind alley of romanticism. Indeed, some of the charm of *Chamber Music* comes, I think, from the impression that these poems give of being a sideline; their daintiness comes into its own only when they are seen as a contrast in size and touch to Joyce's major works. However, the feeling that this kind of poetry was futile grew in Joyce; and the intermittent poetry of his later years shows how totally he became committed to 'real life': the insipid romanticism of many of the poems in *Chamber Music* is almost entirely absent from *Pomes Penyeach*.

The first results of Joyce's attempt to bridge the gap between the world of art and 'the world which his intelligence presented to him with every sordid and deceptive detail' were the brief prose sketches which he called epiphanies. These epiphanies can, I think, suggest an answer to a question which it is natural to ask about the tributes to Ibsen that we find in Joyce's early writings: to what extent is it Ibsen, and Ibsen alone, that caused Joyce to turn to realism?[2] And conversely, to what extent is the Ibsen that Joyce hails a personification of the element of rea-

[1] Robert E. Scholes, *The Cornell Joyce Collection: A Catalogue* (Ithaca, New York: Cornell Univ. Press, 1961), p. 3.
[2] Joyce read other realistic and naturalistic writers, e.g. Flaubert and George Moore. There are interesting parallels to Moore in *Dubliners*. See Graham Hough, *Image and Experience* (London: Duckworth, 1960), pp. 179 ff.

lism and naturalism that was in the air at the turn of the century? We should not expect the epiphanies to give us any full and exact answer to this question. In the last instance it is a question that defies attempts at a complete and definitive answer, for an author is always inextricably connected with his age. Still, the epiphanies present features that can take us some way towards an assessment of Ibsen's share in Joyce's decision to write in a realistic manner.

First, it should be noted that two of the epiphanies are about Ibsen. One is a conversation after the parlour game 'Who's Who':

> [Dublin: at Sheehy's, Belvedere Place]
> Joyce – I knew you meant him. But you're wrong about his age.
> Maggie Sheehy – (*leans forward to speak seriously*) Why, how old is he?
> Joyce – Seventy-two.
> Maggie Sheehy – Is he?
>
> (*Epiphanies*, p. 1)

The other is a picture of the dramatist himself:

> Yes, they are the two sisters. She who is churning with stout arms (their butter is famous) looks dark and unhappy: the other is happy because she had her way. Her name is R. . . . Rina. I know the verb 'to be' in their language.
>   – Are you Rina? –
>   I knew she was.
>   But here he is himself in a coat with tails and an old-fashioned high hat. He ignores them: he walks along with tiny steps, jutting out the tails of his coat. . . . My goodness! how small he is! He must be very old and vain. . . . Maybe he isn't what I . . . It's funny that those two big women fell out over this little man. . . . But then he's the greatest man in the world. . . .
>
> (*Epiphanies*, p. 10. Rina is the name of the elder Miss Tesman in *Hedda Gabler*.)

The sketch describes a dream, but there is no reason to doubt that the tribute to Ibsen obtains on the fully conscious level in Joyce's mind too. And the very fact that Ibsen is the subject of the sketch shows that he was at the forefront of Joyce's mind at the time.

The form of a number of epiphanies reveals an influence directly from Ibsen. So far, forty epiphanies have been recorded;[3] of these, no less that fourteen are dialogues and two are monologues – all complete with stage-directions, the names of the characters as speech-headings, and very often an indication of the tone of a speech in a parenthesis. This gives them exactly the appearance of a page in a play. In the speeches of these 'dramatic' epiphanies there is a great deal of hesitancy and sometimes a conspicuous vagueness. This may be accounted for by Joyce's method of writing down his sketches immediately after he had overheard a conversation he wanted to record; but Ibsen's dialogue with its hesitant speeches and the tendency in so many of his characters to leave sentences half-finished and to approach their point obliquely may have helped Joyce to select just this sort of conversation as an epiphany:

> [Dublin: at Sheehy's, Belvedere Place]
> Fallon – (*as he passes*) – I was told to congratulate you especially on your performance.
> Joyce – Thank you.
> Blake – (*after a pause*) . . . I'd never advise anyone to . . . O, it's a terrible life! . . .
> Joyce – Ha.
> Blake – (*between puffs of smoke*) – Of course . . . it looks all right from the outside . . . to those who don't know. . . . But if you knew . . . it's really terrible. A bit of a candle, no . . . dinner, squalid . . . poverty. You've no idea simply . . .
>
> (*Epiphanies*, p. 2)

Most of these 'dramatic' epiphanies are recordings of conversations that took place (or might have taken place) in Joyce's Dublin; they are real down to trivial details. Only one of them takes us out of Ireland, though without violating the conventions of realistic drama, – to a scene in London with family

[3] Twenty-two epiphanies in the Wickser Collection in the University of Buffalo have been published by O. A. Silverman under the title *Epiphanies* (Buffalo: Lockwood Memorial Library, 1956). Another eighteen, still unpublished, are found in items 15, 17, and 18 in the Cornell Joyce Collection.

relations more scandalous and more frankly reported than those of *Ghosts*. Seen together, the 'dramatic' epiphanies indicate that Ibsen is not just a name for the sum total of what Joyce inherited from the school of realists and naturalists. When Joyce wanted to write in a realistic manner, he thought of this as *Ibsen's* manner, even to the extent of imitating his dramatic style. In content, and in the case of the 'dramatic' sketches also in form, Joyce's early realism reflects his enthusiasm for the Norwegian dramatist.

This impression is not weakened by a study of the narrative epiphanies, of which some are straightforward descriptions of Dublin incidents that Joyce found vulgar, and some recordings of his own thoughts and dreams.[4] Though the style is uneven and sometimes disturbingly highflown, these sketches are all, like those in the former group, realistic in the sense that they are drawn from Joyce's immediate experience and reflections. Even the stilted 'Here are we come together, . . .' (an unpublished epiphany in the Cornell Joyce Collection, Item 17, p. 53) gives the impression of being a slice of life – a poetic moment in Joyce's own life. The frank immediacy of all the epiphanies presents a sharp contrast to the laboured sentiments of the early poems; and it gives some of the sketches a fine poignancy which augurs well for Joyce's later attempts to bring together 'the world ... with every sordid ... detail' and the world of art.

The epiphanies do not all conform to this definition of realism; but seeing them in the light of this programme enables us to account for something which Stephen's Aquinian theories about the epiphany do not explain: the failure of many of the sketches to give artistic expression to something significant. The first half of the lesson from Ibsen is here in abundance – 'I think out of the dreary sameness of existence, a measure of dramatic life may be drawn. Even the most commonplace ... may play a part in a great drama.'[5] It is just this stubborn insis-

---

[4] Cf. Stephen's definition of an epiphany as a 'manifestation, whether in the vulgarity of speech or of gesture or in a memorable phase of the mind itself.' (*Stephen Hero*, p. 211.)
[5] *Critical Writings*, p. 45.

tence on the trivial which in some of the epiphanies stands in the way of a selection of material that could have made them more significant. Joyce never gave up the idea that is was possible to write about trivial matters and shows us in *Ulysses* that a Dublin advertisement canvasser can carry as much human significance as any Roman emperor. And in those epiphanies that find their measure of 'life – real life' in Joyce's own mind, truthfulness to sordid detail does not prevent suggestive richness. Sometimes Joyce finds a conversation which throws light on many aspects of human life; a good example is the epiphany that introduces Stephen's definition in *Stephen Hero*, in which attitudes to sex, religion, and social conventions, as well as a special use of language, are revealed in a brief exchange of words.[6] But without the larger framework of a short story or a novel Joyce could not always draw the dramatic life contained in the commonplace to the reader's attention; and a great many of the early epiphanies are pointless – they do not reveal the 'underlying laws ... in all their nakedness and divine severity'[7] which Joyce had seen behind the commonplaces in Ibsen's work. The lesson had been taken, but only incompletely digested.

Thus, the influence of Ibsen on Joyce can be shown to be a relevant starting-point and a useful background for an analysis of the epiphanies. But they should not, of course, be studied only in the light of this indebtedness; there is something quite original, and a potential virtue, in their very brevity, which presents a clear contrast to the greater breadth and length that the realistic school normally demands of its descriptions of life. In *Stephen Hero* Joyce's approach is realistic in this sense as well; but there is a whish to break new ground in the epiphanies, which are so brief that the reader's own imagination must fill in the necessary background. For this reason the epiphanies make difficult reading: their fragmentary nature asks for a more active participation by the reader than do most realistic novels and stories. It is interesting to note that a discussion of this fragmentary appearance of the

---

[6] See *Stephen Hero*, p. 211.
[7] *Critical Writings*, p. 40.

epiphanies provides a connection in which the Aquinian theories of art make sense: they can justify the 'isolation' – the word
is Stephen's in *Stephen Hero* – of the sketches from a narrative
and social context. However, the theory that Stephen derives
from Aquinas is not related to the actual writing of the epiphanies in a way which makes it a helpful guide for an analysis of
other aspects of the sketches.

  Stephen Hero it not 'epiphanaic' in the sense of the word that
Stephen derives from Aquinas. The detailed description which
it gives of Stephen's life and surroundings is a purer result of
Joyce's acceptance of realism than are the epiphanies; and *Stephen Hero* suffers from a weakness that wholehearted attach-
ment to realism is susceptible to: Joyce indeed used everyday
life as subject-matter, but he is still unable to give it poignant
form. In *A Portrait* and *Ulysses* Joyce concentrates his narrative round focal episodes, often as trivial in themselves as the
chapters of *Stephen Hero*, and by means of this concentration
creates an effect of compactness which is like the one he must
have aimed at – and sometimes achieved – in the early epiphanies. But in *Stephen Hero* the narrative flows evenly and with
little tension, concentration, and rhythm from the first page to
the last. In one way, however, this shortcoming is less disturbing in *Stephen Hero* than in the sketches in the Wickser Collection. In the novel the trivialities have a menial function that
they perform perfunctorily: they contribute to a matter-of-fact
description of the circumstances that Stephen emerges from,
even though they fail to materialize as epiphanies that carry
meaning beyond and above their petty subject.

  Only later, and most notably in *Ulysses,* was Joyce able to
provide a richer and more dramatic context for both the hero
and his antithetical surroundings – a context in which the con-
trasts explain and enrich each other so that they leave little
room in the reader for the stock responses that artists and pillars
of society traditionally trigger. This involved a more sophisticated use of point of view than the simple 'I'-form of *Stephen
Hero,* in which we listen to what the hero says about the hero
all the time. There are only a very few situations in which we

catch a glimpse of Stephen from another angle. Quite inadvertently, I think, Joyce allows us one in Stephen's conversations with Cranly, in which the latter's critical comments enable us to see Stephen through the eyes of another character for
a second. But in *Stephen Hero* all characters other than the
main person are so unimportant in themselves that they cannot
function as effective mirrors in which we could get another
picture of Stephen. We are left with the one he never ceases to
paint for us himself. 'The book', says Mr S. L. Goldberg, 'relies
upon our accepting Stephen's essential rightness, on our immediate assent to the values he is constantly proclaming.'[8] It
does, and it also relies upon our immediate assent to his way of
telling the story. If we start asking ourselves what the Stephen
is like whom Stephen does not tell us about, we shall find that
there is no answer. Stephen Daedalus has not the objective life
that his namesake in *A Portrait* and *Ulysses* gradually achieves.
The use of point of view which enables us to see with the eyes
of the hero, and at the same time see him in the act of seeing, is
essential to this new subtlety.[9] It is also the counterpart, in fiction, to the objective approach that Joyce admired in Ibsen,
who saw all things 'steadily and whole, as from a great
height'.[10] In this respect *Stephen Hero* is a failure, but in
another way it is a more successful attempt to follow the lessons
of the Norwegian: the artist should write about life as he knew
it, even in its drabness. This is reflected in the detailed accuracy
of the account of the daily life of Stephen – something that
gives *Stephen Hero* considerable interest.

Joyce was never a docile disciple; and the first surge of
enthusiasm for Ibsen, which is reflected so clearly in the epiphanies and *Stephen Hero,* was followed by a slow but inexor-
able process which transformed the image of Ibsen from that
of *the* Master to that of a master dramatist. In a letter from
February 1905 Joyce says to his brother, 'Do you not think the

[8] *Joyce* (Edinburgh: Oliver and Boyd, 1962), p. 35.
[9] Cf. S. L. Goldberg, 'Joyce and the Artist's Fingernails', *A Review of
English Literature*, Vol. II, No. 2 (April 1961), pp. 66 ff.
[10] *Critical Writings*, p. 65. See also Chapter VI, where Joyce's use of
point of view is discussed.

search for heroics damn vulgar – and yet how are we to describe Ibsen?'[11] This question is an early manifestation of a trait in Joyce that remained with him for the rest of his days: his reluctance to be a member or an alleged member of any literary school and his insistence on his own originality. When Joyce in later years acknowledged any artistic debts, it was to writers whose works were incompatible with his own. It was essential to Joyce's conception of himself as an artist that the fiery enthusiasm of his teens should give way to a more controlled admiration of Ibsen as a man and an artist.

When Joyce began to rewrite his autobiographical novel, a decade had passed since the time when 'the minds of the old Norse poet and of the perturbed young Celt met in a moment of radiant simultaneity'. He told Stanislaus in September 1907 that 'he would omit all the first chapters and begin with Stephen . . . going to school and that he would write the book in five chapters – long chapters.'[12] Joyce was no longer under the spell of Ibsen. His *alter ego* in *Stephen Hero* had been young and whole-hearted: he 'understood that spirit [Ibsen's] instantaneously'; he saw in Ibsen 'the first among the dramatists of the world' and a mind of sublime power and independence. The new Stephen is almost silent on this point, and Ibsen is mentioned only once in *A Portrait:* on his morning walks across the city Stephen would pass Baird's stonecutting works and remember 'the spirit of Ibsen [which] would blow through him like a keen wind, a spirit of wayward boyish beauty' (p. 176). Other authors had challenged Joyce by now. Starting out from Aristotle, he had become engrossed in the possibilities offered by Thomas Aquinas to a young man struggling with aesthetic concepts and practices; his visits to France had reinforced his interest in Flaubert and Balzac; and in all these years he had read widely, as in his teens.[13] He had outlived the naïve candor and hero-worship which make his early account of Ibsen's power so poignant, and he had opened his eyes to the

[11] Quoted from Ellmann, p. 199.
[12] Stanislaus Joyce's diary, quoted by Ellmann, p. 274.
[13] Cf. Ellmann, pp. 115–284, and *passim*.

limitations of the Master. Typical of this attitude is his 1907 lecture on Mangan, in which his comments on Ibsen – 'the destructive and fiercely self-centred tendency of all Henrik Ibsen's works'[14] – combine admiration with reserve.[15] But Ibsen's plays never ceased to impress Joyce. When he saw *Ghosts* in 1908 he was so moved by Osvald's madness that he 'writhed in pain in his seat and made wild gestures.'[16] In 1915 Joyce 'proved' to an Austrian friend that Ibsen was superior to Shakespeare; and a year later he is remembered to have placed Ibsen above Strindberg, about whom he remarked, 'No drama behind the hysterical raving.'[17]

The first indication that Joyce could use Ibsen without imitating him is found in *Dubliners*, the stories of which were written as early as the years 1904–1907. This venture into short-story writing gave Joyce a measure of freedom from Ibsen's demands that the autobiography had not afforded. The epiphanies were a direct result of the 'real life' ideal; for the 'dramatic' ones Joyce inherited from Ibsen a ready-made and detailed technique; and *Stephen Hero* shows us how mechanical and indiscriminate Joyce's insistence on a realistic approach could be within the loose boundaries of a large novel. In *Dubliners* Joyce profits from the mental exercise that the new *genre* necessitated. He had to accommodate his theories to a literary kind in which it was impossible to emulate *Ghosts* or *Pillars of Society* in detail. He could still write about the sordid and the trivial, but the short story forced stricter form and concentration on him.

We should not conclude that Ibsen is left behind. In nearly all his books Joyce hints at the authors he is indebted to. Such built-in acknowledgements are obvious, though sometimes mis-

---

[14] *Critical Writings*, p. 180.
[15] In an alphabetical notebook which he kept at this time, Joyce jotted down under 'Ibsen (Henrik)': 'He seems witty often because his discoveries at such startling angles to applauded beliefs'. Here, too, is approval of Ibsen's approach tinged with reservation, expressed in the slightly ironic 'seems'. James Joyce, Alphabetical Notebook, Item 25 in the Cornell Joyce Collection, Ithaca, N.Y.
[16] Ellmann, p. 275.
[17] *Ibid.*, pp. 410, 425.

leading, in *Ulysses* and *A Portrait,* where Stephen as Joyce's *alter ego* recalls authors that have impressed him; and they provide a major set of keys to an understanding of literary allusions in *Finnegans Wake.* There are fewer hints of this sort in *Dubliners,* but on one occasion Joyce makes clear his allegiance to Ibsen. The reference is oblique, as so often in the later books, but unambiguous. It is found in a story in the 'I'-form, in which the protagonist can easily be associated with the author: in 'An Encounter' the two boys who play truant from school are fascinated by a Norwegian ship on the Liffey, and the boy who narrates the story,

> came back and examined the foreign sailors to see had any of them green eyes, for I had some confused notion. . . . The sailors' eyes were blue, and grey, and even black. The only sailor whose eyes could have been called green was a tall man who amused the crowd on the quay by calling out cheerfully every time the planks fell:
> "All right! All right!"
>
> (*Dubliners,* p. 23)

Obviously, the cheerful tally-man does not fit the 'confused notion'; the boy is looking for a more portentous sailor. This idea of a Norwegian sailor with green eyes and an ominous appearance leads us straight to *The Lady from the Sea,* where there is such a man. The boy cannot be expected to have read Ibsen's play; in him there is only a vague memory of something he may have heard. But through the 'confused notion' of the boy, Joyce can tell some of his readers that *he* has read Ibsen. An intimate greeting of this sort had been given to Ibsen earlier, when Joyce quoted from *When We Dead Awaken* towards the end of his essay on James Clarence Mangan.[18] In both cases the tribute reveals Joyce's feeling of fellowship with Ibsen.

A point which needs to be made as regards the more mature relationship between Joyce and Ibsen in *Dubliners* is found in James R. Baker's 'Ibsen, Joyce, and the Living-Dead: A Study of Dubliners':

[18] *Critical Writings,* p. 83.

Like Ibsen's 'social' dramas, *Dubliners* is an exposé of the para-
lysis of spirit which binds the urban bourgeois. Less obvious, the
basic themes, the structural design, and symbolism of the stories
parallel Ibsen's work in the group of plays beginning with *A
Doll's House* and ending with *When We Dead Awaken*. ... Joyce
finds in it [*When We Dead Awaken*] the embodiment of his own
preoccupations: the problem of the artist's relationship to a spiri-
tually mean society, the penalties of aloofness from the common
stream of life, and, most pertinent for the stories shaping in his
mind, *a comprehensive dramatization of the pitiful failure of men
to awaken from the somnolence which holds them among the
living-dead.*

(My italics.)[19]

Mr Baker quotes Joyce's own words about Professor Rubek,
'there may be lying dormant in him a capacity for greater life,
which may be exercised when he, a dead man, shall have risen
from among the dead', and comments,

... the final portion of Joyce's comments on Rubeck [*sic*] ...
defines with faultless precision the status of the characters in
Dubliners. Most of them are summoned by these words: the boy
of 'The Sisters' and 'Araby,' Eveline, Little Chandler, Maria, Mr.
Duffy, the wardmen of 'Ivy Day in the Committee Room,' and
Gabriel Conroy. Each of these is 'an outcast from life's feast,' a
member of the great host of the living-dead. For Joyce, as for
Ibsen, 'the timeless passions' are 'lying dormant' in these drab
lives. ... Thus the real unity of *Dubliners* derives from the condensed symbolism of Ibsen's last play.[20]

Only when Mr Baker ventures further into Joyce's career does
he stretch his point unduly. *When We Dead Awaken* does not
provide 'for Joyce a neatly condensed version of the symbolic
parable he was to repeat all his life, from *Chamber Music*
through *Finnegans Wake*'.[21] Joyce's view of the living-dead
changed; he came to see that their lives were often not as
'dead' as he had thought; and he made Bloom the hero of

---

[19] *A James Joyce Miscellany*, Third Series, ed. M. Magalaner (Carbondale: Southern Illinois University Press, 1962), pp. 20–21.
[20] *Ibid.*, p. 22.
[21] *Ibid.*, p. 20.

Ulysses, not Stephen who challenges his inert surroundings. Like the characters Joyce so accurately portrays in the short stories, Bloom is a Dubliner; his is not a life of dramatic emotions and wayward individualism. But in *Ulysses* a veil is lifted from this sort of existence; and Joyce presents to his readers the heroism and poetry that can be found in the apparent lifelessness. Joyce never lost sight of the theme and idea of resurrection (which in itself probably owes much more to his Catholic upbringing than to his reading of plays), but he associated it with Ibsen's raising of the living-dead to a new and full life only in *Dubliners* and the two autobiographies. When Ibsen's last play reappears in *Finnegans Wake* to remind us of a life-death-resurrection cycle, the conflict between the heroic artist and his 'dead' surroundings is conspicuously absent.

The beginning of this change in attitude towards the living-dead is glimpsed in *Dubliners*. In 'The Dead' Gabriel Conroy awakens almost according to the pattern Mr Baker outlines, but not quite. He sees that he has been blind to human passions around him, and that life is not only the placid and conventional existence which he has hitherto regarded as all. But in spite of this he does not break with this society which is blind and dormant, and in which he has been unseeing and asleep. Unlike hawk-like Stephen, he accepts it and realizes that he will never be able to shake himself loose from it. The mellowing of the Stephen-versus-the-world conflict (Joyce's version of the Rubek-dead-and-Rubek-come-to-life dichotomy) is evident in the portrait of Gabriel Conroy's wife, too. Gretta Conroy also changes before our eyes on the last pages of the story, but her metamorphosis is of another kind than her husband's; it lies in Gabriel's and our conception of her, not in any development in her own mind: this doll's house has a passive Nora. Up to the climax Gretta has been as lifeless as any of the shadows in the earlier stories. Then suddenly, Gabriel – and we, the readers – see that her passive life has a rich, secret meaning. This moment of revelation marks the beginning of Joyce's acceptance of – and more than that, his liking for – unheroic, small lives. Even social conventions, which had been anathema to him, become

less repulsive: Gabriel and Gretta remain conventional people
without losing their new-won dignity.

In *A Portrait*, which was completed eight years after 'The
Dead', the theme and the main character provide closer parallels with the earliest short stories. In the conflict between the
living artist and his 'living-dead' surroundings there is no
room for a development of the character-portrayal in 'The
Dead'. But we find it again in *Ulysses* – and there at the very
centre of the book: Bloom is an apparently lifeless creature who
proves to have a surprising amount of life and nobility and
grace mixed with sheer triviality. The elusive Mr Earwicker of
Finnegans Wake also belongs to this band of mediocre heroes,
which is a highly original contribution to the character gallery
of twentieth century fiction (and to which I shall return in my
last chapter). Joyce's Stephen had forbears in Ibsen and in
many a *Bildungsroman* and has many a descendant in later
novelists. But Gabriel Conroy-Bloom-Earwicker belong to a
more exclusive group of 'heroes', portrayed with a fine balance
of dignity and paltriness which is not easily imitated.[22]

What is not lost in this development is something from Ibsen
more basic than a symbolic pattern of characters – the convic-
tion that ordinary lives and drab surroundings could contain
'a measure of dramatic life'. For Joyce retained the belief that
trivial life could be used for significant artistic purposes when
he discontinued the practice of jotting down short sketches of
life around him. And even the characters in Ibsen's plays come
to life again in *Ulysses* and *Finnegans Wake*, in which they
play other parts than they did in the short stories. Ibsen is not
associated in Joyce's mind merely with a jejune rebellion
against all conventional values, as Mr Kenner and others seem
to imply.[23] The Norwegian playwright had other parables –
less conspicuous, but still important – to offer to the mature

---

[22] Cf. S. L. Goldberg, *The Classical Temper* (London: Chatto and Windus, 1961), pp. 120 ff.
[23] Cf. Hugh Kenner, *Dublin's Joyce* (London: Chatto and Windus, 1955),
pp. 80–81 and A. Walton Litz, *The Art of James Joyce* (London: Oxford
University Press, 1961), p. 4.

Joyce. Two of these, two sets of symbols, are found also in his early work.

The hero of *Catilina*, Ibsen's first play, which Joyce reviewed in 1903, cries,

> Jeg drømte at, som Ikarus, jeg højt
> opunder himlens hvælv bevinget fløj;
> (Act II)[24]

Joyce's Icarus, Stephen the 'hawklike man',[25] is both inventor and rebel, whereas Catilina is only presented as an idealist in revolt; but in *Love's Comedy* a bird symbol is used with a double meaning very close to that of Stephen's family name. The protagonist is called Falk (Falcon); and he is at once a 'fabulous artificer', as Joyce repeatedly calls Daedalus, and one who alienates himself from his stolid, conventional surroundings. In Ibsen's poems Joyce found even more conspicuous bird symbols. 'Fugl og Fuglefænger' ('Bird and Birdcatcher') presents the poet as a bird who is caged and dies in the attempt to escape. In 'Ederfuglen' ('The Eider-Duck') the image of a bird which is robbed of its down is combined with the idea of exile; and in 'Lysræd' ('Afraid of Light') the poet sees himself as a falcon, and as Icarus:

> Da trodser jeg hav og flammer;
> jeg sejler som falk i sky,
> jeg glemmer angst og jammer –
> til næste morgengry.[26]

Ibsen's symbolic birds are regularly threatened by prosaic powers, by 'the trolls of day' ('Lysræd'); and Joyce makes use of birds in *A Portrait* for the same purpose – to give a picture of art which soars above the snares of the rabblement. Birds are also found as symbols of authority in European literature;

---

[24] 'I dreamt that, like Icarus, I high / Beneath the vault of heaven winged flew.' (From the 1875 version.)
[25] *A Portrait*, p. 169.
[26] 'I reck not of storm and tempest, / Like a falcon in clouds I soar, / And I laugh at fear and sorrow – / Till the morning breaks once more.' R. A. Streatfeild's translation. I have changed his 'eagle' to the correct 'falcon'.

William York Tindall reminds us that they appear as such in the early parts of *A Portrait*.[27] But in the latter half of the novel, where they are given greater prominence, the birds carry symbolic implications similar to those of Ibsen's winged creatures. Stephen watches the birds outside the National Library and sees in their free flight an augury for himself: he will leave the country as they do, he will live a free life, as theirs is:

> What birds were they? He thought that they must be swallows who had come back from the south. Then he was to go away for they were birds ever going and coming, building ever an unlasting home under the eaves of men's houses and ever leaving the homes they had built to wander. (P. 225)

The combination of the Daedalus myth, birds in free flight, and exile is no very original concatenation of thoughts; and Joyce could of course find it elsewhere than in Ibsen. But similarities in the situations in which we find these symbols and in the emotional implications they are made to convey suggest a debt, and not only a parallel.

Another set of images – less common in European literature but more likely to have reached Joyce through literature than through life – has more direct links with Ibsen: the association of artistic inspiration with mountains. The image is first found in 'Drama and Life',[28] which from beginning to end is a tribute to Ibsen; and it is taken up again in *Stephen Hero*, in which Stephen sees himself as an artist (or as a reindeer) on a mountain-ridge and his enemies as sniffing dogs from the lowlands: 'Let the pack of enmities come tumbling and sniffing to my highlands after their game. There was his ground and he flung them disdain from flashing antlers' (pp. 34–35). The same images are used in 'The Holy Office'; and in that poem their parallels in Ibsen are close enough to leave no doubts about Joyce's indebtedness. This particular symbolic image is conspicuously absent from *A Portrait*, in which symbols are more

---

[27] William York Tindall, *A Reader's Guide to James Joyce* (New York: The Noonday Press, 1962), pp. 89–90.
[28] *Critical Writings*, p. 45.

tightly knit into the general texture of the work than in any of Joyce's earlier books. Joyce may simply not have thought of it while he wrote his second novel about Stephen, or he may have left it out consciously as part of his general plan to tune down literary influences on the young artist. But the fact that *Dubliners* and *A Portrait* are richly symbolical brings us back to Ibsen. For the plays of the Norwegian provide the lesson that realism and symbolism can co-exist in a work of art. *The Wild Duck* and *Ghosts* do not violate the rules the realists – or naturalists – set themselves; still, a number of striking symbols emerge from their precise picture of humdrum life. The author of *A Portrait* is much less concerned with the requirements of the naturalistic school; but he, too, wanted to write a book about 'real life'. When symbols, which are few and inconspicuous in *Stephen Hero*, were given such weight in *A Portrait* Joyce had no need to feel – with Ibsen's example before him – that his writing became less realistic. The notes for *Exiles*, written at the same time as the latter half of *A Portrait*, give further evidence that Joyce had noticed Ibsen's attempt to combine the realistic and the symbolic,[29] and that he himself tried to do the same thing. Indeed, as early as in *Dubliners* Joyce succeeds in making a realistic book rich in symbolic implications. In some stories symbol-hunters find game even in inconspicuous details of the narrative.[30]

It is interesting to note that though Joyce had read Arthur Symons's *The Symbolist Movement in Literature*[31] his use of symbols does not follow the principles that Symons lays down. Symons advocates the claims of the French Symbolists at the expense of realism and naturalism: symbolism is

> an attempt to spiritualise literature, to evade the old bondage of rhetoric, the old bondage of exteriority ... We are coming closer to nature, as we seem to shrink from it with something of horror, disdaining to catalogue the trees of the forest. And as we brush

[29] See Ch. V.
[30] Cf. Brewster Ghiselin, 'The Unity of Joyce's "Dubliners"', *Accent*, Vol. 16, No. 2 (Spring 1956), pp. 75–88.
[31] Cf. Ellmann, p. 79.

aside the accidents of daily life, in which men and women imagine that they are alone touching reality, we come closer to humanity, ...

Here, then, in this revolt against exteriority, against rhetoric, against a materialistic tradition; in this endeavour to disengage the ultimate essence, the soul, of whatever exists and can be realised by the consciousness ... literature ... may at last attain liberty, and its authentic speech.[32]

In his reaction against the traditional techniques of storytelling Joyce must have considered the possibilities of this sort of symbolism; and *Chamber Music* can be seen as an attempt in Symons's vein. But from the epiphanies on, Joyce prefers the symbolism that can be expressed in catalogues of 'trees of the forest'. Symbolism is woven into a texture of firm realism as in Ibsen where everyday things like shawls and pipes carry the symbolism without becoming 'spiritualised'. Symons must probably have felt the force of this approach which is so different from that of Verlaine or Maeterlinck, for in a prefatory letter to W. B. Yeats he smuggles Ibsen in by the back door. But Ibsen does not fit the pattern that one can find in the French Symbolists. Both Ibsen and Joyce saw that in art the essence of things could not be dissociated from their appearance, nor human existence described without scrupulous attention to 'the accidents of daily life'.

The formal structure of *A Portrait* may also be seen to reflect Joyce's interest in Ibsen. To write a novel, and especially a *Bildungsroman*, in only five chapters is unusual. Joyce did so, feeling that his first autobiography was too long and formless and spurred by the wish to concentrate and order the huge mass of personal material that he had put into it. This – Joyce's reaction to *Stephen Hero* when he planned *A Portrait* – goes far to explain the conciseness and relative brevity of the latter, but it does not account for its particular structure. When Joyce cast about for a design that could suit his new concept of the auto-

---

[32] Arthur Symons, *The Symbolist Movement in Literature* (London: A. Constable, 1908), pp. 8–9.

biography, memories of a playwright's (which for him primarily meant Ibsen's) devices must have been at the forefront of his mind. He divided it into chapters of roughly the same size and number as acts in a play, and he drew upon the techniques of drama in his writing of each chapter. Important parts of *A Portrait* are written almost exclusively in dialogue. This dialogue is different from the hesitant, allusive speeches Joyce had admired in Ibsen and used in his early epiphanies. The heat and straightforwardness and speed of the discussion between Dante and Mr Casey over the Christmas turkey in *A Portrait* give evidence of the deft way in which Joyce now utilized the *minutiae* of his own life for his artistic purposes rather than of any memories of *Ghosts*. But the very fact that the whole Christmas dinner 'scene' consists of dialogue and 'stage directions' with only few comments by Stephen reflects Joyce's interest in drama. A preoccupation with the relations of drama to other *genres* is also seen in Joyce's notes from 1903–1904 in which he seeks for a formula by which he could incorporate his theories about drama in a more comprehensive system of aesthetics that would include lyric and epic literature as well.[33] Another resemblance to drama, and more specifically to *Peer Gynt*, is found in Father Arnall's sermons. Neither Peer's situation nor the actual words of the clergyman in the play remind one of Chapter III of *A Portrait;* but the function is similar: in both cases the protagonist and the readers (or audience) are placed side by side; both receive the same treatment, so to speak; and thus the reader's identification with the hero is strengthened. In both works the reactions to the sermons are rich in ironic implications. Peer misunderstands the clergyman who could have helped him to a true understanding of his life; Stephen acts on the words of the priest, but these words throw him so violently in the direction of piety that he recoils and comes to rest at what is almost the opposite extreme.

In the second chapter of *A Portrait* Joyce makes important use of retrospection. Stephen's fight with his schoolfellows after he has been accused of heresy is incorporated as a 'flash-back':

[33] Cf. *Critical Writings*, pp. 141–148.

when Heron strikes him jestingly to have him admit that he is in love, Stephen remembers the first time Heron used physical force to extract a confession. We follow Stephen's memories and in the end come back to the incident that started the train of thoughts in the hero. This use of retrospection is scarcely a result of Joyce's interest in the cinema, as J. S. Atherton assumes.[34] The sophisticated film techniques that Eisenstein discusses were developed too late for Joyce to have been able to use them in the early chapters of *A Portrait*. The use of remembered incidents is related to a more general tendency in *A Portrait* and in *Ulysses* to avoid descriptions of violent action. Thus, some of the striking incidents in the *Odyssey* that we expect to see repeated in *Ulysses* play no part in the *action* of Joyce's book, but are present as memories (or as wishes or fears). The phrase 'retrospective arrangement' is used no less than seven times in *Ulysses*,[35] and it sums up at once the way in which the characters of the book conceive of their own lives and the way in which Joyce presents these people to us (these two aspects are, of course, largely indivisible in a stream-of-consciousness novel). There is remarkable similarity here, not only to Ibsen's dramatic technique, but also to the 'retrospective arrangement' of experience by which his characters reach a fuller understanding of themselves. It is not surprising to find that the young Joyce commented on this aspect of Ibsen's art: 'into the comparatively short space of two days the life in life of all his characters [in *When We Dead Awaken*] is compressed.'[36] The review of Ibsen's last play leaves no doubts about Joyce's awareness of the importance of retrospection in Ibsen.

Within the five 'acts' of *A Portrait* we find another practice that undoubtedly can be traced back to Joyce's Dublin days and to his epiphanies, and, if one accepts the origin I have suggested for these prose sketches, partly to Ibsen: incidents – sometimes trivial, sometimes momentous, always rooted in

[34] See James Joyce, *A Portrait of the Artist as a Young Man*, ed. J. S. Atherton (London: Heinemann Educational Books, 1964), p. xv.
[35] See *Ulysses*, pp. 90, 237, 273, 406, 437, 636, and 709.
[36] *Critical Writings*, p. 50.

Joyce's own experience – are made to carry unexpected emotional and thematic weight. The first chapter of *A Portrait* is, like the epiphanies proper, a series of such incidents, only more successful than the early sketches. The impressions from infancy, the illness at Clongowes, the Christmas dinner, and the pandying are foci from which light is shed on Stephen's life as a whole up to his leaving boarding school. The other chapters are not built round isolated incidents to the same extent. They lead the narrative more continuously through Stephen's adolescence and young manhood, and thereby correspond in form to what they express: the growing intellectual agility of the artist in embryo. But there are focal incidents in these chapters too, often in the form of 'purple' passages, pages of poetical prose that doubtlessly owe something to Walter Pater, but which are essentially Joyce's own in their attempt at a dense concentration of themes, symbols, narrative, and characterization. The revelation on the shore on 'a day of dappled seaborne clouds' in the fourth chapter is a good instance of these 'epiphanies' and so is the beginning of the third part of Chapter V where Stephen stands outside the National Library watching the birds.[37]

The word epiphany, as defined either by Joyce's early practice or by his theories in *Stephen Hero,* may be confusing when applied to an analysis of the focal scenes of *A Portrait.* These scenes are epiphanaic in the sense that they reveal important things, most often with considerable stylistic pregnancy, about the hero; but they are not isolated from either a literary or a social tradition, as Joyce seems to have wanted his early sketches to be. Moreover, the epiphanies proper that are incorporated in *A Portrait* do not make up any of the most central incidents, nor do they stand out as different from the rest of the narrative. But one of them is remarkably effective in the context that the book provides for it. Originally a brief sketch of a nightmare,[38] it has absorbed symbols and still more revealing details that

[37] Cf. Harry Levin, *James Joyce: A Critical Introduction* (London: Faber and Faber, 1944), p. 28.

[38] See Item 17, pp. 57–58, in the Cornell Joyce Collection.

enhance its intensity and make it better suited for incorporation in a greater structural whole:

> Creatures were in the field; one, three, six: creatures were moving in the field, hither and thither. Goatish creatures with human faces, hornybrowed, lightly bearded and grey as indiarubber. The malice of evil glittered in their hard eyes, as they moved hither and thither, trailing their long tails behind them. A rictus of cruel malignity lit up greyly their old bony faces. One was clasping about his ribs a torn flannel waistcoat, another complained monotonously as his beard stuck in the tufted weeds. Soft language issued from their spittleless lips as they swished in slow circles round and round the field, winding hither and thither through the weeds, dragging their long tails amid the rattling canisters. They moved in slow circles, circling closer and closer to enclose, to enclose, soft language issuing from their lips, their long swishing tails besmeared with stale shite, thrusting upwards their terrific faces... (Pp. 137–138)

With its deliberate use of ornate cadences, of rhythmic repetitions of the same phrases, and the overtones in 'soft language' and 'swish' – here used about the creatures of hell, otherwise the very words Stephen returns to in his descriptions of his Jesuit masters at school – this dream vision of hell combines 'real life', for it is real enough as Stephen's tormented thoughts, with a stylistic compactness that is foreign to the early epiphanies. Sordid life has been transformed into art, with greater skill now than in the epiphanies proper, but again along the lines that Ibsen had suggested.

IV
STEPHEN

Joyce's early works (with the exception of *Dubliners*) present as their obvious centre of interest a main character who is a young artist. He holds the stage as Stephen Daedalus in *Stephen Hero* and *A Portrait* (in which his surname becomes Dedalus) and in the early parts of *Ulysses*. Richard Rowan in *Exiles* and Shem in *Finnegans Wake* are further studies of the same hero. In *Ulysses* and *Finnegans Wake* the portrait of this youthful artist is greatly modified by the larger context in which he is described, but at least in *Ulysses* there are no radical changes in the character himself.

It is in this hero that earlier critics have found the most conspicuous debts to Ibsen. Hugh Kenner writes:

> The five chapters of *A Portrait of the Artist as a Young Man* constitute a rewriting of the five acts of *Brand* with infinitely greater local sensitivity and within a richly nourished milieu of classical ethics. It is from Brand that many of the most humorlessly arrogant gestures of Stephen Dedalus are derived: his behavior at his mother's deathbed, his rejection of the Christianity of the clergy, his romantic positives expressed in terms of 'the spell of arms and voices' and of 'exultant and terrible youth,' corresponding to Ibsen's 'flashing eye' and his dawn above the ice-fields.[1]

Mrs Macleod, too, finds similarities to *Brand:*

> And in these type-situations – the hero (superior individual) against the demeaning influence of society; the 'ideal' as against the claims of human, sexual love; the old values against the new (mother against son) – the demands of Brand's ethical slogan always seem to legislate for cruel, loveless, deprivatory action. Brand, in his first meeting with his mother on his return home, states the conflict clearly:

[1] 'Joyce and Ibsen's Naturalism', *Sewanee Review*, Vol. 59, No. 1 (Winter 1951), p. 89.

A child's a steward, you suppose,
Of the parental cast-off clothes;
You've been no mother, I no son.

And the bargain he would make with her, flowing from the 'All or Nothing' touchstone, is strangely like the implied alternative Stephen offers his mother in *A Portrait of the Artist as a Young Man,* ...[2]

The similarities are certainly there; but a closer analysis of Joyce's portrait of Stephen is required to determine whether the parallels are the results of any influence from Ibsen.

Stephen's attitude to his mother country is, of course, ambivalent: 'Ireland is the old sow that eats her farrow' (*A Portrait,* p. 203); but at the same time Stephen is genuinely concerned about her: when he leaves Ireland, it is to 'forge in the smithy of my soul the uncreated conscience of my race' (p. 253). What the editors of Joyce's *Critical Writings* say about one of his Triestine lectures on Ireland, delivered at the time when he worked on *A Portrait,* is equally true about Stephen: 'His attitude ... wavers between affectionate fascination with Ireland and distrust of her.'[3] Stephen's feelings towards Ireland reach a climax in *A Portrait* where the artist versus the various claims of his country emerges as an important theme after Stephen has gone through his initiation on the seashore. Then, busily casting off all conventional values, he feels free to scorn Irish nationalism too; it is against this general reorientation that his satirical words on 'rebellion with hurleysticks' and ' Long pace, fianna! Right incline, fianna!' (p. 202) must be placed. They stem as much from a general fear of all importunating isms as from a specific dislike of anti-English activities in Ireland.

Stephen reflects his creator more accurately here than in most other matters in the book, I think. For Joyce had re-experienced what he writes about at the end of *A Portrait* – his disappointment in Ireland and his departure for the Continent

[2] Vivienne Koch Macleod, 'The Influence of Ibsen on Joyce', *PMLA,* Vol. 60, No. 3 (September 1945), p. 886.
[3] *Critical Writings,* p. 153.

– a short time before he composed Chapter V of the autobiography. With warmer feelings towards his country than he had
nursed for years he had gone to Ireland on three successive
visits (twice in 1909 and then in 1912) only to find what he had
felt more vaguely in 1904: Ireland tried to strangle him; to
Joyce she was the same 'sow' in 1912. Again he took refuge in
'exile, and cunning', though not in 'silence'.[4] He gave vent to
his disappointment in the final chapter of *A Portrait;* and just
as he had written the broadside 'The Holy Office' when he left
his country in 1904 he wrote a fiery poem when he left Ireland
for good in 1912, 'Gas from a Burner'.

The earlier of these poems demonstrates how Joyce, in his
search for words to describe the attitude which is so conspicuous in *A Portrait*, made use of Ibsen. After a description of the
poet as the scapegoat of Ireland, and more especially of the
Irish literary movement, Joyce openly strikes the proud attitude
that is implied in the whole poem: he stands

> self-doomed, unafraid,
> Unfellowed, friendless and alone,
> Indifferent as the herring-bone,
> Firm as the mountain-ridges where
> I flash my antlers on the air.[5]

Two expressions in this poem come from other writings by
Joyce where Ibsen figures. The lines 'every true-born mysti-
cist / A Dante is, unprejudiced' stem from his review of *Catilina;*[6] and the flashing antlers derive from a passage in *Stephen
Hero* where impulses are described that some pages later in the
book are shown to have come from Ibsen.[7] Earlier, in 'Drama
and Life', Joyce had used a related image: he imagines himself
standing 'on the mountains', alpenstock in hand.[8] The alpenstock may have come to Joyce from the first copy he had of
The Masterbuilder, on the cover of which Hilde Wangel was

---

4 Cf. *A Portrait*, p. 247.
5 *Critical Writings*, p. 152.
6 *Ibid.*, p. 101.
7 See *Stephen Hero*, p. 35.
8 *Critical Writings*, p. 45.

drawn with one in her hand.[9] Its reappearance in *Finnegans Wake* (p. 85, 1. 11), with conspicuous sexual connotations, may also hide a reference to Ibsen's play. This vision of the artist alone on the mountain-ridge is so close to Ibsen's portrait of his *alter ego* in 'På Vidderne' ('On the Fells') that one can, with Hugh Kenner, speak of influence, not only of similarities.[10] Joyce has taken over from Ibsen a set of images in which he could clothe his attitude. Ibsen's 'I' looks down into the valley:

> jeg holdt for øjet den hule hånd
> til vinding for perspektivet[11]

and down below he sees the many-coloured wedding-party on their way to church:

> De flagrende skaut, det skinnende lin,
> og mændenes kofter røde,
> . . .[12]

Joyce gives his hero a similar vision and similar words:

> So distantly I turn to view
> The shamblings of that motley crew,
> Those souls that hate the strength that mine has
> Steeled in the school of old Aquinas.

There is the same opposition between the lonely man on the ridge and the vulgar, gaudy crowd below in both poems. And the will of the hero is steeled in Ibsen's poem too:

> Nu er jeg stålsat, jeg følger det bud,
> der byder i højden at vandre![13]

Even a detail like the antlers has probably come from 'På Vidderne' where the hero and *his* Aquinas, the enigmatic rifleman,

---

[9] Cf. Stanislaus Joyce, *My Brother's Keeper* (London: Faber and Faber, 1958), pp. 98–99.

[10] Cf. Hugh Kenner, *op. cit.*, pp. 84–86.

[11] 'I held to my eye my hollowed hand / To get the perspective right.' (F. E. Garrett's translation.)

[12] 'The fluttering snoods, the linen fine / And the men in their jackets red, / . . .' (Garrett's translation.)

[13] 'Now I am steeled; I follow that call / That bids me range the heights.'

go reindeer-hunting. The first time Joyce used this image was in the sketch called 'A Portrait of the Artist' which he offered to the Irish periodical *Dana* in Januar 1904,[14] a time when his adulation of Ibsen was still in its first vigour.

Another Ibsen-poem offers an equally striking resemblance. In his embittered greetings to Norway in 1872 Ibsen says:

> Mit folk, som skænkte mig i dybe skåler
> den sunde, bittre styrkedrik, hvoraf
> som digter jeg, på randen af min grav,
> tog kraft til kamp i døgnets brudte stråler, –
> mit folk, som rakte mig den landflugts-stav,
> den sorgens byldt, de angstens rappe såler,
> det tunge alvors-udstyr til min færden, –
> dig sender jeg en hilsen hjem fra verden!
>
> Jeg sender den med tak for alle gaver,
> med tak for hver en smærtens luttrings-stund.[15]
>
> . . .
>
> ('Ved tusenårs-festen den 18de Juli 1872')

Here are the Katharsis and the chain of painful incidents, as well as the exile, that are implied in 'The Holy Office'. Norway drove Ibsen away: his people gave him his 'landflugtsstav'; and in the concluding couplet of *his* poem Joyce protests that the Irish 'spurn me from their door.' 'The Holy Office' is violent in sentiment and slipshod in execution; but its reaction to Ireland is basically the same as that of the later and very carefully written *Portrait*, though with some difference: what Joyce praised in his review of *When We Dead Awaken* – 'Ibsen's power over two generations has been enhanced by his own reticence. Seldom, if at all, has he condescended to join battle with his enemies' – has gone into the making of Stephen, while it did not bring Stephen's creator to silence.

[14] See M. Kain and Robert E. Scholes, 'The First Version of Joyce's "Portrait"', *The Yale Review*, Vol. 49, No. 3 (March 1960), p. 361.

[15] 'My people who served me in deep bowls / The healthy, bitter cordial from which / As a poet, on the brink of my grave, / I gained strength to fight in the day's broken rays, – / My people who handed me that staff of exile, / That bundle of sorrow, those fleet soles of fear, / That heavy, serious gear for my journey, – / To you I send a greeting from the world. / I send it with thanks for all your gifts, / With thanks for every purifying pain.'

In *A Portrait* Joyce has been careful to make his protagonist's feelings towards Ireland an organic part of a greater fictional whole. Stephen's attitude to his mother country is presented as an integral part of his personality. He turns away from the Irish movement in disgust for idealistic reasons, but also because his Emma coquets with Father Moran who is enthusiastic about it. Ibsen had also recognized the power of slighted love over one's feelings for a country or a community. When the protagonist of 'På Vidderne' finally leaves the tepid life of the valley behind, he does so fortified by his last view down from the ridge: he has seen his girl's wedding to another. As in *A Portrait* disappointment in a romantic, non-realized love and a general feeling of suffocation combine to turn the artist into an exile.

Stephen's uneasiness is further enhanced by the betrayals that seem to lurk everywhere in Irish politics. He says to Davin, 'When you make the next rebellion with hurleysticks . . . and want the indispensable informer, tell me. I can find you a few in this college' (p. 202). The same idea – of a people that is given to proliferating political factions – obsessed Ibsen who sent his greetings home at a time when,

> . . . hjemmets liv et tvesyn slutter inde:
> et folk, som kløver sig i spredtheds splid –
> og flokker sig om samlings-tankens minde.[16]
> ('Ved tusenårs-festen den 18de Juli 1872')

And Ibsen could no more than Joyce help feeling for his divided and treacherous country. The poem ends on a vision of a Norway that has had its 'uncreated conscience' forged, not in the smithy of an artist, but by the exertion of its own willpower.

The conversation between Emma and Father Moran, which is given such emphasis in *A Portrait*, is about one aspect of the Irish movement – the revival of Gaelic. Stephen pours scorn over the cause and the conversation. He is fascinated by Eng-

---

[16] '. . . life at home frames in a double vision: / A people which splits up into straggling factions / And gathers to commemorate the idea of unity.'

lish, which he likes to think of as *his* language as much as that of the English. The fact that 'tundish', which Stephen used and the English Dean of Studies did not know, is another *English* word for 'funnel' makes him remark about the Dean, 'Damn the dean of studies and his funnel! What did he come here for to teach us his own language or to learn it from us?' (P. 251). Mrs Macleod suggests a debt to *Peer Gynt*[17] where Huhu, the mad language reformer, has this to say on the question of a native language versus that of the conqueror:

> Portugiser og Hollænder
> Landet med Kultur bespænder.
> Desforuden boer der Skarer
> af de ægte Malebarer.
> Disse Folk har Sproget blandet; –
> de er Herrer nu i Landet. –
> Men i Tiden længst forgangen
> raaded der Orangutangen.
>
> . . .
> Ak, men saa kom Fremmedaaget
> og forplumret Urskogs-Sproget.
>
> . . .
> Skogen Urlyd er forstummet;
> ikke længer blir der brummet; –
>
> . . .
> Jeg har prøvet paa at fægte
> for vort Urskogs-Maal, det ægte, –
> prøvet at belive Liget, –
> hævdet Folkets Rett till Skriget, –
> skreget selv og paavist Trangen
> til dets Brug i Folkesangen. –
> (*Peer Gynt*, Act IV)[18]

[17] Vivienne Kock Macleod, *op. cit.,* p. 881.
[18] Hollanders and Portugueses [*sic*]
compass all the land with culture.
There, moreover, swarms are dwelling
of the pure-bred Malabaris.
These have muddled up the language,
they now lord it in the country. –
But in long-departed ages
there the orang-outang was ruler.

. . .
Ah, but then the foreign yoke came,
marred the forest-tongue primeval.
(Cont.d.)

Certainly, this bantering satire on the *landsmål* movement in Norway must have delighted Joyce the Irishman; and he cannot have missed the close resemblance between it and the Gaelic movement. But there are, strangely enough, no references, direct or indirect, to this spirited extravaganza from *Peer Gynt* in *A Portrait,* where Stephen's dislike of linguistic puritanism is not represented as stemming from an awareness of its grotesque results or its impracticability.

Indeed, the forces that led Stephen to denounce and leave Ireland, Irish nationalism, and Gaelic are presented as coming exclusively from his experience of life, not literature. He noticed the parochial submissiveness of his fellow-students and was repelled: his peasant friend Davin

> stood towards this myth [Irish mythology] upon which no individual mind had ever drawn out a line of beauty and to its unwieldy tales that divided themselves as they moved down the cycles in the same attitude as towards the Roman catholic religion, the attitude of a dullwitted loyal serf. Whatsoever of thought or of feeling came to him from England or by way of English culture his mind stood armed against in obedience to a password... (p.181)

Stephen saw friends with greater physical vigour and social adaptability than his own take up an Irish nationalist programme, and he turned away partly in envy and partly in a mood of rational criticism. In *A Portrait* he moves among boys and fellow-students who are more boisterous and keener at wild play and games than he is; and he comes to associate 'rude bodily skill', 'Michael Cusack, the Gael', 'grossness of intelligence', 'bluntness of feeling' and 'a dull stare of terror' with his mother country (p. 180).

> (Cont.d.)
> Mute are now the wood-notes primal;
> grunts and growls are heard no longer; –
> . . .
> I have tried to fight the battle
> of our real, primal wood-speech, –
> tried to bring to life its carcass, –
> proved the people's right of shrieking, –
> shrieked myself, and shown the need of
> shrieks in poems for the people. –
> (William and Charles Archer's translation.)

Ibsen had felt himself in a similar opposition to his contemporaries; and Joyce may have known this. But Richard Ellmann makes it abundantly clear that Joyce drew upon his own life rather than his reading when he developed Stephen's attitude to Ireland. Davin, MacCann and the other students that Stephen cannot stomach had their counterparts in University College; and what Emma contributes to Stephen's development corresponds to what – *mutatis mutandis* – Joyce found in his infatuation with Mary Sheehy.[19]

It is equally difficult to find any decisive influence from Ibsen on Stephen's break with the Roman Catholic Church. There is nothing in *A Portrait* to indicate that he was driven to any active anti-clericalism by Ibsen. In *Brand* Ibsen *is* very critical of the established church and makes a point of showing the discrepancy between a clergy that compromises in all matters and the 'All or Nothing' call of the Gospel. But this gap between church theory and church practice, to which Søren Kierkegaard so urgently called the attention of his Scandinavian contemporaries, is never stressed in *A Portrait* and *Stephen Hero*. Taken in a wider sense as a condemnation of all half-heartedness, Kierkegaard's 'All or Nothing' is akin to Joyce's and Stephen's early ideas; but that Joyce was uncompromising and made Stephen uncompromising does not prove any literary influence. It is often in the nature of youth to be consistent; and Stephen is headstrong enough to be so without the reminder from Kierkegaard through *Brand*. Since Stephen so definitely seems to incorporate the important elements of Joyce's own development, we may ask whether Ibsen might have been responsible for *Joyce's*, and thus indirectly for Stephen's attitude to Christianity. However, if the chronology of events that I have outlined in Chapter II is correct, the answer is a definite no. Joyce shook off his allegiance to the Roman Catholic Church first, and then encountered Ibsen in his search for new bearings.

The happiest hunting-ground for critics in search of Ibsen-influence has been another side of Stephen's personality, his

---

[19] Cf. Ellmann, pp. 52–53, 62–66.

attitude to his family, and in particular to his mother. Both Hugh Kenner and V. K. Macleod see it as a result of Joyce's interest in the Norwegian dramatist. Some of the parallels in *Brand* and *Peer Gynt* are indeed highly conspicuous; they should, however, be examined in some detail; for only after an examination of the closeness of the parallels is a discussion of the question of influence possible.

The death-bed scenes in *Brand* and *Peer Gynt* on the one hand and in Stephen's life on the other offer themselves as a natural starting-point. As she lies dying, Mother Åse weakly asks Peer to fetch her a collection of sermons; Mrs Dedalus repeatedly and earnestly tries to lead or lure Stephen back into the Church. And Peer disobeys because, instinctively and by habit, he recoils from a hard fact like death:

> Nej, nu vil vi sammen snakke, –
> men bare om løst og fast, –
> og glemme det vrange og skakke,
> og alt, som er saart og hvasst. –
> *(Peer Gynt*, Act III)[20]

Stephen faces the challenge without flinching and chooses his own way with no thoughts of evasion, as Buck Mulligan makes it perfectly clear: 'But to think of your mother begging you with her last breath to kneel down and pray for her. And you refused. There is something sinister in you' (*Ulysses*, p. 7).

The vehemence and rigour of Stephen's attitude to his dying mother resemble that of the protagonist in the earlier and more severe Ibsen play, *Brand*. Brand, who is the vicar and only clergyman in a secluded little fjord community, sternly refuses to see his miserly mother until she gives her wealth away; and as he is not satisfied that she is willing to sacrifice everything, they are not reconciled; she dies without the comfort her son might have brought her. In this rigour that borders on weak-

---

[20] Nay, now we'll just sit and chatter,
But only of that and this;
Forget there's aught sore the matter,
And all that is sad and amiss.
(F. E. Garrett's translation.)

ness, Stephen and Brand, who are opposites in many ways, meet. But the moral and philosophical considerations with which Joyce decks out Stephen's behaviour are not reminiscent of *Brand*. Stephen is on his guard to defend his individuality and acts accordingly; Brand, on the other hand, is concerned with the ideal of complete renunciation and the All or Nothing call which he finds in his religion. He wants the individual to yield to the ideal. Nor is there any point by point similarity between Mrs Dedalus and the mothers in Ibsen's plays; Stephen's mother is not depicted as a Dublin descendant of Mother Åse, nor of the dying Mrs Brand. But – and this is typical of the use Joyce makes of Ibsen – her *function* is similar to that of many Ibsen characters; she is a reproachful voice from the dead speaking to the living in a way strikingly similar to the one in which Ibsen makes use of Mrs Rosmer, Irene in *When We Dead Awaken*, and the sailor in *The Lady from the Sea*.

Mr Dedalus offers similarities that are equally striking (and intriguing) to Peer Gynt's father. In *Stephen Hero* and *A Portrait* he is a reckless and feckless father and husband, an ageing man who is 'a praiser of his own past' (*A Portrait*, p. 241), and whose sullenness makes the home more unhappy than it need be. In *Ulysses* he is seen at Dignam's funeral with his own generation, and through Bloom's observant and forgiving mind. This portrait is far more pleasant than that of the autobiographical novels: Simon Dedalus has a poise and a *savoir vivre* that impress his friends and give him some dignity. The artist's father in *Exiles*, clearly related to Mr Dedalus of the novels, is almost ideal, 'smiling', 'handsome', liberal in his tastes, and never insistent as a parent.[21] Jon Gynt, Peer's father, was also a boon companion, a lover of ways too expensive for him, and the ruin of his family. And like Simon Dedalus, he is seen from two points of view: as a social success and as a failure at home. But the similarities stop here, for in *Peer Gynt* this man serves as a clear-cut moral warning to the son, whereas in Joyce he is a character with a much more complex moral nature and moral

[21] See *Exiles*, p. 29.

function. Mr Dedalus lacks the dedication that is a supreme
virtue in the son, but at least in one respect, in the liberty he
allows Stephen in *Ulysses*, he is preferable to most of the Dublin characters that surround the young artist. Moreover, he is
very much a live character in Joyce, a man who takes part in
the action of the book and who has surprises in store for the
reader, whereas Jon Gynt, dead long before the first act of
Peer Gynt, is a remembered character.

The parallels between Stephen's father and mother and the
families in *Peer Gynt* and *Brand* are striking, but never exact;
there are not any simple and indisputable borrowings in the
character-gallery of *A Portrait*. Indeed, all the traits in Joyce's
young hero that remind one of the Norwegian dramatist are
indivisible parts of his whole character. As he is presented to
us, Stephen is whole and consistent and he cannot be divided
into an essential core that is purely Joycean on the one hand
and traits patched on from literary predecessors on the other.
Stephen himself thinks that Ibsen is 'like a keen wind, a spirit
of wayward boyish beauty' (*A Portrait*, p. 176), and this is
clearly an acknowledgement of the independence and vigour
and freshness that Stephen finds in the Norwegian. But the
other significant reference that Stephen makes to Ibsen is to his
art, his realism,[22] and Stephen's attitude to his family is never
described as stemming from modern authors that he had read.
Seen against the portrait of Stephen that emerges from all three
books in which he figures, the mention of the spirit of Ibsen
cannot be taken as an indication that Stephen thinks that he has
been decisively influenced in his reaction against his mother by
Ibsen. Ibsen's is a confirming example, but he is not a prime
mover in the liberating process that Stephen goes through.

We may proceed to ask, not how Stephen's reactions are
accounted for within the autobiographical novels, but what
made Joyce include the incidents between Stephen and his
mother in this story about the growth of an artist. Criticism
written before the appearance of Ellmann's biography natur-

---

[22] See *Stephen Hero*, pp. 40–41, and cf. my discussion pp. 42–44.

ally tended to stress the fact that Joyce found similar stories
and incidents in earlier literature, and in particular in Ibsen.
Ellmann's *James Joyce,* however, showed that Joyce had utilized incidents from his own life to an extent which exceeded
all earlier guesses. The parallels between Stephen and Peer
Gynt or Brand can now be shown to be relevant to a discussion
of Ibsen's influence only on the assumption that Joyce modelled
not only Stephen, but his own life on the examples found in
Ibsen's early plays. Hugh Kenner holds that Stephen's attitude
to his dying mother derives from Brand;[23] but Ellmann's research into Joyce's adolesence and young manhood makes it
clear that it is Joyce's experience of life, not of literature, that
gives him the outlines and most of the details that he transforms and transfers to the portrait of Stephen. When he was
twenty-one James Joyce had himself refused to kneel down by
the bed of his unconscious mother and pray for her; and he had
not let himself be persuaded to take communion for her sake
and his own, as she wished.[24] Similarly, Stephen's 'rejection of
the Christianity of the clergy,' which Kenner sees as coming
directly from Brand,[25] is more naturally accounted for by reference to *Joyce's* rejection of Christianity and its priests.

It was his own story and his own ambition that Joyce made
the centre of his early novels; and he did not need much support
from *Peer Gynt* and *Brand* (or *Love's Comedy*) to find it a
worth-while subject. Like the rest of us, Joyce was apt to find
little, if anything, more intrinsically interesting than his own
life-story. In Chapter II I have discussed the question of Ibsen's
influence on Joyce's early life, and the conclusion may be re-
stated here: Ibsen did not make Joyce a writer, but he confirmed
him in his choice of a career and a way of life, and he suggested
to him two useful principles – 'life – real life' as subject-matter,
and an authorial attitude that Joyce calls 'the classical temper'.
Ibsen also helped Joyce the writer in other ways by the ex-

---

[23] 'Joyce and Ibsen's Naturalism,' *Sewanee Review,* Vol. 59, No. 1 (Winter 1951), p. 89.
[24] Ellmann, pp. 134, 141.
[25] Kenner, *op. cit.,* p. 89.

amples of literary art and craft that his plays offered. Joyce's *art* is indubitably indebted to Ibsen, but Joyce's behaviour as a son, a Roman Catholic, and an Irishman can more easily be explained by reference to his immediate surroundings. To say that 'the first three decades (roughly) of Joyce's life were subtly and pervasively, consciously and unconsciously, modeled along the central lines of Ibsen's own biography'[26] is to imply the existence of decisive impulses from Ibsen on the whole of Joyce's life of which there are proofs neither in Joyce's own writings, nor in our present knowledge of his biography. Stephen's reactions against his home, Church, and country are described as prompted by life rather than books; and there are no signs that this does not obtain in the case of Joyce's development, too. I think Mr Graham Greene is right in saying that in adolescence we are past the time when books can easily change the course of our lives:

> Perhaps it is only in childhood that books have any deep influence on our lives. In later life we admire, we are entertained, we may modify some view we already hold, but we are more likely to find in books merely a confirmation of what is in our minds already . . .[27]

The reading of literature can, however, make us more articulate about, and perhaps improve our understanding of, the motivating forces in our minds. There is no doubt, I think, that Ibsen's life and his plays gave Joyce a more vivid understanding of his young life than he had had before he came across the Norwegian. And Joyce's reading of Ibsen probably suggested answers to the question he must have asked himself continually while he was writing about his *alter ego:* What in my stock of experiences is significant and worth incorporating in a novel? From Ellmann's biography it may seem as if Joyce put most of the crucial incidents of his early life into *A Portrait* and *Ulysses;* but it is useful to remember that Ellmann's eminent book is

[26] Vivienne Kock Macleod, 'The Influence of Ibsen on Joyce', *PMLA*, Vol. 60, No. 3 (September 1945), p. 879.
[27] *The Lost Childhood and Other Essays* (London: Eyre and Spottiswoode, 1951), p. 13.

very much a portrait of the artist. The biographer has asked the questions that the novels suggest and given most attention and space to the biographical counterparts to the characters and incidents in Joyce's fiction. This is, of course, no fault in the biography; on the contrary, Ellmann's is a rewarding principle. But it has the side-effect that the portion of Joyce's life that did not provide characters and incidents for his fiction is made to seem less important than it may actually have been. There must have been wide areas of Joyce's life that we do not know about because he did not explore them in his portrait of Stephen, and therefore did not leave clues that biographers can work on. The process in which the personal material was sifted must have been considerably more radical than it will seem from either Gorman's or Ellmann's biography. And Ibsen probably influenced this process in two ways: his early plays offered an interpretation of Joyce's personal history, and they could suggest what sort of incidents he could use in his fiction. Deaths in the family, the individual against a compact majority of mediocrities, moments of day-dreaming – these are all found as highly effective scenes in *Brand* and/or *Peer Gynt*. Joyce puts similar things into his novels; and Ibsen's example must have strengthened his belief that these incidents could be made parts of a work of art.

Stephen is not simply a character in *A Portrait*, he is also the exponent of the view of life that informs the book. This philosophy is similar in a number of ways to that which emerges from some of Ibsen's early plays. Falk in *Love's Comedy* has a fervent wish to be nobody's servant; and Peer boasts in the fourth act of *Peer Gynt* that he has been himself all his life, has known no limits to his self-realization. The phrase 'at være sig selv' – 'to be oneself' – rings through all the acts of *Peer Gynt*, and Stephen echoes it in his conversation with Cranly. His friend asks him whether he was happier as a schoolboy when he still believed in the Roman Catholic faith, and he answers:

– Often happy . . . and often unhappy. I was someone else then.
– How someone else? What do you mean by that statement?

– I mean, said Stephen, that I was not myself as I am now, as I had to become. (P. 240)

In the same conversation Stephen says about his mother:

– . . . She wishes me to make my easter duty.
– And will you?
– I will not, Stephen said.
– Why not? Cranly said.
– I will not serve, answered Stephen.
– That remark was made before, Cranly said calmly. (P. 239)

Though there is something histrionic in the attitude Stephen strikes, his *non serviam* is no empty boast. The whole book builds up to this moment when Stephen utters his credo. We have witnessed his break with the Church, with his fellow students, with Emma who represents domesticity and sentimental love, and finally with his mother, and we are in no doubt about Stephen's honesty when he solemnly states that he will not serve and that he will be himself.

Stephen believes that his idea of freedom is possible, and also that it can serve as a moral ideal, that it is right. Neither Falk nor Peer Gynt arrives at this reassuring faith in freedom. Falk comes nearest to it in that he believes in the rightness of his choice of an artist's free life to the end, but he realizes that his freedom is impossible in society. His departure is symbolic: he leaves the town as one of a group of student singers who are on their way to the mountains. There, in the uninhabited regions of Norway, he will find room for his freedom, but not in the town that he leaves behind. Peer Gynt realizes in the end that the unrestricted liberty he has sought is impossible. He is enmeshed again and again; and, what is more important, he understands that he has been trapped by his own idea of freedom. For him 'at være sig selv' has meant 'at være sig selv nok' – 'to be enough unto oneself'. His freedom has been a cultivation of the self and an indulgence in his own wishes with little or no regard for those whom this sort of freedom might hurt, or those who might have needed his help. And this selfishness has made him a hollow man. In the end the Buttonmoulder explains to Peer what it really means to be oneself:

At være sig selv, er: sig selv at døde.
Dog, paa dig er sagtens den Forklaring spildt;
og derfor, lad det kaldes: overalt at møde
med Mesters Mening till Udhængsskilt.[28]

In this scene Ibsen sets the question of identity firmly in a Christian framework. Man is himself when he 'slays' himself, or, in the words of St. John, 'Except a corn of wheat fall into the ground and die, it abideth alone: but if it die, it bringeth forth much fruit.' Peer's whole history up to the moment when he meets the Buttonmoulder endorses the view that in order to be himself Peer should have presented himself everywhere with his Creator's intention 'displayed like a signboard'.

As in *A Portrait*, there is a greater respect in Ibsen for the man who breaks out in search of freedom than for ordinary people. But the balanced account in *Peer Gynt* of the moral and practical situation of the hero who wants to achieve his freedom is not paralleled in Joyce's portrait of Stephen. The most obvious reading of *A Portrait* is one that finds the book a defiant defence of the artist-hero and an approval of an almost unlimited individualism, derived, according to Hugh Kenner, from Ibsen: 'All Joyce's ruthless honesty didn't dispose of the Ibsenite temptation to be as a god until the writing of *Exiles* in 1914.'[29] On the other hand, since *A Portrait* insists all the time on Stephen's right to be himself – fully and freely – and since it dismisses so perfunctorily the values one might expect to find in Stephen's surroundings, it invites a question that it never asks openly: is not Stephen himself more ridiculous, more limited in his understanding of life, and more doctrinaire than the people around him, and at least as cruel? Support for this reading may perhaps be found in the fact that Stephen's family name is now Dedalus, a name which puns on 'dead'.[30] This

[28] To be oneself is: to slay oneself.
But on you that answer is doubtless lost;
and therefore we'll say: to stand forth everywhere
with Master's intention displayed like a signboard.
(William and Charles Archer's translation.)
[29] *Dublin's Joyce* (London: Chatto and Windus, 1955), p. 39.
[30] See *ibid.*, p. 38.

interpretation seems to me, however, to read the more comprehensive irony of *Ulysses* into an earlier novel in which it does
not make sense. This reading makes *A Portrait* a poorer novel
than it need be in that it sees the book as a slick and total denunciation of all human values – those of society in general through
Stephen, and those of the artist-individual in Stephen. It is possible to find a less categorical discussion of life in the novel
when Stephen is looked upon as a prig and a *poseur*, but still
essentially right in his dedication. This reading mellows the
portrait of the artist as a young man, he is not simply glorified;
but the unqualified denunciation of all other people in the book
remains a disturbing element.

In *Ulysses*, on the other hand, we follow the thoughts of both
Stephen and Bloom – the artist and the citizen. The point of
view shifts from Stephen to Bloom, neither is described solely
through the eyes of the other. Therefore they affect us in much
the same way. Both can irritate and both can be moving, because they share a common humanity and are presented to us
with equal immediacy. However ludicrous, they are engagingly
human in their sufferings and their hopes. It is against a sympathetic presentation of this kind that they are shown to be con-
ceited, small, and ridiculous – Bloom in his lazy and acquiescent
life as husband and citizen, Stephen in his seemingly ineffectual
revolt.

What Hugh Kenner does not mention is the fact that this is a
presentation of the questions of freedom, art, and integrity
which comes very close to Ibsen's manner in *Peer Gynt*. For
Stephen and Peer alike, 'to be oneself' is a dangerous principle
in that it may lead to the way of life that Ibsen calls 'to be
enough unto oneself'; and, conversely, Bloom and the other
characters in *Ulysses* and *Peer Gynt* who do not break out are
shown to be marked, and even crippled, by their captivity.
Moreover, Peer is no real artist and no moral paragon; in a
great many respects he is presented as Everyman. As early as
in 1907, when he first thought of writing a story about a Jew
who should be a Dublin Peer Gynt,[31] Joyce must have realized

[31] See Ellmann, pp. 274–275.

that Ibsen's play could provide a pattern for an examination of life from another point of view than that of Stephen alone. We shall see in the following chapters that Joyce's understanding of Ibsen kept pace with – and aided – the development in his *Weltanschauung* from a relatively naïve glorification of the isolated artist to a richly ironic account of the virtues and shortcomings of artist and citizen alike.

V

EXILES

In appearance *Exiles* is like one of Ibsen's realistic dramas from beginning to end. Joyce's stage-directions begin, as if copied from *A Doll's House* or *An Enemy of the People,* with a minute description of the drawing-room; then follows, in a new paragraph, a sketch of the persons we see on the stage. Throughout the play stage-directions are frequent, often in the form of an adverb to indicate the tone of a speech. Words like 'heartily' or 'shyly' are used as often in *Exiles* as in *The Masterbuilder.* Behind these outer resemblances lies the fact that, like Ibsen, Joyce deliberately chose the present time and the ordinary parlour as the setting for his drama. In his articles on Ibsen's plays Joyce had praised the Norwegian dramatist for his courage to put life – real life – on the stage, without the conventions or embellishments that had often served to veil reality. And this is Joyce's aim, just as in a grim, reformist way it was John Galsworthy's in the plays which he wrote at the time. No purple passages, no farce, no extravagant characters were admitted. *Exiles* was to be a realistic play.

But the notes[1] which Joyce made while he was working on *Exiles* show us that realism was not his only aim. In the notes Bertha is more of a symbol than a real person. She is compared

[1] These notes were first published in the 1952 edition of the play. Their fate is traced by Magalaner and Kain:
'The notes . . . were found among Joyce's effects in Paris after the liberation. On his departure to the south of France in 1940, Joyce entrusted his books, manuscripts, and personal papers to his close friend and volunteer amanuensis, Paul Léon. Despite the tragic death of M. Léon in a concentration camp, most of the materials were preserved. . . . The books and manuscripts were displayed at the La Hune exhibit in Paris in 1949, and a year later the entire collection was sold to the University of Buffalo Library.'
M. Magalaner and R. Kain, *Joyce: The Man, the Work, the Reputation* (N.Y.: New York Univ. Press, 1956), p. 139.

to the moon – her age is twenty-eight, the number of days in a lunar (and menstrual) cycle – and to the earth: 'She is the earth, dark, formless, mother, made beautiful by the moonlit night, darkly conscious of her instincts' (p. 167). As in *Dubliners* and *A Portrait* Joyce wants to transcend the rigid realism for which he praised the old playwright in 1900. This attempt may in itself testify to an influence – not from Ibsen the realist, but Ibsen the symbolist. In 1914 Joyce is consciously aware of these other qualities in the Norwegian: in the notes he mentions 'the Scandinavian women (Hedda Gabler, Rebecca Rosmer [*sic*], Asta Allmers) whom the poetic genius of Ibsen created' (p. 173).

There is more symbolism in the notes than in the play itself, where Bertha's associations with the moon are restricted to Robert's not very original compliment:

> ROBERT: *(Moves his hands slowly past his eyes.)* You passed. The avenue was dim with dusky light. I could see the dark green masses of the trees. And you passed beyond them. You were like the moon.
> BERTHA: *(Laughs.)* Why like the moon?
> ROBERT: In that dress, with your slim body, walking with little even steps. I saw the moon passing in the dusk till you passed and left my sight. (P. 39)

More is made of her likeness to the earth. In the second act, when Robert puts his arm round Bertha's shoulder, he tells her to listen to the summer rain and says:

> The rain falling. Summer rain on the earth. Night rain. The darkness and warmth and flood of passion. Tonight the earth is loved – loved and possessed. Her lover's arms around her; and she is silent. Speak, dearest! (P. 125)

She reminds Robert of the rich, fertile earth; and as the only wife and mother in the cast she might have been shaped into a modern Gea-Tellus, as Molly Bloom was to be in *Ulysses*. But Joyce develops other traits in her. She becomes a bit confused, though she behaves naturally and remains composed when Robert confesses his love and asks for permission to kiss her, but when Richard tells her that he is going to visit the cottage

where Robert has arranged for the *rendezvous* she becomes
furious and miserable. In the second act her bewilderment
grows; and she begs her husband helplessly to tell her what to
do (p. 106). In the last scene, in her concluding words, she is
again the woman who instinctively knows her way – something
of an earth-symbol again – but by then we have witnessed her
realistic misery for so long that the symbolic side of her character has been considerably weakened. The final impression is one
of a beautiful, bewildered, essentially human woman without
the consistently symbolic function of some of Ibsen's 'Scandinavian women'.

The first two lines of Joyce's notes give us the cryptic information that Richard is 'an automystic' and Robert 'an automobile'. Here, too, Joyce has probably had some symbolic
properties in the two characters in mind, but I cannot find that
these are developed in the play. Archie's role, on the other
hand, is left virtually untouched in the notes while in the play
he seems to carry greater symbolic weight than the adults. He
is happy as none of the grown-up people are; he enters the
room through the window twice, obviously a thing Joyce has
included to suggest the atmosphere of sunlight and fresh air
which Archie brings with him. He stands in the play as the
embodiment of the possibilities of the future. 'Perhaps, there,
Richard', says Robert, 'is the freedom we seek – . . . In him and
not in us' (p. 158).

Joyce has tried, it seems, to unite the first impression he had
of the perfect drama which should be realistic as *A Doll's House*
and *Pillars of Society* were and his later understanding of
Ibsen's use of symbols. The result is not a play like *The Wild
Duck,* where there is a symbiosis between parlour-realism and
poetic symbolism. *Exiles* remains a play firmly in the realistic
tradition – with patches of symbolism rather incongruously stit-
ched to it. Again, as in the case of the early epiphanies, Joyce
was not quite successful as an epigone. But that he could master
an interplay between realism and symbolism is evident from
the other work he was engaged on in 1914. Writing *A Portrait*,
Joyce did not feel the same oppressive weight of Ibsen's ex-

ample; and lessons from the master could be incorporated more naturally in these books.[2]

That Joyce's reading of Ibsen influenced the dramatic art of *Exiles* can also be demonstrated in other aspects of the play. The dialogue is strikingly similar to that of Ibsen's later works, as the following example from the first act of *Exiles* can illustrate. Most of the information which the audience can glean from the scene between Richard and Beatrice in Act I is couched in the same evasive dialogue that Ibsen very often used to hint at some important point. Richard asks a question that requires nothing but yes or no for an answer, but Beatrice does not answer straightforwardly:

> RICHARD: . . . Tell me, Miss Justice, did you feel that what you read was written for your eyes? Or that you inspired me?
> BEATRICE: *(Shakes her head.)* I need not answer that question.
> RICHARD: What then?
> BEATRICE: *(Is silent for a moment.)* I cannot say it. You yourself must ask me, Mr Rowan.
> RICHARD: *(With some vehemence.)* Then that I expressed in those chapters and letters, and in my character and life as well, something in your soul which you could not – pride or scorn?
> BEATRICE: Could not?
> RICHARD: *(Leans towards her.)* Could not because you dared not. Is that why?
> BEATRICE: *(Bends her head.)* Yes. (Pp. 21–22)

In the dialogue of Ibsen's later plays a question is often answered by a new question, by a declaration of ignorance or by a blunt unwillingness to answer, as this example from *The Masterbuilder* will illustrate:

> SOLNESS *(closing the folder, getting up, and going nearer to her):* You just see, Aline – in future things will be better with us. Far more comfortable. Life will be easier – espesially for *you.*
> MRS SOLNESS *(looking at him):* In future?
> SOLNESS: Yes, believe me, Aline –
> MRS SOLNESS: Do you mean – because *she's* come here?
> SOLNESS *(checking himself):* I mean, of course – when we've once moved into the new house.

[2] Cf. Chapter III.

MRS SOLNESS *(taking her outdoor coat):* Oh, do you think so, Hal-
vard? That it will be better then?
SOLNESS: I can't believe it won't. And surely you think so too?
MRS SOLNESS: I don't think about the new house at all.
(Act II, Una Ellis-Fermor's translation).

In Ibsen and Joyce alike, the dialogue tends to be long-drawn
with too much mincing of words. Still, at times, both attain a
fine balance between suggestiveness and clarity – Joyce notably in the last scene of *Exiles,* Ibsen through whole plays. At
his best Ibsen escapes flaccid dialogue by introducing richer
overtones than Joyce does. In the extract from *The Masterbuilder* quoted above, the new and the old house of the Solness
family – both heavy with symbolic meaning and effective re-
minders of the past – add significance to a dialogue that would
otherwise be limp, as does the shadow of the intruder, Hilde
Wangel.

Since Joyce sets *Exiles* going with Richard Rowan's return to
Ireland, he has to give the necessary information about the past
in retrospective glimpses. Early in the first act Richard and
Beatrice start recalling the days before Richard left Ireland
and their correspondence during the years when he was away.
What *is* eventually revealed is the story of Richard's elopement
with Bertha. The relationship between the four main persons
was very much the same at that time as it is in the play. In her
intellectual way, Beatrice has been drawn towards Richard all
the time; and Richard has found in her the intellectual companion he could not find in Bertha. Robert has been in love with
Bertha all the time, and lost her when she went abroad with
Richard, as he loses her at the end of the play when she says to
her husband, 'I am yours' (p. 162). As the emotional patterns
and the conflicting forces of the past are just the ones we meet
on the stage, the gradual retrospection becomes no overwhelming revelation to the characters and the audience; it does not
basically change the attitude of the persons while they are on
the stage and therefore leaves *Exiles* without the growth in the
characters and in their understanding of each other which Ibsen
is careful to present. In *When We Dead Awaken* Maja under-

stands how closely Rubek is tied to Irene and leaves him; Rubek gets to know how futile his life has been; and Irene comes nearer an understanding of her role in Rubek's life and at the end loves him again. All this, improbable though it may be, happens as a consequence of the past that is unrolled. Similarly, in *The Lady from the Sea,* the full knowledge of the past – revealed on the stage – alters the lives of Ellida, Dr Wangel, and the Stranger. In *Exiles* the past is only loosely related to the present, and unable to change the characters and motivate the action. We have seen that Joyce was aware of the importance of retrospection as a dramatic device. He praises Ibsen's use of it in his review of *When We Dead Awaken.* At that time, however, Joyce was not aware of the dynamic nature of the past as Ibsen unrolls it; and *Exiles* testifies to no deeper insight into this aspect. As it is revealed in Joyce's play, the past is without sufficient dramatic force.

In dialogue, use of symbols, and retrospective technique *Exiles* presents itself as a hotchpotch of material – partly well grasped and partly not – from Ibsen. The characters and the incidents in the play strengthen this impression, while at the same time they show that it is from Ibsen, and not from nineteenth-century drama in general, that Joyce derived most of his ideas about dramaturgy. The many analogies to the action and the *dramatis personae* in Ibsen indicate that Joyce's imagination drew on the dramatic world of the Norwegian all the time, and that he used this world even when the situation or character remembered seems to us to fit ill into its new place. Indeed, elements from Ibsen are used so indiscriminately that it makes more sense to describe them one by one, as I shall do in the following, than to attempt to discuss them in relation to any thematic core in *Exiles* that might have given them all a coherent meaning in their new context.

The human situation that we meet in the opening scene presents a good example of Joyce's indebtedness. Richard Rowan comes home after years in a foreign country, just like Professor Rubek in *When We Dead Awaken* and Osvald in *Ghosts,* or Gregers Werle in *The Wild Duck,* who returns from a self-imposed exile in an inland mining area. Indeed, almost all Ibsen's later plays are set in motion by some person who returns home. Like Rubek and Osvald, Richard is an artist, even if he is unlike Rubek in that he has completed no acclaimed masterpiece and unlike Osvald in that he has achieved something.

Robert Hand, the friend of the family, has near spiritual relatives in Ibsen, where an important role is often given to such a 'friend', who may set the plot going or be a foil to another character. Good examples are Arnholm in *The Lady from the Sea* and Kroll in *Rosmersholm*. In *Hedda Gabler* Judge Brack wants to seduce the wife of his friend and brings news of a professorship, just as Robert Hand does in *Exiles*.[3]

In his early writings Joyce noticed Ibsen's preference for a set of three characters,[4] and one of Ibsen's triangles is mother-father-only child. Joyce may well have got some impulse towards the introduction of Archie as an only son from Ibsen. Another reason why Joyce gave Richard and Bertha only one child was propably his wish to avoid too conspicuous similarities between the Rowans and his own family, which supplied so much material for *Exiles*.

Bitter conflicts between the generations are revealed in the play. In a tense scene Richard Rowan tells Beatrice about his mother:

> She drove me away. On account of her I lived years in exile and poverty too, or near it. I never accepted the doles she sent me through the bank. I waited, too, not for her death but for some understanding of me, her own son, her own flesh and blood; that never came. (P. 27)

After having prayed for his 'dead mother's hardness of heart', he turns to the memory of his father:

> (*... points to the crayon drawing on the wall.*) Do you see him there, smiling and handsome? His last thoughts! I remember the night he died. (*He pauses for an instant and then goes on calmly.*)

[3] Cf. P. Colum, 'Introduction', *Exiles*, p. 8.
[4] *Critical Writings*, p. 99.

1 was a boy of fourteen. He called me to his bedside. He knew I
wanted to go to the theatre to hear *Carmen*. He told my mother to
give me a shilling. I kissed him and went. When I came home he
was dead. Those were his last thoughts as far as I know. (P. 28)

He goes on to say, 'He will help me, perhaps, my smiling handsome father.' Richard Rowan's parents and his attitude to them
have close parallels in *Peer Gynt*. The spendthrift Jon Gynt,
Peer's father, was smiling and handsome. Mother Åse has nothing of the rigidity of Richard's mother, but is, like her, conventionally religious. Mrs Rowan died 'fortified by the rites of
holy church' (p. 26); Mother Åse asks Peer to fetch her collection of sermons and read to her. *Brand* offers an equally interesting resemblance: the conflict between Richard and old
Mrs Rowan is as bitter and deep as the gulf between Brand and
his mother. In one way the roles are reversed, however. In
Brand the mother is worldly and the son wholly dedicated to
his ideals, while in *Exiles* it is the son who does not conform to
the religious standards of the mother. In both plays the mother
dies without any reconciliation with the son. These similarities
are striking, but the mother-father-son situation in *Exiles* is not
simply an echo from Ibsen. It is an essential part of Joyce's idea
of a family; and its roots can be seen in his own early life.[5]

Exiles offers another similarity to Ibsen in the possibility of
a *renversement des alliances* as we find it in *When We Dead
Awaken*. Professor Harry Levin suggests this[6] and is right, I
think, in saying that it is nothing but a possibility in *Exiles*. The
double set of partners certainly bears a strong resemblance to
When We Dead Awaken, though one must stretch the imagination rather far to find, as Mrs Macleod does,[7] clear correspondences between Ulfheim and Robert Hand, Maja and Bertha,
Irene and Beatrice, Richard Rowan and Rubek. The differences
between them are as marked as the similarities. It is the *situa-*

[5] Cf. Chapter IV.
[6] *James Joyce: A Critical Introduction* (London: Faber and Faber, 1944),
p. 34.
[7] V. K. Macleod, 'The Influence of Ibsen on Joyce', *PMLA*, Vol. 60,
No. 3 (Sept. 1945), p. 894.

tion embodied in *When We Dead Awaken* which is revived
in *Exiles*.

Behind this situation, as well as behind the conflict between
generations, the family-relations in *John Gabriel Borkman* can
be glimpsed. Richard Rowan remembers his mother's 'hardness
of heart'; a similar mother and the same metaphorical description of her heart can be found in Ibsen's play. Mrs Borkman's
heart is 'cold' and 'hard'; and she wants to possess her son and
form him in her own image, but in the end the son chooses a
woman who presents a clear contrast to the rigour of the mother. Though unlike Bertha in most respects, this woman, Mrs
Wilton, serves like her as a symbol of human warmth; and in
her company the young man can live a life in freedom from the
restrictions that his mother wanted to impose on him. The older
generation in Ibsen's play offers another analogy to the lives
of Richard, Bertha, Beatrice, and Robert Hand. Richard has
John Gabriel Borkman's dedication, and like him he has had to
choose between two women, one whom he loved and one who
might further his career. Borkman's choice is not Richard's;
Joyce's hero chooses the woman he loves, and thus the marriages
of the heroes are different in tone and content in the two plays.
In spite of this, there occurs both in *John Gabriel Borkman* and
Exiles the possibility of a *renversement des alliances* – in Joyce
when Bertha and Richard misunderstand each other, in Ibsen
in the renewed understanding and love between John Gabriel
and Ella Rentheim. In *John Gabriel Borkman* the slighted
lover is very much in the background; and the whole analogy
between the two plays is, of course, only moderately close, but
still close enough to provide another illustration of Joyce the
dramatist working on patterns that can be found in Ibsen.

In the themes and attitudes that underlie the various incidents and the individual characters of *Exiles* there are further
similarities to Ibsen.[8] An important theme is brought out in
Richard's attitude to his wife. He wants her to choose between

---

[8] Cf. James T. Farrell, 'Exiles and Ibsen', in *James Joyce: Two Decades
of Criticism*, ed. S. Givens (New York: The Vanguard Press, 1963), pp.
110 ff.

him and Robert in freedom. When Bertha accuses him, 'Because
I am simple you think you can do what you like with me', he
repeatedly answers, 'I have allowed you complete liberty' (p.
73). Even when Bertha appeals to him to decide for her, he
declines:

> BERTHA: ... Why do you not defend me then against him? Why do
> you go away from me now without a word? Dick, my God, tell
> me what you wish me to do?
> RICHARD: I cannot, dear. *(Struggling with himself.)* Your own
> heart will tell you. ... (P. 106)

The resemblances are great between the treatment of this idea
in *Exiles* and in *The Lady from the Sea*.[9] When the Stranger
enters in the last act of Ibsen's play Dr. Wangel first insists on
his right as husband to decide for Ellida. But when he understands that she must feel free to regain her mental health, he
leaves all talk of authority and says hesitantly, but decisively:
'And so – so I'll – cancel the bargain at once. – You may choose
your way now – in full – in full freedom.' The play ends in a
short dialogue between Ellida and her husband about her new
life 'in freedom' and 'under responsibility'.

Both Bertha and Ellida – in their freedom – eventually
choose their husbands, but the situations they are placed in are
widely different. Dr. Wangel has a great capacity for love, but
is conventional and possessive, a pillar of society quite unlike
Richard Rowan. It takes the combined elements of a love that
is refined during the play and a doctor's eye for a cathartic
treatment to change Wangel's attitude so that he allows Ellida
the freedom she needs. Richard, on the other hand, presses freedom on Bertha, who really wants to be guided by her husband.
Richard even wants her to be unfaithful in order to see his
jealousy fulfilled:

> In this play Richard's jealousy is carried one step nearer to its own
> heart. Separated from hatred and having its baffled lust converted

[9] These resemblances have been discussed at length by Mrs Macleod, *op.
cit.*, pp. 894–895.

into an erotic stimulus and moreover holding in its own power the hindrance, the difficulty which has excited it, it must reveal itself as the very immolation of the pleasure of possession on the altar of love. He is jealous, wills and knows his own dishonour and the dishonour of her, . . . (Notes, pp. 163–164.)

Richard's motives are of two sorts, partly concern for his wife that she should be a person in her own right, and partly masochism and even sadism. Joyce was aware of this and calls the play 'a rough and tumble between the Marquis de Sade and Freiherr v. Sacher Masoch' (Notes, p. 172). The idea of love that emerges from the marriage of Bertha and Richard is tragic in its final consequences. The freedom of the individual can never be reconciled to the demands of love. Freedom and love are both fundamental values, and they seem mutually exclusive in the last scene of *Exiles*. As the conclusion of *The Lady from the Sea* is exactly the opposite – freedom and love can coexist and even reinforce each other in a marriage – there is no question of Joyce having taken the denouement of his play from Ibsen.[10]

The theme of freedom for the wife is one among others in *Exiles*, while it is the centre of *The Lady from the Sea*. 'The affirmative doctrine of freedom *und* responsibility' which Mrs Macleod finds in *Exiles*[11] is partly overshadowed by other motifs: jealousy as portrayed in Richard, treacherous friendship as in the relations between Richard and Robert, and what looks like another main theme, the artist's – and man's – loneliness. In *Finnegans Wake* Joyce asks, 'Was liffe worth leaving?'[12] This is just the question Ibsen, in a less oblique way, put to himself and his audience in *When We Dead Awaken*. Richard Rowan in *Exiles* has faced a similar problem: should he leave Bertha (life) to live with Beatrice whose congeniality is of great importance to his art, but who is 'dead' compared to

[10] In his insistence in *Exiles* on the romantic agony of impossible love Joyce may have been influenced by Knut Hamsun and Gunnar Heiberg, the foremost Norwegian exponents of a *fin-de-siècle* attitude to love.

[11] V. K. Macleod, *op. cit.*, p. 895.

[12] *Finnegans Wake*, p. 230, 1. 25. 'Liffe' means life as well as the Liffey, which again is a symbol of Anna Livia, the great paragon of an earthbound, life-giving, non-intellectual woman.

the motherly, earthly, womanly Bertha? Bertha admits readily enough that she does not understand her husband's ideas and adds about Beatrice, 'She will understand it!' (p. 76). But again there is a difference between *When We Dead Awaken* where Irene meant an overwhelming inspiration and at the same time represents life, and *Exiles* where Beatrice's mind, in Joyce's own words,

> is an abandoned cold temple in which hymns have risen heaven-ward in a distant past but where now a doddering priest offers alone and hopelessly prayers to the Most High. (Notes, p. 168.)

The title of the play was meant to stress another side of the same predicament:

> Why the title *Exiles*? A nation exacts a penance from those who dared to leave her payable on their return. The elder brother in the fable of the Prodigal Son is Robert Hand. The father took the side of the prodigal. (Notes, p. 164.)

Like the Prodigal Son Richard Rowan left his country and the conventional life his mother wanted him to live. But the theme of exile is not developed in terms of the artist's estrangement in the play – and Joyce may have felt that the title which he had decided on at an early stage was somewhat incongruous as he gave it supplementary and more matter-of-fact meaning in the notes: 'Exiles – also because at the end either Robert or Richard must go into exile.' (Notes, p. 172.)

Beneath the actual exile to which either Robert or Richard is consigned, as well as beneath the art-versus-life dilemma, there may be the related and more basic theme of 'the ultimate lone-liness and doubt that must possess the soul, the inevitable exile of man'.[13] *Exiles* ends on this note, Richard stubbornly repeat-ing that he has 'a deep wound of doubt' in his soul. Richard is essentially lonely in the play; but other characters like Robert and especially Bertha seem to me to carry rich possibilities of human contact; and Richard's own loneliness is so willed that

[13] M. Magalaner and R. Kain, *Joyce: the Man, the Work, the Reputation* (N.Y.: New York University Press, 1956), p. 137.

it cannot, without a great many qualifications, represent the sort of loneliness that *must* possess the soul. Loneliness in Ibsen is a different thing. In *An Enemy of the People* Dr Stockman finally finds himself triumphantly alone and says, 'The strongest man in the world is the one who is most alone'. But his loneliness is political; he stands happily surrounded by his family with which he feels one when he says this. And even though the heroes of Ibsen's later plays, a Solness or a Rubek, are unique, and therefore to a certain extent lonely men, they respond to, and develop in close fellowship with, another person. Hedda Gabler and John Gabriel Borkman are lonely, but both have been brought by outer forces and their own deceptions into their isolation: their exile is not inevitable in the way Joyce intended Richard's to be.

While Ibsen's later plays generally centre round one motif, *Exiles* has no focus, and the themes in it scarcely fuse in an organic whole. The theme of freedom for the wife is weakened by being centred 'on the fairly negligible matter of a seduction', as Mrs Macleod points out.[14] Even if a seduction is not always a negligible matter, it is so half-hearted in *Exiles* – the only one who seems to want it with some zest is the husband – that Richard's words about liberty become much too grand for the situation. The artist's dilemma is weakened in a similar way: too little is made of Richard as a writer and Beatrice as a source of inspiration to make it a focal theme. And loneliness as an inescapable quality in life is not well exemplified in a man who *wants* to be lonely.

A reason for this lack of a thematic centre may be found in one of the impulses that made Joyce write the play: *Exiles* is a work that grew out of a marital crisis which Joyce felt very acutely; so acutely, I think, that the artistic detachment he had praised in Ibsen and made his programme in *A Portrait* was lost in 'the rough and tumble'. For *Exiles* does not owe almost everything to Ibsen except its poor execution. Joyce has certainly imitated Ibsen's dialogue and retrospective technique;

[14] V. K. Macleod, *op. cit.*, p. 895.

and the characters as well as the action and the ideas of *Exiles* remind one of Ibsen. But the urge to write the play and the basic situation in it came from Joyce's own life: Joyce had gone abroad with a woman without marrying her; he had been away from his country for many years; he had, he thought, been met by treachery when he returned; and he had seen another man make advances to his wife. This man was the Triestine journalist Prezioso, who had been a good friend of Joyce, had helped him with references for applications and had some articles by Joyce published in his newspaper. One of his tributes to Nora is found in *Exiles* where Brigid says to Bertha: 'Sure he thinks the sun shines out of your face, ma'am' (p. 128). Nora told her husband everything, just as Bertha does. But Joyce, unlike Richard Rowan, told Prezioso to keep off. Still, Joyce had allowed Prezioso's endeavours for some time, and, says Ellmann, 'studied them for secrets of the human spirit'.[15]

Further, Joyce's trip to Ireland in 1909 was put into *Exiles*, incident by incident:

> The trip to Dublin had been at once turbulent and pointed. Moving through the events of Joyce's brief stay there are, in phantasmagoria, the outlines of *Exiles* and *Ulysses*. . . . In *Exiles* Robert Hand, Richard Rowan's best friend, cordially tries to help him secure a post as professor of Italian at the University, writes about him in the newspaper, and at the same time tries to cuckold him. The cordiality is Gogarty's, the attempt to help him with a teaching position and an article in the newspaper is Kettle's, the attempt to cuckold him is Cosgrave's.[16]

Thus, incidents, characters, and themes from Joyce's immediate experience were used in *Exiles*. As Ibsen was one of those who formed Joyce's understanding and interpretation of his own life he may be indirectly responsible for the form and emphasis of some of the personal matter in the play; but the raw materials are essentially Irish and personal, rather than literary and Norwegian. It was when he elaborated on his material to fashion the play that Joyce had Ibsen in mind all the time; and

[15] Ellmann, p. 327.
[16] *Ibid.*, p. 300.

it is at this stage of composition – a fairly late one – that most of the Ibsen-elements we have considered found their place in *Exiles*. This lateness is certainly one of the reasons why some of the situations that Ibsen provided would not function as objective correlatives to what Joyce wanted to express.

Another reason why *Exiles* gives us the impression of being a poor attempt to write an Ibsen play is altogether different: Joyce did not set out only to write a realistic play; he also intended to do something that Ibsen had not done: he wanted to write a 'metaphysical' play.[17] Richard Rowan is conceived as an 'automystic'; and enigmatic though the word is, it indicates, I think, that Richard is not primarily seen as a social being whose actions and thoughts influence, and are influenced by, his surroundings, but as an individual separated from human fellowship. He is meant to fight out his problems with forces more general and more mystical than impulses from his wife and friends. In my opinion, Joyce has not succeeded in bringing out this metaphysical dimension in the play; but the intention is there and accounts for much of the solipsism present in the portrait of Richard Rowan.[18]

Exiles is sometimes seen as a landmark in Joyce's relations to Ibsen – as far as *Exiles* apprenticeship, after the play artistic independence. A. Walton Litz says, 'In *Exiles* he exorcised the spectre of Ibsen, . . .'.[19] It is true that Ibsen is nowhere more immediately recognizable than in this play; but this is due to the fact that *Exiles* is a work in the same *genre* as Ibsen's. Joyce could take over ready-made techniques and situations as he had done in his 'dramatic' epiphanies. But the adaptability of Ibsen's devices is no true measure of the influence of the Norwegian on Joyce. This influence is equally well, or better, illustrated in *Ulysses*, to the style and structure of which Ibsen's plays contributed even though none of the devices of a playwright could be used without modifications in that book.

[17] Cf. Francis Fergusson's introduction to *Exiles* (Norfolk: New Directions, 1945), pp. v–xviii.
[18] Cf. Harry Levin, *James Joyce: A Critical Introduction* (London. Faber and Faber, 1944), p. 34.
[19] *The Art of James Joyce* (London: Oxford Univ. Press, 1961), p. 4.

If Stephen is a character made of the sum total of the characteristics of the heroes in Ibsen's early plays, or if he is built on Joyce's early life and this life was decisively influenced by Ibsen, then it may be true to say that *Exiles* marks the end of a period of dependence. For *Exiles,* and *A Portrait* which was completed in the same year (1915), are the last works in which the rebellious artist (Stephen and Richard) is a main character. But if one tends to think that the raw materials for Stephen came from Joyce's own life, and that his youth and early manhood was determined largely by other forces than a dramatist whom he chose as his idol, then *Exiles* presents no evidence of being a watershed in Joyce's relations to Ibsen. From the first epiphanies to *Ulysses* Ibsen provided equally important help on another plane, that of literary art and craft; and, what is highly significant, there were parallels to be found in Ibsen, not only to Stephen and Richard Rowan, but to Bloom and HCE, who represent Joyce's altered attitude to artists and common men.

VI

ULYSSES - A DUBLIN
PEER GYNT?

Ibsen's name is mentioned only once in *Ulysses*. As they walk through Dublin late at night Bloom and Stephen pass the police station in Store Street, and,

> Between this point and the high, at present unlit, warehouses of Beresford Place Stephen thought to think of Ibsen, associated with Baird's, the stonecutter's in his mind somehow in Talbot Place, first turning on the right, while the other, who was acting as his *fidus Achates* inhaled with infernal satisfaction the smell of James Rourke's city bakery, situated quite close to where they were, the very palatable odour indeed of our daily bread, of all commodities of the public the primary and most indispensable. (P. 598)

Stephen's association links this passage with the corresponding one in *A Portrait,* where the spirit of Ibsen is defined as one of 'wayward boyish beauty'. Drunk and tired at this stage in *Ulysses,* Stephen does not follow the train of thoughts which was set in motion by Baird's, but the mention of Ibsen is certainly an acknowledgement of these youthful impulses. Further, by the juxtaposition of Stephen's thoughts about Ibsen and Bloom's about bread Joyce may hint at 'the primary and most indispensable' nourishment Ibsen provided to Stephen's artistic needs.

As we have seen, Ibsen's importance in the creation of Stephen may not have been as fundamental as a number of critics have thought. But an obvious and basic fact may be emphasized again about Ibsen's influence on Joyce: he confirmed the Irishman in his reaction against conventionality and in his dedication to art, and thus in the waywardness that is so prominent in Stephen. And the example of the Norwegian contributed to Joyce's own literary 'waywardness': the ventures into new and bold novelistic techniques in *Ulysses* found moral support in *Ghosts* and *When We Dead Awaken*.[1]

As early as 1906 Joyce toyed with the idea of writing a short story about a Dublin Jew under the title of 'Ulysses'; and, if we can rely on what Stanislaus Joyce told Ellmann nearly fifty years later, Ibsen was in his mind at the time: he felt unable to write more stories for *Dubliners*, he said, because he was, 'unlike Ibsen, not enough of an egoarch'.[2] Nothing came of the idea in 1906, but it was not forgotten; and in the next year, on November 10, Stanislaus Joyce has an interesting note in his diary: 'Jim told me that he is going to expand his story "Ulysses" into a short book and make a Dublin "Peer Gynt" of it'. Ellmann, from whom this is quoted, comments:

> In what sense *Ulysses* was to be a *Peer Gynt* is not altogether clear, except that the hero was to sample all aspects of Dublin life. How he could be at once the clear-eyed Ulysses and the self-deceived Peer Gynt is also unexplained.[3]

When Joyce was casting about for an outline structure for *Ulysses* I suppose he knew, consciously or unconsciously, that, like Shem in *Finnegans Wake*, he had to write 'over every square inch of the only foolscap available, his own body' (p. 185). His writing of verse, and of *Dubliners* as well as the autobiographies, had taught Joyce that his own life and his memories of Dublin were the materials he could make use of and had to make use of. So, once he had decided that Homer's wandering hero was to provide the mythical background to his story he had to face an inescapable problem: How could he weld into one the aging man of action, Odysseus, and the artist-*persona* he had utilized in his autobiographies? Certainly, Joyce must have felt and seen that the Stephen of *A Portrait* for all his wars against everything Irish was too young and inexperienced to be the counterpart to the august warrior from the siege of Troy – and still this Stephen was an indispensable part of

---

[1] Cf. *Critical Writings*, pp. 48–49.
[2] Ellmann, p. 238.
[3] *Ibid.*, pp. 274–275.

Joyce's fictional raw materials! This is, I think, the stage at which *Peer Gynt* offered help. In Ibsen's play the protagonist is a reckless, unconventional, imaginative young man in the first three acts, and then in the rest of the play an old man – still essentially the same person, but now rich, experienced and wary. This presentation of two different phases in the life of the same man could, and in my opinion did, teach Joyce that he could find room for himself both as a young artist and as a husband and father, a mature man who might well have Homer's hero as a foil, within the framework of the *Odyssey:* Stephen could correspond to Telemachus, and Joyce the family man could find a *persona* in Odysseus.

Peer Gynt also suggested, I think, a way in which Stephen, while remaining the same young artist as in the earlier novels, might be presented in a new light. For the young Peer Gynt is only fully understood when he is seen against the portrait of the successful elderly business man and of the disintegrating old man in Acts IV and V: this is the terrifying consequence of the brilliant and erratic life of the young Peer. The elder hero of *Ulysses* has a similar function. Bloom serves as a mirror in which Stephen is presented to the reader, a welcome change from *Stephen Hero* and *A Portrait,* in which Stephen himself provides the only point of view so consistently that the author's sporadic irony seems curiously ineffective. Even more important is the reassessment of the role and nature of the artist that the relatively sympathetic portrait of an ordinary citizen like Bloom implies. In *Peer Gynt* and *Ulysses* alike a middle-aged or old man gives us a new understanding of the young hero. In this respect *Peer Gynt* served a purpose similar to that of the *Odyssey,* which Joyce, in T. S. Eliot's words, used as 'a way of controlling, of ordering, of giving a shape and a significance to the immense panorama of futility and anarchy which is contemporary history.'[4] One of the things that Joyce had to control and order was his own changing attitude to the artist as a young man. Telemachus in Homer's poem was definitely a minor

---

[4] 'Ulysses, Order and Myth', *The Dial,* Vol. 75 (Nov. 1923), p. 483.

character and would not serve as a vehicle for what Joyce
wanted to express; but when reinforced and slightly modified
by *Peer Gynt* the *Odyssey* could serve as an ordering and controlling frame for Joyce's mature view of citizen and artist.

The idea that *Peer Gynt* could serve as a subsidiary structural framework for *Ulysses* may have come to Joyce the more
readily as the hero in his story, in Ellmann's words, 'was to
sample all aspects of Dublin life', just as Peer is a cross-section
of Norway such as Ibsen saw it in his indignation. And there
are other similarities between the two protagonists; Peer Gynt
and Odysseus are both wanderers; both leave their homes, roam
abroad for many years, and return in the end. Both return to
their wives, after amatory experiences in other quarters. Both
find that their wives have been faithful. Solvejg has nothing of
the practical resourcefulness that we admire in Penelope – she
is altogether more etherial, but shares with her Homeric counterpart a soul of sterling virtue. And in both works the woman
is given a small part. She appears in person at the beginning
and at the end, but remains for the greater part of the life of
the wandering hero a background figure.

Neither was Joyce blind, at this time, to the points of contact
between Dublin and Norway. In a letter to Stanislaus in 1905
he had said, 'Is it not possible for a few persons of character
and culture to make Dublin a capital such as Christiania has
become?'[5] In a lecture Joyce gave at the Universita Popolare
in Trieste in 1907 on Irish history he devoted a paragraph to
the Scandinavian invasions, which he rounded off by a significant comment:

> The Scandinavians, however, did not leave the country, but were
> gradually assimilated into the community, a fact that we must
> keep in mind if we want to understand the curious character of the
> modern Irishman. (*Critical Writings*, p. 160.)

This is why, in *Ulysses*, the word 'Dane', otherwise a mere
alliterative jingle, is used by Stephen in 'Scylla and Charybdis':

[5] Ellmann, p. 216.

'. . . Dane or Dubliner, sorrow for the dead is the only husband from whom they refuse to be divorced' (p. 210). Joyce's awareness of the ties between Ireland and Scandinavia was to grow steadily until, in *Finnegans Wake*, HCE becomes both the 20th century Irish innkeeper and the first Scandinavian invader.[6]

So, when the Dublin Jew stirred in his mind again in 1914, Joyce did what we might have expected: he bought a new copy of *Peer Gynt*, which he had read in his undergraduate days but probably not brought with him from Ireland in 1904.[7] Then, doggedly for seven years, as Joyce notes with some pride at the end of *Ulysses*, he laboured to clothe his image of the Homeric Dublin Jew and his family and surroundings in words. We shall see that *Peer Gynt* did not, all in all, contribute much to this elaboration of the basic plan it had helped to form; but some stylistic features, a couple of incidents, and some of the prominent traits in Bloom and Stephen may have come to Joyce the more naturally because he remembered similar features in Ibsen's play.

A number of similarities between Stephen and Peer had become established in Joyce's mind when he wrote and rewrote his autobiography. The protagonists had similar fathers and mothers, both challenged the conventionality of their surroundings, and both were potential, and subsequently real, exiles.[8] In *Ulysses* new sides of the two personalities provide resemblances to a reader who is at home in Ibsen's verse play:

Both Stephen and Peer are essentially poets, men of imagination; both refuse or evade religious obedience at the death-bed of their mothers, both are tempted by incontinence and self-sufficiency,

---

[6] Stuart Gilbert cites historians who think they have found close racial links, not only between Vikings and Dubliners, but also between these and Homer's Acheans. Such theories would, of course, have pleased Joyce inordinately; but I doubt that he made much use of the sources Gilbert mentions. The only correspondences in *Ulysses* between all three races seem to me to be the ones Joyce *himself* creates in his Homeric book about Dubliners in the old Norse stronghold. See Stuart Gilbert, *James Joyce's* Ulysses (London: Faber and Faber, 1952), pp. 72 ff.

[7] Ellmann, p. 788.

[8] Cf. Chapter IV.

both turned into beasts in the den of Circe (or the trolls), both
haunted by guilt and both saved by their friends.[9]

These parallels are, of course, not always close. We have already seen how the attitudes of the heroes to their mothers differ in emphasis; other parallels between Stephen and Peer, for
instance the incontinence, are closer and will be investigated
below. But if it is possible that Ibsen's play provided Joyce
with the idea that two characters, one young and one middle-
aged, together could become his *persona,* and thus make more
homogeneous a work about Odysseus where he was to give a
disproportionately great part to Telemachus, we should be entitled to look for another set of parallels – this time between
Peer and Bloom.

In spite of the almost overwhelming differences between the
mild advertisement canvasser of 7 Eccles Street, Dublin, and
Ibsen's impetuous jack-of-all-trades, there are also significant
similarities. Bloom has taken over from the *Odyssey* some of
the significant traits that Homer's hero had in common with
Peer: both Peer and Bloom return, though late, to their homes
after a peripatetic day and life, and both – Bloom grudgingly,
Peer pathetically – are welcomed by their stay-at-home wives.
Bloom receives a letter from his pen-'love' during his day, and
Peer has his Anitra. But both have been half-hearted in their
enjoyment of these affairs and in the end know where they
belong: Peer in Solvejg's lap and Bloom in the marital bed
with Molly. Both men are inventive. Peer thinks out a grand
plan for leading water into the Sahara, and sees himself as
ruler of a hedonistic paradise on a luscious island in the new
sea. There is in Bloom a *Drang nach Osten,* but his imagination
works on a smaller scale and in another way: his plans do not
always and necessarily end in a vision of himself as a Croesus.
It is an indomitable practical sense that sets his thoughts
going.[10] But the pleasure in devising new schemes is equally
great in the heroes of both books.

[9]Kristian Smidt, 'Joyce and Norway', *English Studies,* Vol. 41, No. 5
(Oct. 1960), pp. 318–319.
[10] See *Ulysses,* e.g. pp. 69, 90, 107.

Even more interesting is a similarity between Peer and Bloom that they do not share with Odysseus. Neither is satisfied as a father. Quite unlike the Odysseus-Telemachus relationship, Bloom's and Peer's relations to their children are uncertain and pathetic. Bloom loves his daughter with a persistent and moderate love, but has lost the son that meant so much to him and Molly the few days he lived. Peer has the Bastard, which is as repulsive to him as is the Green-clad, its mother. Even more significantly, both Peer and Bloom end their days having established a new and all-important parent-child relation. Bloom has 'got' a son in Stephen – has become a father by acting like a father for an hour or two. And as he falls asleep later that night, Bloom is still seen in the same frame of reference, though now – after a day as man and father – he is allowed a child's part in sleep: 'the childman weary, the manchild in the womb' (p. 722). Peer in Solvejg's lap becomes a child too, and, shedding the years in which he has squandered his life, he can be saved from the Buttonmoulder as the boy who has lived in Solvejg's mind, as the child of her imagination. Molly, 'in the attitude of Gea-Tellus, fulfilled, recumbent, big with seed,' (p. 721) is certainly not reminiscent of the very spiritual Solvejg of Act V in *Peer Gynt* who, a blind, old woman on her way to church on Whit Sunday, receives Peer without surprise. But they have been given one trait in common: both are passive, and much more so than Penelope with whom they share the role of the stay-at-home.

Typical of Joyce's feeling that he was, and his *persona* had to be, a family man is the shift of a favourite Ibsen-image from Stephen to Bloom: the deer-image from *Stephen Hero* and 'The Holy Office' is attributed – with a change in meaning – to Bloom in 'Cyclops'.[11] The 'stags' horns' which are included in the 'gigantic' description of Martin Cunningham's blessing (p. 333) do not remind us only that Bloom is a cuckold and that he will be chased out of the public house. He is also a free man, one who is hunted, but not hunted down. He belongs to the low-

[11] See also Ellmann, p. 452.

lands, but in an unassuming way he can 'flash his antlers' with a less ludicrous effect than Stephen/Joyce in 'The Holy Office'.

I do not contend that all the parallels discussed above are debts to Ibsen or even that Joyce was consciously aware of them all; but their sum total supports the theory that *Peer Gynt* contributed to the character-drawing of *Ulysses* at an early stage and later offered scattered hints for the detailed elaboration of the main characters.

The only hint of this kind which Stuart Gilbert mentions in his *James Joyce's* Ulysses is the similarity between the thirteenth mourner in 'Hades' and Gregers Werle in *The Wild Duck:*

> One sees this M'Intosh as one of those ominous and more-than-unnecessary persons in an Ibsen play – Gregers Werle in the *Wild Duck*, for instance, which concludes:
> 'GREGERS *(looking straight before him).* In that case, I'm glad my destiny is what it is.
> 'RELLING. Excuse me. What is your destiny?
> 'GREGERS *(going).* To be the thirteenth at table.
> 'RELLING. The devil it is!'[12]

As there are no further points of similarity between M'Intosh and Gregers Werle which can substantiate what Stuart Gilbert says, it is more reasonable to conclude, I think, that Joyce got the idea directly from the common fund of European folklore in which the thirteenth of a party is subject to bad luck.

Another episode in *Ulysses,* 'Circe', has more conspicuous traits in common with *Peer Gynt.* It is written in dialogue; and it resembles (it may even parody) Ibsen in its lavish use of stage-directions which, however, goes far beyond anything in the plays of the Norwegian to establish a vaudeville atmosphere and style. Stephen's situation in 'Circe' is like Peer's at the end of the second act of *Peer Gynt.* Both are drunk, both drift into sexual incontinence, and both have to fight, Peer against the trolls and the Boyg, Stephen more prosaically against the soldiers. Both are saved by the intervention of

---

[12] Stuart Gilbert, *op. cit.,* p. 171, footnote.

others: the Boyg dwindles when he hears the church-bells and Solvejg's singing, Stephen is rescued through Bloom's faithful chaperonage and Corny Kelleher's incidental intervention. In both works these nightly riots are presented in a series of fleeting 'shots', like visions in a dream; and both versions of the nightmarish incidents are crowded with fantastic beings, trolls and monsters as well as veiled sibyls and personified sins of the past. In this technique Ibsen and Joyce both found a medium that could serve as a vehicle for the presentation of the boozy, half-paralyzed brains of their protagonists. And both utilized the dream-atmosphere to stress another side of their works: the main moral and religious implications of Peer's self-sufficiency are brought out directly in 'Dovregubben's Hall' for the first time in the play; and the moral stamina of Bloom is nowhere so clearly established as in the den of Circe where he takes upon his medium-sized shoulders the responsibility of fatherhood, and patiently and firmly asserts his genuine concern for his neighbour.

Peer does not change his personality in 'Dovregubben's Hall', as Stephen and Bloom do in 'Circe', though he is on the point of becoming a troll himself. He remains the same irresponsible nondescript through the greater part of the play, and in the fourth act he has to face difficulties that resemble the predicament of Stephen and Bloom in 'Circe'. In the lunatic asylum Peer is surrounded by people who change in very much the same way as Bloom and Bella Cohen undergo metamorphoses in 'Circe': Bloom becomes a woman and Bella a man for a time, and in Ibsen's asylum people become the opposite of what they were. The sane go mad, and the patients are thought normal.[13] These changes in *Ulysses* and *Peer Gynt* are different from the less radical magic of Homer's Circe who simply converts men who lack wits and restraint into animals with the corresponding deficiencies.

Further, Peer in Act IV and Bloom in 'Circe' are both seen in their roles as ridiculous and pitiable lovers. At the beginning

[13] Cp. Vivienne Kock Macleod, 'The Influence of Ibsen on Joyce', *PMLA*, Vol. 60, No. 3 (Sept. 1945), p. 892, footnote.

of the episode the women in Bloom's life hover round him, remind him of their encounters, magnify them, and accuse him of inconstancy: and Bloom is pleased to see that his amorous life has been so full of adventures, but also willing to be punished. *'With desire, with reluctance'* (p. 517) he humiliates himself in front of Bella. Peer is just as proud of his affairs and has a similar wish to be mastered. Like Bloom under Bella's fan, he has given the lash to Anitra and wants to lead her horse as a slave. He asks for – and promptly gets – punishment.

This body of incidents and techniques that 'Circe' has in common with *Peer Gynt* is so substantial that one can conclude, I think, that Joyce had Ibsen's play in mind when he wrote and rewrote it the nine times that he prides himself on in a letter to John Quinn.[14] There is no mention of *Peer Gynt* in Joyce's letters from this time, which are all full of news about the writing of *Ulysses;* and Joyce has not acknowledged any debts to Ibsen by putting references to his name or to his *dramatis personae* into the text of 'Circe'. But a grain of external evidence can perhaps be found. Throughout the autumn of 1920 Joyce waited for a case containing books and papers to arrive from Trieste:

> Circe has been very much delayed by a number of causes – . . . also the fact that the case of books and documents which I sent on to Paris from Trieste on 28 June to enable me to write the two episodes *Circe* and *Eumeus* here went astray. After a great deal of writing, wiring and interviewing it was at last discovered at a station on the Franco-German frontier. It arrived a few days ago . . .
> (Letter from Nov. 10, 1920; *Letters*, p. 149.)

It is likely that *Peer Gynt,* which Joyce had bought in Trieste with *Ulysses* in mind, was in this case. Once it arrived, Joyce probably refreshed his memory of it and used it for the final drafts of 'Circe', which was not completed till around Christmas the same year. The fact that there are a number of resemblances to Ibsen's play in the next episodes too, supports the guess.

[14] *Letters*, p. 156.

At the beginning of the last act of *Peer Gynt* Ibsen has placed Peer on board a ship which is wrecked on the Norwegian coast. The last episode but two of *Ulysses*, 'Eumaeus', makes use of a great many references to navigation: and its main symbol, according to the author, was that of sailors. In *Peer Gynt* we witness the ship being wrecked, and in 'Eumaeus' the clientele of the cabman's shelter recollect a similar catastrophe, an 'illfated Norwegian barque' which went down on the East coast of Ireland (p. 622). The name of the ship is *'Palme'*, and this may be a reference to another Ibsen play, *Pillars of Society*, in which there is a ship called 'Palmetræet'. There is mention of alms at this stage in both works: Stephen gives money to the idle Corley who does not deserve it; Peer first promises to give money to the poor and deserving cook, then, out of envy of a family man, changes his mind.

Ibsen's play and Joyce's novel both give each stage of their heroes' journey home a special tone and style: just as Ibsen lets Peer escape from the wreck only to be closely interrogated by the Buttonmoulder and the Devil, so Bloom and Stephen are led from the nautical atmosphere and language of 'Eumaeus' to the severely catechising style of 'Ithaca'. The rigidity of this episode – which, in Joyce's own words, lets the reader 'know everything and know it in the baldest and coldest way, but Bloom and Stephen thereby become heavenly bodies, wanderers like the stars at which they gaze'[15] – has a counterpart in Peer's words,

> Hils fra Peer Gynt, Broer Stjernerap!
> Lyse, slukkne og forgaa i et Gab – – –
> *(Peer Gynt*, Act V)[16]

and in the outrightness and flatness with which the Buttonmoulder and the Devil discuss Peer. Peer is not, like the two wanderers in *Ulysses*, exalted into a heavenly body (the only

---

15 *Ibid.*, pp. 159–160.
16 'Here's from Peer Gynt, Brother Shooting-Star!
Shine, flash down, and disappear –'
(Rolf Fjelde's translation.)

heavenly thing he is compared to is a *falling* star), but by a similar stylistic process he is reduced to a case. And at last – Bloom in 'Penelope' and Peer in the meeting with Solvejg – the heroes are made more intimately personal and human again, seen as they are through the thoughts of the women who have the last word in both books: Molly has her 'yes I will yes', and Solvejg a song that is equally affirmative, though different from Molly's soliloquy in most other respects.

These points of similarity represent nothing like a complete analogy between the styles and situations of Acts IV and V of *Peer Gynt* and 'Circe' plus the 'Nostos' part of *Ulysses;* but they indicate that Ibsen's dramatic world must have been a persistent presence at the back of Joyce's mind, a fund that could provide incidental help at times when Joyce used major patterns from other sources. The tone and style, as well as the incidents, of the last episodes were of course determined by Joyce's over-all plan for the novel – a plan which necessarily limits and modifies the inclusion of material from literary sources. There may, however, be a relationship that is worth studying between some of the basic concepts that guided Joyce through all the eighteen chapters of his novel and his reading of Ibsen. We have already seen how *Peer Gynt* contributed to Joyce's creation of the Stephen-Bloom-Molly triangle. But what about the considerations that made the stylistic innovations of *Ulysses* possible?

With Robert Martin Adams I think that 'we may assume that Joyce's frequent purpose, like Ibsen's, was to present both a solid surface and a luminous symbol at the same time.'[17] The aspect of the 'solid surface' that has struck readers of *Ulysses* with perhaps the greatest force, the bold use of interior monologue, owes little or nothing in itself to Ibsen. Joyce grandly pointed to the French writer Édouard Dujardin as the man from whom he had got the main impulse towards the stream-of-consciousness technique; and even if Joyce liked to simplify and dramatize the origins of his novelistic methods, and over-

[17] Robert Martin Adams, *Surface and Symbol: The Consistency of James Joyce's* Ulysses (New York: Oxford Univ. Press, 1962), p. xvii.

emphasized his debt to Dujardin, a case can scarcely be made for any influence from Ibsen's dialogue – which here and there, and notably in some of Peer's soliloquies, tends towards the interior monologue. But in one respect the use of interior monologue is a direct result of Joyce's interest in Ibsen's realism. The stream-of-consciousness method is the logical extreme to which psychological realism can be taken. Ibsen taught Joyce to use life around him in all its drabness as subject-matter. Then, when Joyce later in his career wanted to explore in detail the workings of the mind, the nearest he could come to a similar 'real life' approach was a description of thoughts – trivial, drab, and sometimes poetic and grand – as they actually come and go in the human mind.

But the surface of *Ulysses* is not only interior monologue. From 'Telemachus' to 'Hades' we do follow the stream of consciousness of Stephen and Bloom respectively. In 'Eolus' Joyce still gives us the ebb and flow of Bloom's and Stephen's thoughts when they are on the 'stage'. But when they are not, the style changes into that of a newspaper report; and all through the chapter the lay-out is that of the front page of a newspaper with headlines like 'MEMORABLE BATTLES RECALLED' or 'YOU CAN DO IT!'. Towards the end of the chapter the headings become increasingly parodic. 'SOPHIST WALLOPS HAUGHTY HELEN SQUARE ON PROBOSCIS. SPARTANS GNASH MOLARS. ITHACANS VOW PEN IS CHAMP' and 'VIRGILIAN, SAYS PEDAGOGUE. SOPHOMORE PLUMPS FOR OLD MAN MOSES' are far from the principle of psychological verisimilitude which governed the inclusion of material in 'Hades';[18] but 'Eolus' does, like the preceding chapters, add to the solidity of the surface by its facetious and apt imitation of the Dublin newspaper world.

Other chapters where Joyce abandons the 'traditional' interior monologue for some other medium have the same effect of grounding the story in what was said and what happened in Dublin on 16 June 1904: in spite of all that is fantastic and grotesque in 'Circe', the episode describes what happens to

[18] Cf. Kristian Smidt, *James Joyce and the Cultic Use of Fiction* (Oslo: Oslo Univ. Press, 1959), p. 84.

Stephen and Bloom and what occupies Bloom's mind in a way that is factual enough. For all the ridicule that 'Ithaca' pours on a naturalism as a literary principle,[19] it is in itself a treasure-house of naturalistic information, the importance of which Joyce sincerely believed in. Even the developmental style of 'Oxen of the Sun' may find a tenuous factual equivalent in the growing booziness of the medical students, so that the main immediate impression *Ulysses* leaves in the reader is one of a minutely faithful and surprisingly direct presentation of a Dublin day.[20]

This solid surface is different from the conventionally realistic or naturalistic. Ellmann was the first to point out one of the most striking of Joyce's idiosyncrasies:

> Joyce's surface naturalism in *Ulysses* has many intricate supports, and one of the most interesting is the blurred margin. He introduces much material which he does not intend to explain, so that his book, like life, gives the impression of having many threads that one cannot follow.[21]

Another stratagem, which also goes much further than traditional naturalism and which may be seen as a further development of the blurred margin, is the technique of collage: to his picture of Stephen, Bloom, and Molly, Joyce glues odds and ends from Dublin life that make up a considerable body of intrinsically trivial bric-à-brac which is largely irrelevant to the delineation of the main characters and to most of the moral and philosophical issues of the book, but often brilliantly evocative of an ordinary day in the Irish city.[22] Thus, Joyce's realism is not identical with Ibsen's, but the whole surface of *Ulysses* may well be summed up in the words Joyce employed to praise Ibsen, 'life – real life'.[23] This lesson from the Norwegian that

---

[19] See Hugh Kenner, 'Joyce and Ibsen's Naturalism', *Sewanee Review*, Vol. 59, No. 1 (Winter 1951), pp. 75–76.
[20] Joyce may have remembered similar stylistic experiments in Jonas Lie's *Østenfor sol*.
[21] Ellmann, p. 377.
[22] Cf. Robert Martin Adams, *op. cit.*, pp. 247–248.
[23] *Critical Writings*, p. 44.

life in all its sordidness and triviality can and should be used as fictional subject-matter, is reflected everywhere in *Ulysses*. Joyce's views of his literary practice had matured since his teens, and since the writing of *A Portrait;* and when he wrote *Ulysses* they included, needless to say, a great many other ideas and ideals than those from Ibsen. But the use of detailed explorations into the mind, of trivial incidents, as well as of bric-à-brac, was first and most decisively justified in Joyce's mind by the Norwegian dramatist.[24]

Another line runs equally firm from Joyce's early writings on Ibsen through *A Portrait* to *Ulysses*. We have seen that Joyce praised Ibsen for his 'impersonal' attitude to his characters:

> Ibsen treats . . . all things, with large insight, artistic restraint, and sympathy. He sees it steadily and whole, as from a great height, with perfect vision and an angelic dispassionateness, with the sight of one who may look on the sun with open eyes.
>
> (*Critical Writings*, p. 65.)

Joyce never lost sight of this authorial attitude which he found demonstrated in *When We Dead Awaken,* and later in Flaubert. Stephen defines the dramatic form (for him the most perfect of all *genres*) in *A Portrait:*

> The dramatic form is reached when the vitality which has flowed and eddied round each person fills every person with such vital force that he or she assumes a proper and intangible esthetic life. The personality of the artist, at first a cry or a cadence or a mood and then a fluid and lambent narrative, finally refines itself out of existence, impersonalises itself, so to speak. The esthetic image in the dramatic form is life purified in and reprojected from the human imagination. The mystery of esthetic like that of material creation is accomplished. The artist, like the God of the creation, remains within or behind or beyond or above his handiwork, invisible, refined out of existence, indifferent, paring his fingernails.
>
> (P. 215)

This is the 'classical temper' on which Joyce complimented

[24] Cf. Ch. II.

Ibsen in the review of *Catilina*, and on which Stephen discourses in *Stephen Hero*.[25] The classical temper was a more exacting ideal than realism; and in *A Portrait* it remains an aspect of the theories of the youthful Stephen rather than a practice which Joyce adheres to throughout the book. At times he does view his Stephen from above: in parts of the final chapter he gives a description of the perceiver together with what is perceived by our informant. The conversation with Lynch is a good example of this. We follow Stephen, see what he sees, hear what he hears; but while we see *with* him we see *him* too, and in this perspective he 'assumes a proper and intangible esthetic life' for a time. In the chapters that were written earlier, and notably in the first two, there is a disconcerting identification with Stephen on the part of the author which tends to give the protagonist the same glorified hero-status as he had in *Stephen Hero*. This is most obvious in the places where Stephen for some reason or other suffers. When Stephen is ashamed of his father in Cork, Joyce does not attempt to give his protagonist to the readers as an aesthetic object. Joyce and Stephen merge in the picture of the humiliation:

> They had set out early in the morning from Newcombe's coffeehouse, where Mr Dedalus' cup had rattled noisily against its saucer, and Stephen had tried to cover that shameful sign of his father's drinkingbout of the night before by moving his chair and coughing. One humiliation had succeeded another: the false smiles of the market sellers, the curvettings and oglings of the barmaids with whom his father flirted . . . (*A Portrait*, p. 93)

In Chapter I there is the same personal intensity in the description of the pandying at school. Joyce's prose is effective; it drives home forcibly the idea of a sensitive boy suffering – but the revelation of suffering as an 'object' together with an equally factual description of the sufferer had to wait until *Ulysses* for its full realization.[26]

The ideal, that 'The personality of the artist . . . finally re-

[25] See *Stephen Hero*, pp. 78–79, and my discussion in Ch. II.
[26] Cf. S. L. Goldberg, 'Joyce and the Artist's Fingernails,' *A Review of English Literature*, Vol. 2, No. 2 (April, 1961), pp. 61–71.

fines itself out of existence . . .', is reached, as S. L. Goldberg notes, when Joyce in 'Hades' lets the readers 'participate in Leopold Bloom's view of the funeral' and 'see *through* Bloom's consciousness as well',[27] and thus gives Bloom life both as narrator and looker-on and as the main subject of the narrative. Bloom, the 'esthetic image' in this case, has been 'purified in and reprojected from' Joyce's imagination, and he acquires a full, independent life that Joyce could not – at least did not – give the Stephen of *A Portrait*. But in *Ulysses* Joyce's portrait is successful on his own terms. Right from the first page of the book the touch is sure:

> Stately, plump Buck Mulligan came from the stairhead, bearing a bowl of lather on which a mirror and a razor lay crossed. A yellow dressinggown, ungirdled, was sustained gently behind him by the mild morning air. He held the bowl aloft and intoned:
> – *Introibo ad altare Dei.*
> Halted, he peered down the dark winding stairs and called up coarsely:
> Come up, Kinch. Come up, you fearful jesuit.
> Solemnly he came forward and mounted the round gunrest. He faced about and blessed gravely thrice the tower, the surrounding country and the awaking mountains. Then, catching sight of Stephen Dedalus, he bent towards him and made rapid crosses in the air, gurgling in his throat and shaking his head. Stephen Dedalus, displeased and sleepy, leaned his arms on the top of the staircase and looked coldly at the shaking gurgling face that blessed him, equine in its length, and at the light untonsured hair, grained and hued like pale oak. (Pp. 4–5)

First, the features of Buck Mulligan are firmly established. He is described in bold, clear outlines; the point of view is, technically speaking, objective: we see him from the outside. Only when we have read some fifteen lines does Stephen appear, and the point of view changes. We are at once introduced to Stephen's mind. He is 'displeased and sleepy' and we see Mulligan's face, 'equine in its length', through his eyes. Then, some fifteen lines further down, by the word 'Chrysostomos', Ste-

---

[27] *Ibid.*, p. 66.

phen's stream of consciousness breaks through for the first time
to be our principal guide through the rest of 'Telemachus'. This
oblique introduction to the main point of view has the effect of
a stage-direction before a monologue; the scene – one that is
more 'objective' than Stephen's mind – is set before the hero
is allowed to start his roaming soliloquy. In this way Joyce
achieves for Stephen in 'Telemachus' what he does for Bloom
in 'Hades': Stephen becomes a character that we see and see
with at the same time. He is the centre of interest, an object,
but also the informant. Thus the author removes himself from
the surface of his novel, hiding behind the character whose
consciousness is the point of view.

The less conventional chapters – the attempt to find a literary
equivalent to the fugue in 'Sirens', the catechising of 'Ithaca',
or the excursion into the history of the English language in
'Oxen of the Sun' – have the same effect of hiding the author.
It is only a very protean Joyce who can stand behind the many
and widely different styles of the book and say, 'Le style est
l'homme même' or 'Le style, c'est moi'. Joyce attains the illusion
of an *incognito* by disguising himself first behind his special
use of the stream-of-consciousness technique, then behind a
number of stylistic extravagances that are usually thought im-
compatible within one novel. The fact that some of the styles of
Ulysses are parodies, or in parts parody other writers, tends in
the same direction: towards a reading that will not immediately
or easily discover the personality of the artist. Joyce is of course
not absent from his work. He has put a part of himself into
Stephen, another has gone to Bloom; and most of *Ulysses* is
built, incident by incident, character by character, on his own
experience of life and his memories of Dublin people and hap-
penings. But in his presentation of these incidents and characters Joyce is 'impersonal': he does not comment in his own
voice; and the authorial management of the narrative is made
unobtrusive by the use of the stream-of-consciousness method
which makes the brain a stage on which thoughts come and
go like characters in a play. Moreover, Joyce avoids making
any one character his own mouth-piece, and the moral values

in *Ulysses* lie firmly embedded in the whole picture of human life that the book offers. This approach is a remarkably close parallel in fiction to the 'temper' of Ibsen's mature plays.

In the other themes, theories, and practices at the roots of *Ulysses* I can find little similarity to Ibsen. Indeed, the writing of *Ulysses* was, for Joyce, a move away from his earlier techniques to a method of composition that finally resulted in the night-language of *Finnegans Wake*. A. Walton Litz writes:

> The late work on *Ulysses* reveals a process almost the opposite of that which transformed *Stephen Hero* into *Portrait of the Artist*. In revising *Stephen Hero* Joyce exercised a rigorous selectivity, discarding the multiple events and elaborate expository passages of the earlier work in favour of a few scenes or 'epiphanies' which embody the essential characteristics of Stephen's development. . . . But the revisions of *Ulysses* undertaken during the last years of its composition were seldom selective. They were almost entirely expansive, and the economy Joyce exercised in achieving isolated effects was overshadowed by the incessant elaborations.[28]

This new method does retain some of the effects of the earlier: something like the early epiphanies is found at this later stage, too – not in a dramatic, meaningful incident, but in a single word or a short sentence that Joyce thought could be made to carry as much meaning as any revelation on a sea-shore. And words are used in the new scheme with the same acute awareness of their rhythmical quality as before. But, as Dr Litz was the first to demonstrate in detail, essentially it is a venture into a new linguistic and stylistic territory which neither Ibsen nor Flaubert nor Dujardin had explored.

That Ibsen supplied important material to *Finnegans Wake*, written consistently along the new lines and so different from the earlier work, tells us how persistent was Joyce's fascination with the Norwegian dramatist. Joyce freed himself completely from the limitations of an epigone that are so conspicuous in *Exiles;* but he continued to draw upon his reading of Ibsen just as he made use of all his experience of life and litera-

[28] *The Art of James Joyce* (London: Oxford Univ. Press, 1961), pp. 35–36.

ture. Thus *Ulysses*, though no gargantuan Dublin copy of *Peer Gynt*, would not have been quite the same book without Ibsen. In Joyce's stock of raw materials the Norwegian had secured a share that never slumped. And as Joyce worked himself into steadily bolder experiments, he still found moral support in his Ibsen, whose morality, he said to a German Ibsenite in 1936, 'consisted not only in the proclamation of his ethical ideals, but in the fierce struggle for the perfection of his work.'[29]

[29] Ellmann, p. 701.

VII

FINNEGANS WAKE

The nature of *FW* studies, made as they are by people whose linguistic and cultural backgrounds are narrower than, or in any case different from, the background that Joyce drew upon so freely, seems to forbid any progress but a slow one in which stone is added to stone, now by an Englishman, now by an Italian, then perhaps by a Norwegian. The general list of allusions at the end of this chapter illustrates this gradual process. I include about 250 references,[1] some of which are uncertain, to Ibsen and his works; of these some 50 were first noticed by Mr J. S. Atherton in *The Books at the Wake*,[2] while an additional 30 are found in Mr M. Carlson's article, 'Henrik Ibsen and *Finnegans Wake*'.[3] Some parts of my discussion of Joyce's *use* of the allusions have also profited from the work of these two scholars. Both seem to be handicapped by scant acquaintance with Ibsen's works in the original; they have missed many interesting points, but have, on the other hand, reached a number of conclusions which I can confirm and the relevance of which I might indeed not have noticed without their writings. Mr Atherton's book especially is of great help to *FW* studies because it reveals some of the main ways in which Joyce utilized his reading. A spirited alphabetical list by an American scholar, Mrs Glasheen's *A Second Census of* Finnegans Wake,[4] has taught me much about the way Joyce manipulates his minor characters and has enabled me to place a number of Ibsen's

---

[1] The figures are approximate as it is sometimes only arbitrarily that one can say what a 'unit' allusion is.

[2] London: Faber and Faber, 1959, pp. 257–258.

[3] *Comparative Literature*, Vol. 12, No. 2, (Spring 1960), pp. 133–141. The less numerous finds of Mrs D. B. Christiani are acknowledged in the general list of allusions.

[4] Evanston: Northwestern Univ. Press, 1963.

characters in what I hope are their correct places in the Ear-wicker family.

In *FW* Joyce asks for the 'ideal reader suffering from an ideal insomnia', but he is wise enough to do so in jest. For the ideal reader of a work of art does not exist; as human beings we are all conditioned and limited in all our responses by our individual backgrounds. These limitations are, of course, felt with a particular acuteness by readers of *FW*. The ideal – and in the last instance inconceivable – reading of that book is one which finds and enjoys all possible allusions to all things, and places each in the over-all pattern that a complete understanding of everything can produce. The best reading which one can think of as possible today, on the other hand, is one which distinguishes well between major and minor allusions against our present, and probably highly superficial, conception of the whole work. Without a sense of proportion, a reader of *FW* can make anything out of any sentence in the book. An unlimited inventiveness in the reading is a mental exercise that traits in the structure and style of *FW* can encourage; but for this there is neither world enough, nor time, in our present dispensation. Indeed, to attempt the impossible may even be harmful in that what one reader finds by a close analysis of one passage is easily made to carry greater weight than it would when judged against a similarly thorough examination of the rest of the book. Discussions of allusions become useful and reliable only when the inventiveness of the critic is restrained by his or her awareness of the proportions of the rest of the book. Some studies of Joyce's use of allusions are nearly as satisfactory in this respect as *FW* allows its secondary sources to be; Mr Atherton, for instance, treats his allusions with an even degree of ingenuity, very rarely allowing a reference more than its due. Other works are examples of the less judicious approach to details that results in pictures of *FW* distorted far beyond what any given angle makes unavoidable.[5]

---

[5] See e.g. D. B. Christiani, *Scandinavian Elements of* Finnegans Wake (Evanston: Northwestern Univ. Press, 1965) and F. M. Boldereff, *Reading* Finnegans Wake (Woodward, Penn.: Classic Nonfiction Library, 1959).

Proportion, then, is my aim in the following pages. But even making proportions relatively clear is at times nearly impossible; FW is so gargantuan that one has to draw a line, often arbitrarily, beyond which one cannot take the discussion of the place in the whole work of a single reference. Since this chapter is a study of Ibsen-allusions in FW my discussion of a given passage in which Ibsen figures cannot – and is not meant to be – an exhaustive explanation of the total meaning of that passage. Other references – literary or non-literary, obvious or not so obvious – have been mentioned only where they throw light directly on the role or meaning of references to Ibsen. Anyone who has read FW will know that a literary reference is sometimes in the foreground and carries the main part of the meaning in the passage where it occurs; sometimes it shares equally with another reference; it may be definitely present, but in the shadow of another meaning; or it may be so faint that its presence is doubtful, though a case can be made for it. These are no hard and fast categories; the references are distributed evenly rather than in groups along the line from the striking to the faint and doubtful. In the discussion of references to Ibsen I have often given some indication of how prominent each is in its context, but I have not tried to be exhaustive. FW is so rich in allusions on all levels that a full discussion of the rank of each Ibsen-reference would be inordinately long. In the general list of references at the end of the chapter I have indicated by question-marks which entries I find doubtful; but again, the borderline between background allusions and those whose presence is doubtful is really a borderland; and the number of entries marked as questionable is bound to be arbitrary.

'Work in Progress'

There is a great deal of external evidence that Joyce had things Norse in his mind when he wrote FW. In the nineteen-twenties he brushed up his knowledge of Norwegian, obviously because he intended to make use of it in 'Work in Progress'. He studied under at least four Norwegian teachers in Paris in 1926–27.[6] One of his teachers in Paris, Mr Haakon Meyer, remembers him trying out puns in the no-man's land between English and Norwegian:

> Kjærringer sitter og drikker kaffe, de helder kaffe på skålen, den ene løfter skålen og sier: saucer! Saucer er en skål, skål er et ord man sier i Norden, når man løfter glasset.
> (Letter to Kristian Smidt, 5. 6. 1963.)

He had already employed some words from this territory in the first pages of 'Anna Livia Plurabelle'; and his interest in Norwegian is conspicuous in his letters to Harriet Shaw Weaver in the nineteen-twenties.[7] In 1932 he translated a poem by James Stephens into five languages, among them Norwegian. The original runs:

> The wind stood up and gave a shout.
> He whistled on his fingers and
>
> Kicked the withered leaves about
> And thumped the branches with his hand
>
> And said he'd kill and kill and kill,
> And so he will and so he will.

This is the Norwegian version:

> Vinden staar op med en vild Huru,
> Han piber paa fingerne og nu
>
> Sparker bladenes flyvende flok.
> Træerne troer han er Ragnarok.
>
> Skovens liv og blod vil han dræbe og drikke.
> Hvad der bliver at goere, det ved jeg ikke.[8]

---

[6] Cf. Kristian Smidt, 'Joyce's Norwegian Teachers', *English Studies*, Vol. 44, No. 2 (April 1963), pp. 121–122.

[7] See *Letters*, pp. 213, 225, 227, 230, 247, 252, 254, 277.

[8] Quoted from Ellmann, pp. 668–669.

The translation is unidiomatic and slightly absurd in a couple of places, and the concluding line is far from the original; but the mood of the poem is well rendered into Norwegian and there are fine poetic effects in all three stanzas.

In *FW* there are Norwegian words on almost every page; and in 'The Norwegian Captain' episode as well as in some shorter passages elsewhere the density is remarkably great. On a number of pages, for instance 315 and 317, there are more than fifty words with an unmistakable element of Norwegian. The appendix – 'A List of Norwegian Words in "The Norwegian Captain"' by Clive Hart and B. J. Tysdahl – shows in greater detail how conspicuous the use of Norwegian can be in the book. Besides its semantic value in each particular context this sprinkling of Norwegian serves at least three specific purposes: it reminds us of the multi-lingual nature of the language of *FW;* it provides an atmosphere of Vikings and early Irish history; and it can prepare for a reference to Ibsen. A good example of this last effect is the fifth question in 'Twelve Questions' where a quotation from *Peer Gynt* follows a sudden increase in the ratio of Norwegian words. Joyce's use of Norwegian in *FW* could itself be the subject for a book larger than the present one; and to keep this study within reasonable length I have limited my discussion of Norwegian words and phrases to those that appear in – and sometimes in the immediate context of – the allusions to Ibsen.

Joyce's use of other Norwegian authors is another subject of considerable interest to a student of *FW*. Joyce had read Bjørnstjerne Bjørnson, Olaf Bull, Knut Hamsun, Gunnar Heiberg, Jonas Lie, the historian P. A. Munch, and Sigrid Undset; and most of these authors, perhaps all, are alluded to in *FW*. Bjørnson appears frequently as a bear, Olaf Bull as a bull. Munch's *Norrøne Gude- og Heltesagn* is an important source for Old Norse mythology in *FW*. Certain books by these authors may have influenced Joyce's earlier works, too. The discussion of love in *Exiles* is similar to that in Heiberg's plays; and the contrapuntal styles of Lie's *Østenfor sol* may have contributed to the stylistic changes in *Ulysses.* The situation of the hero in

Lie's novel is not unlike that of Stephen.[9] An examination of Joyce's interest in these writers would go beyond the scope of the present study, but an awareness that Joyce's fascination with Norway was not restricted to his reading of one author adds an interesting perspective to the relationship between Ibsen and Joyce.

Dublin's Scandinavian history became more and more important to Joyce. He calls HCE 'le gros norvégien' (*Letters*, p. 401); and even a trivial detail like the furnishing of his flat is coloured by his preoccupation. He commissioned a carpet from a friend who, he told Miss Weaver, 'is making a wonderful carpet for me representing the Liffey flowing through Dublin into the Irish Sea with the arms of Norway, Dublin, Ireland and my own woven into the scheme' (*Letters*, p. 268). The parallels between Joyce's description of the carpet and *FW* are obvious.

In 1934 Joyce was so impressed by a production of *Ghosts* that he supplied it with a facetious extra speech by the ghost of Captain Alving in a poem he called 'Epilogue to Ibsen's "Ghosts"'. The poem will be discussed later, but the remark about it which he dictated to Gorman reveals his attitude: though the poem makes fun of the play, it 'is not to be interpreted, however, in the sense that he [Joyce] does not consider Ibsen to be the supreme dramatic poet'.[10] Joyce is known to have discussed Ibsen with the German critic Alfred Kerr in 1936;[11] and when he went to Copenhagen in August that year he was asked by a Danish journalist how high he ranked Ibsen and answered:

He's the greatest playwright I know. No one can construct a piece as he can. There's not a superfluous word in his plays. It was wonderful to see what Lugné-Poë achieved as Old Ekdal in *The Wild Duck*. I'm sorry never to have seen *Little Eyolf;* the first act is pure wonder. ... He [Ibsen] towers head and shoulders above

[9] Cf. Kristian Smidt's notes 'Joyce and Norway', *English Studies*, Vol. 41, No. 5 (Oct. 1961), pp. 318–321, and 'Joyce's Norwegian Teachers', *English Studies*, Vol. 44, No. 2 (April 1963), pp. 121–122.
[10] Quoted from Ellmann, p. 681, footnote.
[11] *Ibid.*, p. 701.

him [Shakespeare] when it comes to drama. No one approaches him there. It's very difficult to believe that Ibsen will grow stale; he will renew himself for every generation. His problems will be seen from a new angle as time goes on.[12]

When he came back to Paris he mentioned his admiration of *Little Eyolf* to James Stephens, too.[13]

Joyce's steady interest in Ibsen is also reflected in the collection of books from his personal library which is now the property of the University of Buffalo. It includes the following plays by Ibsen:

Bygmester Solness in a first edition from 1892, inscribed 'Jas. Joyce April. 1901'.

Vol. XI of the *Collected Works of Henrik Ibsen* (Heinemann, 1929) containing translations of *Little Eyolf, John Gabriel Borkman,* and *When We Dead Awaken.*

A Doll's House and Two Other Plays (J. M. Dent, 1932) The two other plays are *The Wild Duck* and *The Lady from the Sea.*

John Gabriel Borkman in a first edition from 1896.

Little Eyolf, also a first ed., 1894. Many check marks in the margin of this book show that it has been read with great interest.

Peer Gynt, tr. by R. Farquharson Sharp (J. M. Dent, 1934).

Joyce also owned the 1891 edition of *Digte (Poems)*[14] and a biography of Ibsen, A. E. Zucker's *Ibsen the Master Builder* (London, 1930).[15] As we have seen earlier, and as will be abundantly demonstrated below, these are not the only works by and about Ibsen which Joyce read and made use of in his career, but it is interesting to note that he kept *Bygmester Solness,* bought in the early days of his Ibsen-enthusiasm, through

---

[12] *Ibid.,* p. 707.
[13] See also below where *Little Eyolf* is discussed.
[14] See R. E. Scholes, *The Cornell Joyce Collection* (Ithaca, N.Y.: Cornell Univ. Press, 1961), p. 212.
[15] See Thomas E. Connolly, *The Personal Library of James Joyce: A Descriptive Bibliography* (Univ. of Buffalo, 1957), pp. 20, 47.

all the decampments of his erratic life, and that he added to his collection of Ibsen's plays as late as in the thirties. The last in-dication of interest in the Norwegian playwright that I have been able to trace dates from 1939 when he acquired a copy of Barrie's *Ibsen's Ghost* – too late, of course, for his reading of it to influence *FW*.[16]

When he had finished *Ulysses,* Joyce started to take down notes in a large notebook, published in 1961 under the title *Scribbledehobble: The Ur-Workbook for Finnegans Wake*.[17] Though notes were entered into this book as late as in the years 1933–1936, a great many of the entries precede the first frag-mentary draft for the narrative of *FW* which Joyce wrote in 1923.[18] *Scribbledehobble* is divided into sections, each with a title from Joyce's earlier works. In 1922 or '23 Joyce jotted down under 'Scylla and Charybdis': 'Peter Ibsen (†1766), c, Henrik Ib. = Wendu [the editor's incorrect reading of "Wen-che"][19] Dishington, c, Henrik Ib = Xm' (p. 103). This note reveals a surprising knowledge of Ibsen's family. One of the dramatist's forefathers was a Peter Ibsen who died in 1766; his son was called Henrik, and he married a Scotswoman, Wenche Dishington. She became a widow a year after her marriage; and her son, the dramatist's grandfather, who was born after the death of his father, was given the same name. This explains the repetition of 'Henrik' in Joyce's notes. All this information is not found together in any Ibsen-biography that was available in 1922; and Joyce may have read a Norwegian treatise by Johan K. Bergwitz, *Henrik Ibsen i sin avstamning. Norsk eller fremmed?* (Kristiania: Gyldendal, 1916), where all the facts are found. Though it is uncertain where Joyce got his informa-tion, the entry testifies to his interest even in the *minutiae* of Ibsen's biography at the time when he began his work on *FW*.

    Little Eyolf is remembered some lines further down in *Scrib-*

---

[16] *Ibid.,* p. 8.
[17] For particulars see the bibliography.
[18] See *Scribbledehobble*, pp. vii–x.
[19] I have checked it against a photostat copy of the MS page, kindly lent to the British Institute, Univ. of Oslo, by the State University of New York at Buffalo.

bledehobble: 'Land of Heart's Desire = Little Eyolf: 4th wall of theatre'. The '4th wall of theatre' may refer to the parlour-realism of Ibsen's later plays: one of the four walls of a sitting-room is taken away to let the audience see and hear what happens. The link between *Little Eyolf* and *The Land of Heart's Desire* is obvious; in both the youngest member of the family is lured to death by a mysterious visitor. There is probably also a third mention of Ibsen in *Scribbledehobble.* Under *'Exiles'* in the notebook, we read, 'H. I never saw a pair of bellows in Italy' (p. 76). As *Exiles* is a hash of the drama-turgy and partly of the themes Joyce had found in Ibsen, this is a natural place for the dramatist to be found in *Scribble-dehobble,* and I guess that Joyce forgot to put the full stop after 'I', though I cannot explain the meaning of the entry. I cannot find that any of these entries have been used in *FW*. Ibsen's name and his *Little Eyolf* figure there, but not in the same contexts as in *Scribbledehobble.* Still, the notebook brings out Joyce's steady preoccupation with Ibsen, which was to co-lour his last novel as it had given impetus to his earlier works.

To elucidate the genesis of Ibsen-material in *FW* itself, I have traced fifty-five allusions to Ibsen's name or his plays to their first appearance in the *FW* manuscripts in the British Museum. Every chapter of the book is represented in this collection of sample allusions, which cover the portions of *FW* that were written early as well as the intermediate and late episodes. They are all clear and unquestionable references to Ibsen with the exception of those from Book III, Chapters 1 and 2, in which Ibsen and things Norse are kept very much in the back-ground.

The writing of *FW* began in 1923, when Joyce composed six short fragments: 'Roderick O'Connor', 'Tristan and Isolde', 'Saint Kevin', 'St. Patrick and the Druid', 'Here Comes Every-body', and 'Mamalujo'.[20] Later, these sketches were incorporat-ed in *FW,* and they mark the real beginning of 'Work in Pro-gress'. One of our sample allusions is found in 'Tristan and

[20] Cf. *Letters,* pp. 203–204.

Isolde': 'duckhouse' (395.29) has the same function in the first draft[21] as in the final version: it reminds us of *Et dukkehjem* (*A Doll's House*), and it serves as a Joycean word for the *pudendum muliebre*.

BOOK I

In late 1923 and early 1924, Joyce wrote rough drafts, and then almost immediately fair copies and typescripts with substantial additions, of what was to become six of the eight chapters of Book I.[22] Chapter 6 was written later, in 1926 and the beginning of 1927, and Chapter 1 in the autumn of 1926, Then, in 1927, Joyce revised Book I for publication in *transition*, where the eight chapters appeared in Nos. 1–8, April–November, 1927. Of the twenty-one allusions I have checked on in Book I, fifteen are found in the *transition* text from 1927, while three were added when this text was revised to become the manuscript from which the galleys for *FW* were set up. Of these three, two are variations on the 'bygmester' motif,[23] and one is a reference to *The Pretenders*.[24] The last allusions – to *A Doll's House*, *The Masterbuilder*, and *Peer Gynt* – were added on *FW* galleys.[25] The fifteen sample allusions that are present in *transition* testify to the same interest in a wide range of Ibsen works. 'Gibsen's teatime salmon' (170.26–27),[26] 'holding doomsdag over hunselv' (199.04–05),[27] and references to *Peer Gynt*, *Rosmersholm*, and *The Wild Duck*[28] can be traced back to the

---

[21] British Museum Additional Manuscript No. 47481, p. 94 (bound with Add. Ms. 47485).
[22] The chronology of the manuscripts is here and in the following taken from David Hayman, ed., *A First-Draft Version of Finnegans Wake* (Austin: Univ. of Texas Press, 1963), pp. 288 ff.
[23] *FW* 37.35 – Add. Ms. 47475, p. 17 verso.
    FW 111.21 – Add. Ms. 47475, p. 134 v.
[24] *FW* 133.36 – Add. Ms. 47475, p. 237.
[25] *FW* 62.03 – Add. Ms. 47476A, p. 177 v.
    FW 75.17 – Add. Ms. 47476A, p. 186 v.
    FW 138.34 – Add. Ms. 47476A, p. 81.
[26] Add. Ms. 47474, p. 4.
[27] Add. Ms. 47474, p. 107.
[28] *FW* 124. 20 – Add. Ms. 47473, p. 28.
    FW 203.01–05 – Add. Ms. 47474, pp. 129, 148.
    FW 200.06–07 – Add. Ms. 47474, p. 108.

initial work on Book I completed by the late summer of 1924. Other allusions were added in 1926 when Joyce wrote Chapters 1 and 6 and when he made Book I ready for *transition* the next year. 'Bygmester Finnegan' (4.18), 'peer yuthner' (7.29–30), and 'Here is viceking's graab' (18.13)[29] are first seen in early versions of the first chapter. Chapter 6 was given references to *Ghosts* (*Gengangere*) and a two-line quotation from *Peer Gynt*.[30] Four of our sample allusions are first found in revisions made before the *transition* text was submitted to the printer,[31] while 'our misterbilder' (77.03) was added to the proofs.[32]

BOOK III

Ibsen material was woven into the next part to be written of 'Work in Progress' in just the same way. Book III was composed in 1924–1926 and appeared in *transition* Nos. 12, 13, 15, and 18 (March 1928, Summer 1928, February 1929, and November 1929). Of the twelve allusions in Book III that I have traced to their origins, five belong to the years 1924–1926,[33] three were incorporated in the revisions that immediately preceded the publication of the book in *transition*;[34] and the remainder were added either when the *transition* text was enlarged to serve as manuscript for the final edition, or on *FW* galleys. The long list of Ibsen plays on p. 540 as well as a

[29] Add. Ms. 47482A, p. 86.
Add. Ms. 47472, p. 9.
Add. Ms. 47471A, p. 31.
[30] *FW* 126.15 – Add. Ms. 47473, p. 117.
FW 141.24–26 – Add. Ms. 47473, pp. 128–129.
[31] *FW* 57.13–14 – Add. Ms. 47472, p. 179.
FW 96.31 – Add. Ms. 47472, p. 285.
FW 170.18 – Add. Ms. 47474, p. 39. This allusion may have been added as early as June, 1925. Cf. Hayman, *op. cit.*, p. 301.
FW 191.34–35 – Add. Ms. 47474, pp. 80–81.
[32] Add. Ms. 47472, p. 368.
[33] *FW* 530.23–24 – Add. Ms. 47482B, p. 105.
FW 535.16–19 – Add. Ms. 47484A, p. 28.
FW 568.17 – Add. Ms. 47485, p. 11.
FW 572.02–03 – Add. Ms. 47482A, p. 6.
FW 587.02 – Add. Ms. 47482A, p. 16 v.
[34] *FW* 471.01 – Add. Ms. 47483, p. 228 v.
FW 487.29–30 – Add. Ms. 47484A, p. 182.
FW 493.36 – 494.01 – Add. Ms. 47484A, p. 189.

reference to *An Enemy of the People* two pages later must have been added to this manuscript.[35] Two doubtful allusions in Book III, 1 and 2, from which the dramatist is almost totally absent, are first found as additions on the galley-proofs.[36] HCE reappears at the inquest-seance in III, 3; and then Ibsen allusions as well as the use of Norwegian become frequent again. The reason for the absence of Ibsen in III, 1 an 2, seems to be that Shaun, the philistine, who dominates the first two chapters of this book, has little affinity with the Norwegian, while HCE, on the other hand, is conceived as an Ibsen hero (and as a thousand and one other heroes) and his role as a viking makes Norwegian a native language for him.

BOOK II

Book II has a more complicated history. Three of the six sketches from 1923 found their final form and allocation in it; and 'The Muddest Thick That Was Ever Heard Dump' from 1926 became part of II, 2. The main work on this book was done in the years 1930 and 1932–1938, in which Joyce wrote what, with last-minute additions on proofs, became the final version. The fourteen sample allusions from the four chapters of Book II cover all the stages of this development with the exception of the short 1926 story. Though some of the dates are uncertain and some manuscripts can only be dated within the frame of two or three years, a list of these allusions and the time of their first appearance can serve as an illustration of the steadiness of the flow of Ibsen material into 'Work in Progress':

FW 395.29	Add. Ms. 47481, p. 94	Spring 1923.
FW 224.22–23	» » 47477, p. 9	Prob. November 1930.
FW 222.08, 11–12	» » 47477, p. 86 v.	Jan. 1931–Jan. 1933.
FW 274.11	» » 47478, p. 134	1934.
FW 284.F4	» » 47478, p. 68 v.	Prob. between 1934 and 1937.
FW 294.F1	» » 47478, p. 75	Prob. between 1934 and 1937.

[35] Add. Ms. 47487, p. 233.
    Add. Ms. 47487, p. 234.
[36] *FW* 425.24 – Add. Ms. 47487, p. 17.
    FW 440.03–04 – Add. Ms. 47487, p. 26.

FW 323.36	»	»	47479, p. 34 v.	1935.
FW 310.17	»	»	47479, p. 78	Prob. December 1936.
FW 309.13	»	»	47479, p. 80	Prob. December 1936.
FW 252.15–16	»	»	47477, p. 180 v.	Prob. late 1937.[37]
FW 347.07–08	»	»	47480, pp. 13, 49	1937.
FW 330.08	»	»	47479, p. 129	Prob. late 1937.
FW 364.28–29	»	»	47480, p. 189 v.	Early 1938.
FW 390.14	»	»	47481, p. 121 v.	Prob. August 1938.

BOOK IV

Another two of the 1923 sketches were incorporated in Book IV, where Anna Livia's letter, first written in 1924, also found its final resting place. The book got its present form in the years 1937–1938. Seven of eight allusions were put in at this time, when Joyce wrote the bulk of the book.[38] In late 1938 or early 1939 Joyce honoured Ibsen for the last time by adding to the galley-proofs a reference to *Brand:* 'We'll have a brand rehearsal' *(FW 617.16).*[39]

*

Though I have traced only a selection of Ibsen allusions to their first appearance in the manuscripts, there is one conclusion that this check seems more than sufficient to warrant: it was not by a sudden impulse or a flash of memory that Joyce included Peer Gynt, Halvard Solness, and the other brainchildren of the Norwegian dramatist in *FW*. From the first fragments to the proof-reading for the final version – and through all the major stages in between – Joyce enriched his work by allusions to Ibsen. He did so because he wanted to put all his world into the nutshell of his last novel; and, like the sun and the moon, Henrik Ibsen was by then an inescapable part of that world.

[37] 'obscindgemeinded', which comes immediately after the ref. to *The Pretenders*, probably dates back to early 1934. See Add. Ms. 47477, p. 180 v.
[38] *FW* 601.26 – Add. Ms. 47488, p. 13.
FW 602.35 – Add. Ms. 47488, p. 34 v.
FW 608.29 – Add. Ms. 47488, p. 89.
FW 613.32 – Add. Ms. 47488, p. 95.
FW 624.10–12 – Add. Ms. 47488, pp. 136, 142, 189 v., 219 v.
FW 626.34 – Add. Ms. 47488, p. 174 v.
FW 628.10 – Add. Ms. 47488, p. 180 v.
[39] Add. Ms. 47488, p. 215 v.

Ibsen - Obscene and Creative

Mr M. J. C. Hodgart has suggested that '"The keys to. Given!"
. . . tell[s] us, among other things, that all the keys to the meaning have been offered to us in the text.'[40] The keys are not
always to be found, I think; but there is no doubt that Joyce
very often acknowledges his use of other authors by referring
directly to their names or the titles of their works.[41] The titles
of nearly all Ibsen's plays are mentioned in *FW*, but Joyce also
admitted his indebtedness by allusions to Ibsen himself. Ibsen
shares with Shakespeare the first place among the dramatists
(and, of course, kings) that Joyce alludes to on page 138:
'woollem the farsed, hahnreich the althe, charge the sackend'
(lines 32–33). To Joyce he is 'alt' – German: old; Norwegian:
everything; Latin: high – and he comes, as in Joyce's early
essays, before Gerhart Hauptmann, who lurks in 'charge the
sackend'. Mr M. Carlson has noticed that Ibsen's name is found
in a passage 'delightfully recalling the catalogued invectives on
Ghosts compiled by Shaw [*sic!* The list was compiled by William Archer and is quoted by Shaw.] in his *Quintessence of
Ibsenism*':[42]

> The spiking Duyvil! First liar in Londsend! Wulv! . . . Such
> ratshause bugsmess so I cannot barely conceive of! Lowest base-
> meant in hystry! Ibscenest nansence! Noksagt! . . . The broker-
> heartened shugon! Hole affair is rotten muckswinish porcupig's
> draff. Enouch! (535.15–21)

'Noksagt!' means literally 'Enough said!' and is used in Norwegian as a term of abuse, or to end some critical remark with
the implication that enough has been said to prove the point
though more might have been produced if needed.[43] There are
allusions to Ibsen also in the description of Shem who 'pre-

---

[40] 'Shakespeare and *Finnegans Wake*', *The Cambridge Journal*, Vol. 6
(Sept. 1953), p. 735.
[41] Cf. J. S. Atherton, *op. cit.*, p. 20.
[42] M. Carlson, *op. cit.*, p. 139.
[43] Cf. the discussion of *The League of Youth* below.

ferred Gibsen's teatime salmon tinned' (170.26–27),[44] in two passages in which G. B. Shaw is also mentioned, 'Shaw and Shea are lorning obsen' (378.24–25) and 'doomster ... a Northwegian and his mate of the Sheawolving class' (49.17, 28–29), and in 'her crown pretenders, obscindgemeinded' (252.15–16), which combines Ibsen's name with a reference to *The Pretenders*. In three of these instances there is an obvious pun on Ibsen and 'obscene' – a quibble which may refer 'both to Ibsen's initial reception and his bringing to light of fundamental questions.'[45] Since the combination of Ibsen with 'obscene' is driven home in no less than three places, we are probably meant to see, and justified in seeing, the shadow of Ibsen also in the passages where 'obscene' occurs without any further allusions to the dramatist. Such a reading makes good sense in a case like Shaun's words about his brother who 'shall produce ... from his unheavenly body ... obscene matter not protected by copriright in the United Stars of Ourania' (185.29–31). Joyce, who had such difficulties in getting out a copyright edition of *Ulysses* in the United States, merges with Shem, whose defecation gives him an affinity with Leopold Bloom of *Ulysses;* and the whole concatenation of characters and incidents is defended by the memory of Ibsen, whose magnificence was acknowledged only after an initial wave of outrage in which his plays were denounced as filth.[46]

In his young manhood and again in the last years of his life Ibsen lived in Oslo, then called Kristiania. Mr Atherton quotes 331.31–32, 'by neuhumorisation of our kristianiasation', and rightly calls it,

---

[44] Cf. the discussion below in 'Tea, *Love's Comedy*, and the Last Word in *FW*'. 'Gibsen' is Ibsen's spelling for 'plaster of Paris': and there is a chance that Joyce knew a poem by Bjørnstjerne Bjørnson, 'Gamle Heltberg', in which 'Ibsen' and 'gibsen' form a conspicuous pair of rhyme-words:
Anspænt og mager, med farve som gibsen,
bag et kul-sort, umaadelig skæg Henrik Ibsen.
(Tense and meagre, with a colour like plaster of Paris
Behind a pitch black, enormous beard, *Henrik Ibsen*.)
[45] M. Carlson, *op. cit.*, p. 140.
[46] I have not included all the occurrences of the word 'obscene' and its mutations in the general list, only those discussed in this paragraph.

a phrase which is obviously intended to point out ... [Joyce's] youthful idolizing of Ibsen, which is now somewhat tempered by his mature realization of the somewhat humourless nature of his former idol.[47]

One more possible allusion to Ibsen's name deserves mention: The Four ask Shaun about HCE, 'His producers are they not his consumers?' (497.01–02); and Shaun answers with a long list of producers/consumers said to come from,

> Rathgar, Rathanga, Rountown and Rush, from America Avenue and Asia Place and the Affrian Way and Europa Parade and besogar the wallies of Noo Soch Wilds and from Vico, Mespil Rock and Sorrento ... (lines 11–14)

'Vico' and 'Sorrento' are names of places at Dalkey, but they also emphasize the importance of the Neapolitan Giambattista Vico to the production of HCE; and one may perhaps imagine a rough anagram in 'Mespil' of Ibsen, another guiding star for Joyce.

Names of some of Ibsen's followers and one of his forerunners are commemorated in *FW*. Søren Kierkegaard, whose denunciation of half-heartedness and compromise is reflected in *Brand* and *Peer Gynt,* is mentioned,[48] but none of these references seem to go beyond what can be found in a short entry in any encyclopedia. Joyce would know a little about Kierkegaard through Ibsen, who is so often seen as a disciple of the Danish philosopher, but I doubt that he had any first-hand knowledge of his work or biography. Kierkegaard contains great possibilities as a character in *FW*: he was almost a hunchback and he was a Dane (as is the Norwegian Captain); he attacked the conventional thinking of the 'compact majority' (as did Joyce, HCE, and Ibsen); he had the same feeling of, and fear of, being cornered by the philistines as have Stephen and Shem; and there is that story which his father told him of how he had once climbed a hill in a rage and cursed God. Much could have been made of these points in *FW* – but Joyce never did. This is

---

[47] Atherton, *op. cit.,* p. 155.
[48] See *FW,* 201.31, 246.01, 281.26–27, 336.02–03, 388.02, and 596.31.

not to say, however, that there are no parallels between Kierkegaard's philosophy and Joyce's view of life.[49] In *Scandinavian Elements of* Finnegans Wake (pp. 63–67) D. B. Christiani discusses a number of passages in which she finds allusions to Kierkegaard. But all her alleged references are questionable; and as external evidence is lacking, a case for any intimate acquaintance with Kierkegaard on Joyce's part remains unproven. The only Kierkegaard that we can know for certain that Joyce knew is the one that is reflected in Ibsen's plays.

William Archer, who translated Ibsen into English and was a champion of the new drama in the British Isles, is remembered in 'William Archer's a rompan good cathalogue' (410. 03–04). The primary allusion may be to an Irish librarian with the same name,[50] but the catalogue of abusive terms which William Archer compiled from the reviews of the first performance of *Ghosts* in London is present in 'a rompan good cathalogue'. 'gosse' (325.16) may be Sir Edmund Gosse, the first to write about Ibsen in England. "twould grig' (139.19) and 'grig' (279.F1) may be Edvard Grieg, the composer whose music to *Peer Gynt* has helped to make it famous.

Ibsen the lyric poet is conspicuously present in a number of passages in *FW*. In 'Anna Livia Plurabelle' one washerwoman tells the other that HCE is being difficult, 'hungerstriking all alone and holding doomsdag over hunselv' (199.04–05). This is a near-quotation from Ibsen's poem 'Et vers' ('A Verse'):

> At leve er krig med trolde
> i hjertets og hjernens hvælv.
> At digte, – det er at holde
> dommedag over sig selv.[51]

With the original meaning of the lines in mind, Joyce probably implies that HCE is an author (though he is no man of letters); in his own version he tells us that HCE pronounces doom over

---

[49] Cf. A. Goldman, *The Joyce Paradox* (London: Routledge and K. Paul, 1966).

[50] See M. Carlson, *op. cit.*, p. 139.

[51] 'To live is – war against trolls / In the vaults of heart and brain. / To write, – that is to bring / Oneself to Judgement (literally: to hold / Doomsday on oneself).'

'hunselv', which is Norwegian for 'she herself', and further
gives us a quibble on 'elv', which is the Norwegian word for
river. Thus, the blame is clearly put on Alp. This fits the context well, for at this point the washerwomen make the most
they can of a crisis in the marital life of the Earwickers.[52]
Ibsen's doomsday is mentioned elsewhere, too. HCE is said to
have had 'a tussle with the trulls' (134.33) and Ibsen is once
called 'doomster' (49.17). The day Buckley shot the Russian
general is called the 'moist moonful date man aver held
dimsdzey death with' (347.07–08). It is typical, not only of *FW*,
but also of Joyce's new attitude to the lonely artist that 'Et vers'
is treated facetiously. Ibsen the 'doomster' throws out his words
'in loquacity lunacy' (49.17); and on the doomsday that HCE
mentions it is his wife who is judged, not himself. He is not giv-
en to the kind of introspection found in Ibsen's poem. Joyce no
longer sees eye to eye with the artist as a prophet and navel-
gazer. The new hero, HCE, embodies more than purely artistic
gifts; he is a creator in a way less subtle but more fundamental
than that of an artist like Stephen who proudly nourishes a
feeling of splendid isolation from ordinary men. It is an early
Joyce and only one side of Joyce's Ibsen that are ridiculed in
the play on 'Et vers' in *FW*. But the fun is often serious in *FW;*
and there remains behind the facetious references to the poem
a picture of Ibsen as an assessor. To the middle-aged Joyce he
was a standard of integrity;[53] and his doomsday in *FW* reminds
us that there are moral imperatives – different from those of
the wayward artist as well as from those of the stolid majority –
against which the characters of the book can be seen.

A poem which Joyce made more extensive use of in *FW* is
'Til min Ven Revolutions-Taleren' ('To My Friend the Revolu-
tionary Orator'), a poem that Joyce first echoes in *Stephen
Hero:*[54]

---

[52] Strangely enough, Joyce was at one time unaware of the existence or
meaning of the word 'dommedag' in Norwegian. He says to James Stephens
in a letter: 'They [Danes and Norwegians] have no word for . . . the Last
Day or General Judgement.' *Letters,* p. 318.
[53] Cf. Ellmann, p. 701.
[54] See *Stephen Hero,* p. 210.

De siger, jeg er bleven 'konservativ'.
Jeg er, hvad jeg var mit hele liv.

Jeg går ikke med på at flytte brikker.
Slå spillet overende; da har De mig sikker.

En eneste revolution jeg husker,
som ikke blev gjort af en halvheds-fusker.

Den bær for alle de senere glorien.
Jeg mener naturligvis syndflods-historien.

Dog selve d e n gang blev Lucifer luret;
thi Noah tog, som De ved, diktaturet.

Lad os gøre det om igen, radikalere;
men dertil kræves både mænd og talere.

I sørger for vandflom til verdensmarken.
Jeg lægger med lyst torpédo under Arken.[55]

Ibsen tells his friend, the revolutionary orator, that there is only one thorough-going revolution he can remember – the Deluge, though even that revolution was not quite complete: Noah got through with his family and the animals. In the last

[55] The following translation is by F. E. Garret:

They say I'm becoming conservative;
No; still in my life-long creed I live.

Your changing pawns is a futile plan;
Make a sweep of the chess-board, and I'm your man.

Was never but one revolution unfaltering
That was not marred by half-hearted paltering.

To that, all since were but idle menaces.
I allude, of course, to the Deluge in Genesis.

Yet Lucifer tripped, even then; by a later ship
Came Noah, you remember, and seized the dictatorship.

Let us go, next time, to the root of the matter.
It needs men to act as well as to chatter.

You deluge the world to its topmost mark;
With pleasure I will torpedo the Ark.

stanza Ibsen suggests, with ironic overtones, the perfect plan: the revolutionary orator and his likes can drown the world in their speeches, thus providing the water for the deluge, while Ibsen contributes with a torpedo under the Ark. HCE protests that this is what he will do, too: 'They seeker for vannflaum all worldins merkins. I'll eager make lyst turpidump undher arkens' (364.28–29). In III, 4 the Four call Sockerson in, and he testifies:

> – *Day shirker four vanfloats he verdants market.*
> *High liquor made lust torpid dough hunt her orchid.*
> (530.23–24)

Two pages later HCE appears in person; and it is his voice that is heard through Sockerson's, I think.[56] In Joyce's versions Ibsen's nihilism is qualified by less destructive hints – to sexual activity: Joyce's hero will 'eager make lyst' ('lyst' is Norwegian for 'desire' and the adjective 'light'), '*hunt her orchid*' (I take the flower to be a euphemistic expression for the female pudend), and lie drunk (Norwegian 'ligger' (lies) is hidden in 'liquor' and 'I'll eager') in bed with his woman. This may imply a certain turpitude on his part ('turpidump'), but HCE is beyond the censure of conventional morals. The attitude of the publican is asocial, but not nihilistic.

The last time this poem is heard it also comes from the mouth of HCE. He defends himself against the accusations levelled at him in 'Yaun' by crying, 'Man sicker at I ere bluffet konservative? Shucks! Such ratshause bugsmess . . . Ibscenest nansence!' (535.16–19). The innkeeper reacts strongly against the allegation that he has become conservative, and by implication explains and justifies himself as Ibsen did: 'I am what I have always been.' An additional reason for Joyce's interest in this poem is found in its biblical reference. Noah and the Ark provide a prominent *ricorso* stage for *FW;* and Joyce no doubt associated Ibsen's suggested revolution with the beginning of a new Viconian cycle.

[56] Cf. J. Campbell and H. M. Robinson, *A Skeleton Key to* Finnegans Wake (London: Faber and Faber, 1947), pp. 259–260.

Ibsen's exquisite little lyric, 'Borte!' ('Gone!'), has not escaped Joyce:

De sidste gæster
vi fulgte til grinden;
farvellets rester
tog nattevinden.

I tifold øde
lå haven og huset,
hvor toner søde
mig nys beruséd.

Det var en fest kun,
før natten den sorte;
hun var en gæst kun, –
og nu er hun borte.[57]

As day comes and Alp glides out to sea 'in the wake of the blackshape' Joyce quotes three words from it, '*Nattenden Sorte*' (608.29), and refers to it again in the next line, 'the week of wakes is out and over'. The poem adds to the note of sadness that is present in this chapter by its mood of resignation and loss and its suggestion of on-coming death in the words Joyce picks out ('the dark night'). Indeed, the last stanza of the poem is a surprisingly apt summing-up of the life of Mrs Earwicker, captured at the moment when she flows into Dublin Bay, accompanied by a simple and grave poetry that is not allowed into other parts of *FW*. Further, it is a moving tribute to Anna

[57] Garret's translation spoils a couple of fine points in the original, but I cannot make a better one:

The last, late guest
To the gate we followed;
Good-bye – and the rest
The night-wind swallowed.

House, garden, street,
Lay tenfold gloomy,
Where accents sweet
Had made music to me.

It was but a feast
With the dark coming on;
She was but a guest, –
And now, she is gone.

Livia, whose death is made more poignant by the little quotation from Ibsen. The end of one cycle and the beginning of a
new is a painful experience. Combined with the story of *The
Lady from the Sea,* 'Borte!' adds a similar poignancy to an
earlier passage in *FW:* on page 371 the question, 'You here
nort farwellens rouster?' (line 28), hides 'farvellets røster' or
'rester' ('voices saying good-bye' or 'the shreds of good-bye')
and reminds us – and the stay-at-home wife who has here been
tempted to leave her family – of the sadness of the break with
the sailor from the unknown.

There are glimpses of other Ibsen-poems in the novel. Mrs
Christiani rightly finds an echo of 'Ederfuglen' ('The Eider
Duck') in 'Thus faraclacks the friarbird. Listening, Syd!' (595.
33).[58] 'Ederfuglen' is one of Ibsen's poems on the plight of the
artist by the narrow and dark fjords of Norway – a poem for
Shem in one of his plaintive moods. But in *FW* it is clearly
related to Anna Livia's return to the sea. When she glides out
as the Liffey into Dublin Bay, she is presented as Ibsen's bird,
which, having been robbed of its feathers once too often, left in
the night 'mot syd, mot syd til en solskins-kyst!' ('Southwards,
southwards to a sunny shore!') Ibsen's poetry cannot be contained in little Shem; the power of his lines is so great that they
can more naturally be used in descriptions of the lifegiving
parents in *FW* than about the children whose creativity is potential only.

After HCE, according to the washerwomen, has been 'holding doomsdag over hunselv', he is seen 'droming on loft till the
sight of the sternes' (199.06–07). Words similar to 'droming',
'loft', and 'sternes' are found together in the first verse of Mar-
grete's 'Cradle Song' in *The Pretenders*:[59]

> Nu løftes laft og lofte
> til stjernehvælven blå;

---

[58] D. B. Christiani, *op. cit.,* pp. 222–223.
[59] Now light the roof is lifted
Up the blue starry skies;
And now my little Haakon
Puts dream-wings on and flies.
(Garret's translation.)

nu flyver lille Håkon
med drømmevinger på.

If the song is there at all, it may provide a parallel to 'Et vers'
and 'Ederfuglen' by mentioning another aspect of the poet's
life: he suffers, but he also soars to the stars in dream and
fantasy. Ibsen's 'På Akershus' may appear in HCE's description of ex-Colonel Communicator, probably an earlier incarnation of himself: 'Guestermed with the nobelities, to die
bronxitic in achershous! So enjoying of old thick whiles, . . .'
(536.12–13). Although not of bronchitis, two noblemen are seen
dead within the thick walls of Akershus Castle in this poem,
which hails the martyrs of Norwegian history whose blood gave
strength to later national movements. The probability of this
allusion is supported by the mention of another royal castle in
Oslo, Oscarshall, eight lines further down, and by the presence
of the Norwegian dramatist himself. Though no Nobel Prize
winner, Ibsen was 'Guestermed with the nobelities', and he died
a lingering death in Akershus, for that is the name also of the
county in which Oslo (Kristiania) lies.

It is significant that the 'I' (or the implied speaker) of nearly all the poems Joyce quotes is Ibsen himself, and that they are
spoken by HCE in *FW*. HCE may praise Wordsworth, Dante,
Goethe, and Shakespeare, but he is himself a Norwegian, a
'Nearwicked' poet: 'on my honour of a Nearwicked, I always
think in a wordworth's of that primed favourite continental
poet, Daunty, Gouty and Shopkeeper, A.G.' (539.04–06). Recalling Joyce's work up to *Exiles,* we might have expected
Ibsen to be part and parcel of the portrait of Shem the Penman.
But the change in Joyce's attitude to the artist, first seen in
Ulysses, is even more obvious in *FW*. The hero is now a middle-
aged family man, an advertisement canvasser or a publican;
and to Joyce Ibsen is powerful and multifarious enough to keep
the new hero company. Joyce's Ibsen is not only the artist in
rebellion, he is also an artist-creator with dimensions commen-
surable with those of the protean HCE. He has not become a
philistine, but nor is he without contours in *FW*. It is 'obscene

10

nonsense' to say that he has become conservative, he is more
deeply radical than political revolutionaries. And he is obscene,
not only in the sense that he brought to light such problems as
venereal disease, promiscuity, and frigidity, and was denounced
as an indecent writer, but because in him were combined artistic
creativity and an acknowledgement of the force and complexity of sexual life. This idea, conveyed by the pun on Ibsen's
name, is repeated and reinforced by another symbolic pattern
in *FW:* with Halvard Solness Ibsen is the masterbuilder who
builds a tower;[60] the tower is clearly a phallic symbol; sex and
creativity are indivisible. Joyce never tried to 'purify' sex as
D. H. Lawrence so insistently attempted; to Joyce sex is always somewhat obscene; but in *FW* 'obscene' is at the same
time a significant word of praise. Though coarse (and at times
even loathsome), the creativity that asserts itself in the portrait
of HCE is a fundamental and good power.

'Bygmester Finnegan'

Just as composers, and notably Wagner, make use of *Leitmotivs* in their music, Joyce employs a number of words and
phrases as recurrent pointers with a similar function. The analogy with Wagner is particularly close since he makes his *Leitmotivs* either allude to extra-musical dramatic themes or cha-
racterize persons or incidents. Just as a *Leitmotiv* is not usually
the theme of the part of a composition where it appears, it is
not always the primary concern of the passages where it may
occur in *FW*. It may come in music and, metaphorically speaking, in literature as part of the orchestration or accompani-
ment. Thus, Joyce can make use of these organized recurrent
hints to remind us of other aspects of the book than what the
tenor of the narrative at a given moment is about. As implied in Mr Hart's definition of *Leitmotiv* in Joyce, it does not
necessarily consist in the repetition of exactly the same word or

---

[60] Cf. D. B. Christiani, *op. cit.*, pp. 46–56.

words, but is rather 'a short verbal construct characterized by certain easily recognisable patterns of rhythm, sound, form and, sometimes, sense.'[61] The same motif may have as different forms as 'bygger muster' and 'myterbilder' and may be combined with other meanings, as in 'Mastabatoom';[62] but once it has been noticed it is most often easily recognized.

Ibsen's *Bygmester Solness (The Masterbuilder)* is the source of a major *Leitmotiv* in *FW*, present right from the beginning when HCE is called 'Bygmester Finnegan' (4.18) to Alp's words of farewell to her husband, 'Amid the soleness. Tilltop, bigmaster! Scale the summit! You're not so giddy any more' (624. 10–12). The motif is built up of the elements 'bygg' or 'builder' and 'mester' or 'master'; and some 35 variations of it are found in *FW*.[63] It is always HCE who is alluded to in the 'bygmester' motif.[64] And indeed, the similarities between him and Bygmester Solness are many and striking. Both have an elderly wife and boy twins (though Solness's died as babies), both are infatuated with younger women, both are afraid of being overtaken and beaten by the next generation. Ibsen's masterbuilder and HCE as Tim Finnegan both climb up a ladder and both tumble down to their death.

The *Leitmotiv* leaves us in no doubt that HCE is a great builder. Bygmester Solness has built churches, houses, and fi-

---

[61] Clive Hart, *Structure and Motif in Finnegans Wake* (London: Faber and Faber, 1962), p. 20.
[62] Mastaba tomb, an early Egyptian tomb, provides a hint to the fall of the builder.

[63] 4.18	152.26–29	337.18–19	560.29–30	613.32–33
6.08–11	167.18	358.18	565.22–23	622.25
37.35	191.34–36	361.25	568.17	624.10–12
58.16–17	274.11	377.26	568.35–36	
62.03,08	291.F4	393.08	576.18	
77.03	296.07	506.02–08	576.28	
111.20–21	309.13	530.32–35	587.32–33	
126.10–11	324.27–28	535.17–18	607.30–31	

These are all cited in the general list. Like the rest of Joyce's verbal motifs, 'bygmester' has no hard-and-fast limits, and a number of instances from its frontiers might have been included. Some of its appearances suggest Maeterlinck's *The Burgomaster of Stilemonde* besides *The Masterbuilder*.
[64] This is also revealed in the fact that the motif does not occour in III, 1 and 2, in which HCE lies dormant while his son Shaun addresses the girls' school.

nally a tall tower for his new house;[65] and everything he has done has aspired towards heaven; there have been towers and spires on the homes he has built for his clients, he says. And Bygmester Solness argued with God on top of the church spire he had built, proclaiming that he would now build for himself and for people, not churches any more; he intended to challenge the Almighty the second and last time he climbed a tower, too. This does not reveal Ibsen's hero as a crazy megalomaniac. He *is* an inspired builder; and his name is Solness – made up of the Norwegian words for sun and promontory. This grandeur is very much in evidence in the 'bygmester' *Leitmotiv*. Joyce's protagonist stands 'Amid the soleness' (624.10–11); he is called 'Solsking' (607.28), and is not *any* masterbuilder but 'biggermaster Omnibil' (337.18–19) – the man who builds everything. He is said to be one of 'our visionbuilders, Baaboo, the bourgeoismeister, who thought to touch both himmels' (191.34–36; 'himmel' is Norwegian for 'heaven'). The tower of Babel (glimpsed in 'Baaboo') and Solness's tower are of the same sort, presumptious and doomed.

For HCE is not divine in the sense that he is perfect; like Solness, he is 'Mester Begge . . . human, erring and condonable' (58.16,19). This is reflected in the stuttering of the 'bygmester' in *FW*. He is 'Bygmester Finnegan, of the Stuttering Hand' (4.18), and, says Joyce, 'Then inmaggin a stotterer. Suppoutre him to been one biggermaster Omnibil' (337.18–19). Stuttering reveals guilt; and on p. 587 the *Leitmotiv* comes as the answer to Shaun's questions about his father, 'Who has sinnerettes to declare? . . . Who trespass against me? . . . That's him . . . Mister Beardall, an accompliced burgomaster' (587.24, 30–33). This sin that the Masterbuilder has committed is once or twice specified as arson, which links it with the burning down of Solness's house, for which Ibsen's hero feels guilty.[66] But more

---

[65] Mr M. Carlson thinks that for Joyce this may have indicated Vico's cycles: 'Halvard Solness recapitulates the three ages, his life suggests the sacred customs – the churches (religion), the houses (marriage), and the tower (burial).' *Op. cit.*, pp. 135–136.

[66] See 357.03 and 328.10. Cf. the more doubtful reference which Mr Carlson (*op. cit.*, p. 134) finds in 127.05.

often the sin has been committed with 'sinnerettes' (tempting young girls like Hilde Wangel in *The Masterbuilder*); and most significantly it is seen as the sin of *hubris*, of a presumption that tries to challenge God.[67] When Bygmester Finnegan's presumption grows out of proportion, he is called down; and the *Leitmotiv* becomes 'Mastabatoom' (6.10) which echoes 'mastaba tomb'. HCE falls with a bang that re-echoes through all the 628 pages of *FW*; indeed, 'our myterbilder his fullen aslip' (377.26). The outcome of the climbing was his own downfall: he is 'Topsman to your Tarpeia! This thing, Mister Abby, is nefand' (167.18–19); and we see him with Tim Finnegan of the ballad when 'His howd feeled heavy, his hoddit did shake . . .' (6.08–09).

But this fall does not come at the same point in the plot of *FW* as in *The Masterbuilder*. Halvard Solness's fall is the conclusion, the final word. The Joycean masterbuilder tumbles down in the very beginning (4.18 ff); and again and again throughout the book he falls and springs up again, so that the last time he is hailed as 'bygmester' Anna Livia thinks he will reach the top without the fatal giddiness (624.10–12).[68] When we come to the final 'the', which leads on to the beginning of the book again, we know that the success is not lasting: it is 'Finn, again!' (628.14) in repeated failure and repeated success; though in so far as a main impression can be gathered from the varied and variously reported feats and freaks of Mr Earwicker, it is definitely not one of tragedy as in Ibsen's play.

Other characters in Ibsen's play are also brought into the *Leitmotiv* and into other references to *Bygmester Solness*. There are no strong ties between Mrs Solness and Mrs Earwicker, widely different as the two are; but the latter is once called 'Alina' (608.18) in acknowledgement of her tenuous relationship to Aline Solness. Hilde Wangel, the girl who tempts Solness to his final triumph and downfall, is mentioned by name as one of the leap-year girls who accompany (or are aspects of) Issy ('Hilda', 147.12); and her arrival is remember-

---

[67] Noticed by Carlson, *ibid.*, p. 135 and by Atherton, *op. cit.*, p. 156.
[68] Cf. J. S. Atherton, *op. cit.*, pp. 156–157.

ed in 'When the youngdammers will be soon heartpocking on their betters' doornoggers' (572.02–03). Solness, who is afraid of the knocking on the door by a new generation, is cheered for some time when he finds a young lady on his doorstep, and not a young architect, a rival. The similarities between Hilde in *Bygmester Solness* and Issy are striking. Both are seen as daughters and prospective sexual partners at the same time; both displace an elderly wife; and both descend from the hills; they are representatives of a new generation, and at the same time they cause a rejuvenation in the elderly heroes. But Hilde makes the masterbuilder giddy in spite of the confidence she pours into him – and Joyce remembers this in 'a lovelooking leapgirl, all all lonely, Gentia Gemma of the Makegiddyculling Reeks' (92.25–26). She injects reckless courage into Joyce's 'Bygmester', who is here seen with Jacob (Genesis 28):

> Norganson? And it's we's to pray for Bigmesser's conversions? Call Kitty the Beads, the Mandame of Tipknock Castle! . . . He's cookinghagar that rost her prayer to him upon the top of the stairs. She's deep, that one. (530.31–35)

In the moment of calm before the fall in *The Masterbuilder* Hilde thinks she hears song in the air, but is corrected by Ragnar Brovik. 'It must be the wind in the treetops', he says. And in *FW* this becomes:

> there's a windtreetop whipples the damp off the mourning. . . . And the lunger it takes the swooner they tumble two. He knows he's just thrilling and she's sure she'd squeam. The threelegged man and the tulippied dewydress. (331.05–09)

This 'tulippied dewydress' is not only a temptress. To quote E. M. Forster on Hilde, she is both 'a lure and an assessor';[69] for Solness, and in *FW* for HCE, she is the supreme test. As the prankqueen, coming to a twin boys-daughter-father family similar to that of *The Masterbuilder*, she challenges HCE alias Jarl van Hoother, and asks him the great riddle about beer and

---

[69] *Abinger Harvest* (London: Edward Arnold, 1940), p. 84. The idea was suggested to me by A. Glasheen.

urine and women and fertility that echoes through the later parts of FW. Both Jarl van Hoother and Solness accept the challenge and answer by asserting their manhood, HCE successfully and Solness with tragic consequences.

The dialogue from the final scene of *The Masterbuilder* is resumed towards the end of Book II, 3. Hilde sees Solness on top of the tower and says, 'Now I see him great and free again'; and when he waves his hat, she cries to the ladies around her, 'Oh, send him up a greeting in return!' Then, as Solness falls down, Ragnar gasps, 'He must be smashed to death. Killed on the spot.' Joyce's version, in which the Hanged God of *The Golden Bough* may also be present, runs,

> Isn't it great he is swaying above us for his good and ours. Fly your balloons, dannies and dennises! He's doorknobs dead!
> (377.36–378.02)

By including the knocking on the door ('doorknobs'), Joyce stresses an aspect of the scene which is essential to his use of it: the advent of a new generation. The ascent of the tower 'for his good and ours' gives the climber a similarity with Christ which is very much in the background in Ibsen, but which Joyce needed in the picture of *his* masterbuilder. Ragnar Brovik, who is Solness's young rival, is also quoted in 'Loab at cod then herrin or wind thin mong them treen' (587.02), which combines his words to Hilde about the wind in the treetops with a German hymn of praise.[70] His name is found with Ragnarrock in the 101-letter word on page 424: '-rackinarockar!' (line 22) where his function in Ibsen's and Joyce's works is emphasized by the mention of the old Norse word for the end of the world. Thus, the end of an old cycle and the beginning of a new are presented in a cosmic as well as in a personal perspective. The same combination, with the same function, is found in 'ragnar rocks' (19.04) and 'Rocknarrag' (221.23–24).[71] What position Ragnar Brovik has in relation to the Earwickers is not altogether clear. Mrs Glasheen thinks that he stands for the new generation in

---

[70] The first to notice this was J. S. Atherton. See *op. cit.*, p. 156.
[71] Cf. M. Carlson, *op. cit.*, p. 133.

general and that he is thus Shem as well as Shaun.[72] But if he and the Viking Ragnar Lodbrog merge, his role in *FW* is probably Shem's, since Shem is said to be 'an outlex between the lines of Ragonar Blaubarb and Horrild Hairwire' (169.03–04).[73] The most satisfactory answer may lie between the two above: he may be both twins, but Shem may have got a little more of him than Shaun. Joyce was not always concerned with the elaboration of detailed minor correspondences like this (though he would like his readers to find them) and may have left a loose thread here.

*

The Masterbuilder is not used only for detailed elaboration and ornament. The play provides *FW* with one of its most pregnant *Leitmotivs*, and it takes part in the shaping of basic traits in HCE himself. If there had been no *Bygmester Solness* to contribute to the novel the hero would have been a different man in some respects: he would have been only a hod-carrier and not a great builder, and his protestations on pp. 540–546 would have sounded like empty boasting. He would have fallen down from a ladder as Tim Finnegan does and not from a tower on top of which he had challenged God. In *FW* this divine (or quasi-divine) quality in Mr Earwicker is also expressed in other ways, for instance in his ubiquitous presence and in his role as father. But his challenge to God is first and foremost expressed in terms of his being a masterbuilder. This challenge seems to have been as central to Joyce's conception of himself as an artist as to his plans for *FW;* in the words of Kristian Smidt: 'He [Joyce when he wrote *FW*] would no longer be merely the creator of his art, but the Author of all things.[74]

The father-figure in *FW* had to be more than a man, and Ibsen helped Joyce to create a modern – and within the framework of the *Wake*, a timeless and quite successful – counterpart to the god of his childhood. There is no aspiration towards the

---

[72] See A. Glasheen, *A Second Census* of Finnegans Wake (Evanston: Northwestern Univ. Press, 1963), p. 1x.

[73] Cf. M. Carlson, *loc. cit.*.

[74] Kristian Smidt, *James Joyce and the Cultic Use of Fiction* (Oslo: Oslo Univ. Press, 1959) p. 66.

throne and sceptre of Heaven in Tim Finnegan, the builder's hand, or in the innkeeper who humbly accepted his name from his king. But when Earwicker, *pater familias* and fallen man, is realized through Solness who did set himself up as a rival to God, his fall as well as his achievement takes on metaphysical proportions. He becomes one who,

> with ambitious aim
> Against the Throne and Monarchy of God
> Rais'd impious Warr in Heav'n and Battel proud

though his perdition is not so bottomless, nor his stature quite as majestic, as that of Milton's heavenly prince. There is always a streak of triviality in HCE – a heritage from Leopold Bloom – that prevents him from becoming exalted or downcast for very long at a time. And HCE is not at any time a Miltonic Satan in the sense that he cannot create, only destroy.[75] He sins, but he also builds.

In *FW* and *Bygmester Solness* alike the masterbuilder builds a tower; and at least in Joyce's version this construction is not only a ladder towards heaven, but also a phallic symbol. HCE is well and convincingly portrayed as a potent man in his primary manifestation as Mr Earwicker, father of three children, still desiring his wife, and constantly tempted by younger women. But the tower Solness built provided Joyce with a most forceful demonstration of the sexuality of his protagonist. The 'Bygmester' is a 'threelegged man'; and his tower is called 'his risen stiffstaff' (191.36) so as to make all aware of the phallic symbolism involved. The tower as a sexual symbol and as a Tarpeian Rock ('Topsman to your Tarpeia!' 167.18) links the sex life of HCE with his fall. He is a 'bygger muster of veirying precipitation and haralded by faugh sicknells' (324.27–28); and by this combination of rise and fall Joyce can drive home one of his theories about the origin of man's guilt: he is tempted by a girl, yields, and falls. But something even more important is demonstrated in the symbol of the tower: creativity seen as the

[75] Cf. M. Carlson, *op. cit.*, p. 135, where HCE is called Satan without this qualification.

conception and birth of a new generation and as the building of civilization is one and the same. HCE the builder of cities and HCE the sensualist cannot be separated. Thus, the tower becomes another expression of the comprehensive idea of creativity which underlies the Ibsen-obscene pun. There is little contrast and no conflict between the erection of cities (or the writing of poetry) and the act of copulation in *FW*, for 'Bygmester Finnegan [who] lived in the broadest way immarginable' (4.18–19) encompasses everything.[76] However, because he is so multifarious he is not perfect as a creator: his cities are like himself, 'human and erring.' Just as Solness's tower was left only nearly finished, HCE's civilization lacks finish: and like Solness's love for Hilde which was never consummated, HCE's sexuality does not always lead to the act of creation. It often peters out in bawdy talk about varieties of sexual perversion; and when HCE and Anna Livia go to bed together in Book III, 4, a contraceptive is used (cf. *FW*, pp. 585 ff). The symbolic patterns of *FW* are never exclusive of the details of 'life – real life'; Joyce is as steadfast in his insistence on the artistic value of the trivial in his last book as in his earlier writings. HCE is not only grand, he is also common.

Joyce's Revenants

The idea of cyclical recurrence, in new generations or in the lives of individuals, is a prominent theme in a number of Ibsen's plays. Ragnar and Hilde of *The Masterbuilder* are joined in

---

[67] I can find little reason for believing, as Mrs Glasheen does, that the Masterbuilder in *FW* is a symbol of the artist in his ivory tower:

> Ibsen's Masterbuilder Solness was, for Joyce, the symbol of the Artist-Father who does not come down from his tower until he is thrown down by the conjunction of youth and a jealous rival – God. Halvard Solness is a horrid warning against futile, lonely death upon lonely life that overtakes the Artist who isolates himself in pride of his powers.

A Second Census of Finnegans Wake (Evanston: Northwestern Univ. Press, 1963), p. xiii.

This idea may well be present in Ibsen's play; but if Joyce noticed it, he kept it to himself and used other sides of Solness in *FW*, in which the Masterbuilder's fall is the beginning rather than the end.

FW by other *dramatis personae* who represent a shift from one generation to another. In 'Anna Livia Plurabelle' the late Mrs Rosmer of *Rosmersholm* is remembered twice. Her fate (she was drowned in an eddy under a bridge), as well as that of Rebekka West, is incorporated in what one of the washer-women has to say about Alp:

> It was ... before she ever dreamt she'd lave Kilbride and go foaming under Horsepass bridge, with the great southerwestern windstorming her traces and the midland's grainwaster asarch for her track, to wend her ways byandby, robecca or worse, ...
>
> (202.35–203.05)

And her replacement by a younger woman – the fate Alp gladly suffers at the end of the *Wake* – is woven into,

> Do you know what she started cheeping after, with a choicey voicey like waterglucks or Madame Delba to Romeoreszk? You'll never guess. Tell me. Tell me, *Phoebe, dearest, tell, O tell me* and *I loved you better nor you knew.* And letting on hoon var daft about the warbly sangs from over holmen: *High hellskirt saw ladies hensmoker lilyhung pigger:* ... (200.07–13)

Besides the mention of Rosmersholm, we are reminded of the plot of the play by the 'warbly sangs' ('sang' is Norw. for song) which hides the Norwegian sentence, 'Jeg elsker saaledes den smukke lille unge pige' ('I thus love the pretty little young girl').[77] This is just what Rosmer did, but did not say or even realize himself; and it is just what Mrs Rosmer pretended she was deaf and blind to (the first two words of 'hoon var daft' resemble Norw., 'hun var' ('she was')). She then flung herself down from the bridge into the river; and that decorous Issy, Rebekka West, thought she could take her place.[78] In a paragraph about 'the politish leanings and town pursuits' of HCE there may be a faint glimpse of Rosmer himself, whose final

---

[77] Cf. British Museum Additional Ms. No. 47471B, p. 68, which clearly shows us the Norwegian sentence which is present but obscured in the final version.

[78] There are probably further references hidden in the Norwegian words in this passage, perhaps to Ibsen, but I cannot identify them.

tragedy was prompted not only by Rebekka West's plans and presence but also by the hardening of the political climate around him: 'by Butt's, most easterly (but all goes west!) of blackpool bridges' (85.14–15). There is a black pool, indeed, under the bridge in *Rosmersholm;* and the narrowmindedness of Headmaster Kroll creates a link with Dublin – another black pool – in which Joyce felt coerced by similar forces.

The two young rivals of *The Pretenders* (*Kongs-emnerne*) are present in this account of Issy's wooers: 'The bivitellines, Metellus and Ametallikos [the Earwicker twins], her crown pretenders, obscindgemeinded biekerers . . .' (252.15–16). Ibsen himself is pressed into 'obscindgemeinded'; and the winner in the play, the extrovert, charming Haakon, is probably Shaun, while the doubting Skule serves well as a contribution to the picture of Shem. The word 'pretenders' or *Kongs-emnerne* is quoted as 'kongsemma' (133.36), reminding us of the shift from one generation to the next in a royal family.

The League of Youth (*De unges Forbund*) is mentioned by its full name once, 'the Ligue of Yahooth o.s.v.' (310.17 – 'o.s.v.' Norw. for 'etcetera'), and is probably woven into three other passages (224.22–23, 283.19, and 378.28). There is only one indication[79] that Joyce makes use of anything but the title, which is used because it serves the same purpose as the title of *The Pretenders*. There is a touch of irony in the references to *The League of Youth*. The young people are also Swift's Yahoos, and in the play the new generation is defeated by its own crooked ways, whereas in *FW* the sons, embodying and becoming their father, are successful.

The title of *When We Dead Awaken* (*Når vi døde vågner*), provided a particularly succinct expression of the theme of recurrence. The title appears in the list of Ibsen-plays on p. 540 as 'dudder wagoners'; earlier in the book it has had the forms 'for my deading is a? Wake?' (24.14), 'when wee deader walk-

---

[79] 'Noksagt!' (535.19) – Enough said! – is Daniel Hejre's catchword in *The League of Youth*. It is mentioned by William Archer as a word particularly difficult to translate (p. x of his 'Biographical Introduction' to *Henrik Ibsen's Prose Dramas*, Vol. I, London: Walter Scott, 1890).

ner' (170.18), and 'teto-dous as a wagoner' (230.12); and it is possibly hinted at in 'his dode canal sammenlivers' (100.30) and in 'like the dud spuk' (323.36) where it follows a mention of *Ghosts*. There is, however, nothing to be gleaned from these allusions but the obvious: a reminder that in *FW* people come back to life, changed but still the same.

Writing a book about death and resurrection, Joyce naturally found Ibsen's *Ghosts* useful. The Norwegian title, *Gengangere* (literally: 'revenants'), could – and does – serve as an epithet for HCE in his many manifestations. The first of the twelve questions in I, 6 speaks of HCE as a 'chainganger' (126. 15) to remind us of his return as well as of his having been a prisoner; and merging into HCE, Shaun protests, 'gangin I am. Gangang is Mine and I will return' (487.29–30). As the Norwegian Captain, HCE comes 'ghustorily spoeking, gen and gang, dane and dare' (323.35–36), where the idea of return is stressed in 'spoeking' too, in which English 'speak' and 'spook' and Norwegian 'spøke' (to joke or to be a ghost) are combined.

Captain Alving, whose sins live on in *Ghosts*, was tempted by (or himself tempted) a girl and fell. He is thought of as a villain by nearly all the characters in the play, but Joyce lets him defend himself. In 'Epilogue to Ibsen's "Ghosts"', which Joyce wrote in 1934, the ghost of the Captain comes forth to lay part of the blame on his wife, who is the tragic heroine of the play, and on Pastor Manders, the upholder of hollow conventions. He does not consider himself innocent,

> I gave it up I am afraid
> But if I loafed and found it fun
> Remember how a coyclad maid
> Knows how to take it out of one.

But there is one thing he cannot quite understand:

> My spouse bore me a blighted boy,
> Our slavey pupped a bouncing bitch.
> Paternity, thy name is joy
> When the wise sire knows which is which.
> . . .

> The more I dither on and drink
> My midnight bowl of spirit punch
> The firmlier I feel and think
> Friend Manders came too oft to lunch.[80]

Captain Alving is allowed a similar defence in *FW*, though the novel is true to itself in letting HCE utter what is a parody not only of Ibsen's play but also of Joyce's epilogue. 'Arise, sir ghostus!', say the Four at the inquest; and as usual HCE does not require much asking. In a voluble monologue he says:

> as a matter of fict, by my halfwife, I think how our public at large appreciates it most highly from me that I am as cleanliving as could be ... On my verawife I never was nor can afford to be guilty of crim crig con of malfeasance trespass against parson with the person of a youthful gigirl frifrif friend ... (532.14–20)

HCE makes a clean sweep here: he has had intercourse neither with his wife nor with girl friends, he says. But his guilt (in *FW* the memory of the sexual act, in or outside marriage, conveys a feeling of guilt) cannot be hidden; when he mentions the maid it bobs up in a stammer he cannot control. In all the three acts of *Ghosts* the feeling of guilt, as well as the assignment of guilt by the author, is spreading so that in the end virtually no one in the play is innocent. The 'Epilogue to Ibsen's "Ghosts"' shows us that Joyce had noticed this, and Richard Ellmann correctly comments that 'the poem parodies Ibsen's familiar devices of Spreading the Guilt and the Horrible Hint'.[81] But as often elsewhere, Joyce pokes fun at something he has himself adopted: the guilt spreads in *FW*, too; and there are literally thousands of horrible hints in the novel for us to laugh at or be shocked by.

There are a number of incidents in *FW* that may reflect the last act of *Ghosts*, in which Osvald goes mad. Osvald's dementia is due to syphilis; and Joyce may have had him in mind as well as his father, from whom he had caught the disease, when he wrote one of the slanderous accounts of HCE's death pre-

---

[80] *Critical Writings*, p. 272.
[81] Ellmann, p. 681, footnote.

sented in 'The Lion' (I, 4): 'An infamous private ailment (vul-govarioveneral) had claimed endright, closed his vicious circle, snap' (98. 18–19). Osvald is the subjected of the gossip on pages 56–57, too. We see him in the guilty HCE:

olover his exculpatory features ... the ghost of resignation diffus-ed a spectral appealingness, as a young man's drown o'er the fate of his waters may gloat, similar in origin and akkurat in effective to a beam of sunshine upon a coffin plate. (56.15–19)

('Akkurat' is Norwegian for 'exactly'.) A page later he and Pastor Manders are found in a

flashback in which he sits sated, gowndabout, in clericalease habit, watching bland sol slithe dodgsomely into the nethermore, a glo-bule of maugdleness about to corrugitate his mild dewed cheek ... (57.25–28).

There is a reference to Lewis Carroll (C. L. Dodgson) here; but the sun ('sol'), the 'clericalease habit' (of Pastor Manders), and the illness all have their conspicuous counterparts in *Ghosts* and point to that play. So may this description of Shem as Shaun sees him: 'his rotten little ghost of a Peppybeg, Mr Him-myshimmy, a blighty, a reeky, a lighty, a scrapy, a babbly, a ninny, dirty seventh among thieves . . .' (173.26–28).

In these passages Osvald is seen as both HCE and Shem. Osvald is a painter, and it is natural that he should contribute to Joyce's portrait of Shem, who is an artist. And since Captain Alving returns in his son and Shem grows into his father, Os-vald can serve as a representative of two generations without any violation of theme or plot in either Ibsen's play or Joyce's novel. HCE's, alias Captain Alving's, vindication of his morals implies that the maid (and her daughter! Nearly everything is the 'same anew' in *Ghosts* and *FW)* is Issy, and that Mrs Alving is Anna Livia. But the latter identification is not sup-ported by further evidence in *FW*. Nor do I know who, if any-body, Pastor Manders is in the multifarious Earwicker family.

Since three ideas at the very roots of *FW* (the Horrible Hint, the Spreading of Guilt, and the Recurrence of Everything) are found as prominent parts of *Ghosts* it is tempting to assume that Ibsen's play may have influenced Joyce's basic ideas about his book. But for two of them this is hardly so. The Spreading of the Guilt is inextricably connected with the nature of the character-gallery of *FW*. Because HCE has fallen and because he impersonates all fallen heroes, the guilt spreads to a great number of characters. Because the sons, Shem and Shaun, become their father, they do not escape their share in his sins; and through them all artists and philistines appear with their innocence lost. This is such a natural consequence of the main pattern in the character-portrayal in *FW* that no Ibsen is needed as source for it. Similarly, the Horrible Hint is one of the by-products of Joyce's new language. In a book where the greater part of the characters are guilty and where, by a peculiar language and logic of its own, each sentence is to fathom the meaning of the book as a whole, hints, horrible and pleasant, are unavoidable.

The most important literary impetus towards the third idea that *Ghosts* and *FW* have in common, the cyclic recurrence of everything, probably came from Giambattista Vico. His *Scienza Nuova* is a useful guide to *FW* in more ways than one, for Vico has relevant things to say about the relationship between gossip and the acquisition of knowledge, about myth as a way to an understanding of human history, and about the meaning of creation in life and art. Joyce had read Croce's summing up of this last point, which is a surprisingly apt comment on *FW:*

> Man creates the human world, creates it by transforming himself into the facts of society: by thinking it he re-creates his own creations, traverses over again the paths he has already traversed, reconstructs the whole ideally, and thus knows it with full and true knowledge.[82]

Another idea equally central to Vico's and Joyce's understanding of their worlds is the conception of time and history as cyclical recurrence. Joyce makes use of Vico's cycles both in the

[82] See Ellmann, p. 351.

history of the world that is built into *FW* and in the structure of the book. Though he modifies Vico's historical ages on one or two points, they provide him with a pattern without which *FW* would have been another book altogether.[83] But Vico's ideas were not tailored to Joyce's purposes: Vico wrote a philosophy of the history of civilization, Joyce was writing a book about a Dublin innkeeper, his wife, daughter and twin sons, and their doings from about noon one day to the early morning of the next – in short, a novel. And in a novel the primary material is individual human lives, not the history of civilizations. There are some few glimpses in Vico of correspondences between the ages of history and the stages of an individual life from birth to death, but his concern is all the time with the development of the man-made world – with civilizations, arts and sciences – and not with the God-given facts of birth, reproduction and death. Joyce finds the primary manifestation of cyclical recurrence in the family, which for him is the fundamental social and historical unit. But the Earwickers are described over a period of time too brief to give room for any extended treatment of the cyclical theme; and Joyce had to see to it that they merge with other characters and stories that span the thirty years from one generation to the next.

Ibsen's plays provide some of the most important of these stories and characters used to reinforce the idea that the members of the Earwicker family will return in the next generation. Tim Finnegan of the ballad did not provide much help in this respect; he dies and comes to life again as the same individual. But as '*Bygmester* Finnegan' (my italics, *FW* 4.18) he stands for an old masterbuilder that must yield to a new architect of the next generation, a Solness and a Ragnar Brovik; and he is loved by an elderly wife and a new daughter-wife – by Aline and Hilde. HCE is 'sir ghostus! As long as you've lived there'll be no other' (532.04–05), for he will return in the next generation just as men and maids return in *Ghosts. Ghosts, The Masterbuilder, Rosmersholm, The Pretenders, The League of*

---

[83] Cf. Clive Hart, *Structure and Motif in Finnegans Wake* (London: Faber and Faber, 1962), Chapter II.

Youth, and *When We Dead Awaken* all contribute to this same pattern in *FW*, either by adding a history to the five Earwickers or by titles that serve as *Leitmotivs* on the same theme.

So far I have followed the traditional approach to Joyce's use of circular recurrences in *FW:* taking it to derive from Vico and to have been fashioned into a novel by the help of secondary sources such as Ibsen. But the compactness and coherence of the body of references to Ibsen may tempt one to reconsider this development and ask whether Ibsen could be the earlier source. Joyce read Ibsen in his teens, a time when fundamental attitudes and ideas about life are formed; he came across Vico only after the decisive exile from Ireland in 1904. However, the abundance of literary echoes in *FW* does not prove that the experience on which the novel is built is purely or even primarily an experience of books. Indeed, it is likely that Joyce embraced Vico because the Neapolitan offered a philosophical framework for ideas that he already nursed. Nor should we leave Ibsen with all the credit for the cyclical theme and structure of *FW*. The primary manifestation of the theme as we find it in *FW* is the family; and the family (and births, marriages and deaths) is a social fact for which there is no need to search in books. Life itself tells us again and again that new generations take over from old, that sons resemble their fathers, and that most often there is no new thing under the sun. This observation was, I think, Joyce's starting-point. It may never in the first instance have been formulated in writing, or even consciously defined, but it represented a personal experience around which Ibsen's families and Vico's philosophy could make sense – and therefore appeal to Joyce.

Tea, *Love's Comedy*, and the Last Word in *FW*

The word 'tea' and its mutations appear often and sometimes in conspicuous positions in *FW*. Mr C. Hart's *Concordance to Finnegans Wake* lists 'tea' (with its variants) some 60 times whereas 'beer' and 'ale', words central to Earwicker's occupation, are recorded only about 50 times.[84] The prominence of the word is reminiscent of the use of 'coffee' in Swift's letters to Vanessa. Mr Atherton comments, 'The corresponding puzzle in the *Wake* is Joyce's use of the phrase, 'A tea set' (262.16, 17, 18 and 308.2), which is probably a key to a cryptogram in the 'Night Lessons' Chapter (pp. 260–309)'.[85] The phrase 'a tea set' is an enigmatic *presentation* of the puzzle (hiding the word 'tease' and suggesting a meaning like 'the problem is posed'); but the puzzle itself is the word 'tea'. Scholars still disagree on the meaning of Swift's 'coffee'; and, examining a work more puzzling than Swift's, I shall not claim that following interpretation of 'tea' (which does not radically challenge Mr Atherton's) is exhaustive or final. Nevertheless, a number of points can be established with a fair amount of certainty.

Joyce was no doubt aware of the existence and significance of tea and tea-drinking in Ibsen's plays. We know that he praised *Love's Comedy*,[86] in which a central scene is a tea-party. The play is alluded to in 'What a surpraise, dear Mr Preacher, I to hear from your strawnummical modesty!' (493. 36–494.01): Pastor Strawman is the spokesman of the tea-drinking ladies in the play. To him and his likes, the youthfully romantic ideas of the hero, Falk, are indeed 'Outragedy of poet-scalds! Acomedy of letters!' (425.24).[87] Falk ironically hails the tea-party with the words, 'Hurra/ for Venskab, Thevand, Kjærlighed og Tanter!' ('Hurrah/ For friendship, tea-water, love, and aunts!') In this party, where Falk and his Svanhild feel themselves to be the only representatives of passion and truth, the conversation turns into an extravagant comparison of love to plants. Falk sums it up in a scornful speech where he presents

[84] See Clive Hart, *A Concordance to* Finnegans Wake (Minneapolis: Univ. of Minnesota Press, 1963). I have not included what Mr Hart calls syllabifications in the figures above.

[85] J. S. Atherton, *op. cit.*, p. 118.

[86] Ellmann, p. 79. Joyce was probably introduced to the 'tea-scene' in *Love's Comedy* by C. H. Herford's 'A Scene from Ibsen's "Love's Comedy"' in *The Fortnightly Review*, Vol. 67 (Feb. 1, 1900), pp. 191–199. Professor Herford does not comment on the symbolism of the word 'tea'.

[87] This is, of course, also a reference to *A Comedy of Errors*.

his simile: love is like tea. It comes from the East, where its taste – as well as love itself – is still fresh and pure. But on the way to Europe and to Norway the fine fragrance is lost, just as what might begin as love in the members of the tea-party will lose its name and substance by being forced through a never-ending treadmill of demands from society. Tea is the proper image for a 'love' that has been drained of all spontaneity, all passion, all natural ease – of everything, so that only a hard shell of social demands is left.

In Ibsen's later plays tea recurs from time to time with a similar and an equally clear-cut symbolic meaning. Peter Stockmann, the real enemy of the people in *En folkefiende*, drinks tea with his lonely evening meals. He cannot understand his brother's, Dr Stockmann's, pleasure in a savoury meal or a strong drink any more than he can fathom the passion for truth or the wayward, boyish impetuosity which the doctor so charmingly displays. In *Rosmersholm* tea is promised to Headmaster Kroll. But when Rosmer declares his conversion to a new morality Kroll leaves; and, appropriately enough, no tea is ever served in *Rosmersholm,* in which true love between Rosmer and Miss West grows before our eyes. It is with scorn that Hedda Gabler – high-strung and passionate, though frigid – suggests tea for Løvborg who to her seems to have lost much of his taste for the other sex. In *The Masterbuilder* the insipid Mrs Solness invites her doctor to a cup of tea; and in *John Gabriel Borkman* the lively Mrs Wilton tauntingly orders the young and loving Erhart back to his fossilized mother and her tea. In all these plays tea is Ibsen's drink for the 'living-dead', those in whom there is no life left, but who have not yet been collected by Death, and linger on by clinging to conventions and old habits.

'Tea' is closely connected with Ibsen's name in *FW:* 'Shem ... preferred Gibsen's teatime salmon tinned' (170.25–27). This may mean that Shem (the artist) likes the neat way in which Ibsen serves up the emptiness of a life without love and passion, or it may imply that Shem prefers the life he finds in books to that around him, that he is so bookish that he belongs with the tea-drinking shadows in Ibsen's plays. In either case Joyce makes use of the symbolic meaning of tea which he found in the Norwegian dramatist. It is with this sort of tea in mind that he calls the Irish 'the most . . . theobibbous paùpulation in the world' (140.12–13). Ireland's tea is 'tamelised' (110.11), tamed, just like the tea that lost its fine taste on the way to Norway in *Love's Comedy*. In keeping with this, and quite in character, is Shaun's comment on Shem, 'all the teashop lionses of Lumdrum hivanhoesed up gagainst him' (177.36–178.01), in which he boasts that Shem has been affronted by the tea-drinking lions of London (and turned out of Lyons's teashops). The ass which narrates III, 1 may well refer to *Love's Comedy* when it says of Shaun: 'Ever of thee, Anne Lynch, he's deeply draiming! Houseanna! Tea is the Highest! For auld lang Ayternitay!' (406.27–28). If so, Shaun is Lind; and the 'Anne' or 'Anna' he is dreaming of is not only Anna Livia but also Anna in *Love's Comedy* who becomes Lind's fiancée and is content to be a housewife ('Houseanna!') in sharp contrast to the other young couple, Falk (Falcon) and Svanhild (the first element in her name is 'swan'), who aspire towards free and perfect (and, as it turns out, unrealizable) love. Lind completely succumbs to the pressure from aunts and mother-in-law and becomes a philistine, a Shaun. An echo of the tea in *Love's Comedy* may also be heard later in Book III in HCE's description of 'an illfamed lodginghouse'. As Mr Atherton has shown, many of the details are taken from Rowntree's *Poverty*,[88] but Ibsen's play may have been in Joyce's mind when he lets his hero go on to say, 'teawidow pension but held to purchase . . . head of domestic economy never mentioned . . . reputed to procure' (545.04–06). Mrs Halm in *Love's Comedy* keeps a 'teawidow pension', her late husband ('head of domestic economy') is never mentioned, and she marries her daughters to her lodgers.

But as may be expected of Joyce, he does not make a faithful disciple's use of Ibsen's 'tea'. The drink itself and the part of its meaning which we have discussed above are inherited from Ibsen; but the main function of 'tea' in *FW* is original and

[88] Atherton, *op. cit.*, pp. 75–79.

typically Joycean: 'tea' becomes a euphemism for semen. And
since all words in *FW* sprawl in a number of directions it has
a group of secondary significations associated with the idea of
fertility: urine, wine, and baptismal water.[89] Joyce may have
been aware of the medical information Mr Atherton reminds
us of in *The Books at the Wake*, that one teaspoonful is 'the
amount of the male ejaculation';[90] but he may also have got an
impulse towards the new meaning from *Love's Comedy*, in
which Falk, though without any specifically sexual connotations, mentions a tea 'de beuf' that is found in novels and said
to be extremely powerful. Joyce mentions this sort of tea twice
in *FW*, and both times with the possible meaning of semen. In
'MAWMAW, LUK, YOUR BEEEFTAY'S FIZZIN OVER!' (308.R1), the
Four are invoked; and they stand for much the same social
'chorus' as the tea-drinking ladies in *Love's Comedy*, but their
never-absent lechery makes an allusion to sexual orgasm more
than pure guesswork. The other reference to beef-tea occurs in
the description of the letter Shaun carries. The letter has a
tea-stain which is accounted for by the words 'His Bouf Toe is
Frozen Over' (421.09), the meaning if which seems to be that
Shaun's ejaculation (or urination) has stained the letter.[91]

This meaning of 'tea' is conspicuously present in other passages in *FW*. On page 240 we find 'polentay' (line 16) where
the presence of pollen makes it clear that this tea is, among
other things, semen. Moreover, the word 'egg-', which appears
in the preceding line, has prepared us for the male counterpart
to be mentioned. This combination of egg and Joyce's variation
of tea occurs elsewhere in *FW*, too: in III, 2 Jaun mentions one
of 'Mary Liddlelambe's flitsy tales ... *Egg Laid by Former
Cock*' and says, 'Trip over sacramental tea into the long lives of
our saints and saucerdotes ...' (440.18,20–21). 'Sacramental

---

[89] Cf. Clive Hart, *Structure and Motif in Finnegans Wake* (London:
Faber and Faber, 1962), pp. 206–208.
[90] Atherton, *op. cit.*, p. 154.
[91] Cf.: 'It [the letter] may not inconceivably have been what is known in
England as a "French letter" and in France as a *capote anglaise*'. Harry
Levin, *James Joyce: A Critical Introduction* (London: Faber and Faber,
1944), p. 116.

tea' is sex and marriage, which he asks the schoolgirls to trip over to become more saintly. 'Tea' sometimes takes part in an elaborate sexual word-play, e.g. 'Hennery Canterel – Cockran, eggotisters, limitated; we take our tays and frees our fleas round sadurn's mounted foot' (137.07–09).[92]

The ironic *double entendre* in tea (semen and frigid conventionality) is one of the remnants in *FW* of Joyce's early view of life as a conflict between the artist and his surroundings. But the artist-creator on the lonely mountain-ridge, surrounded by birds and called Daedalus, does not hold the stage alone in Joyce's last books. He becomes one aspect only of man-as-creator; and the new symbol, semen, expresses the more fundamental act and idea of creation that HCE represents. Thus, the word 'tea' becomes a compressed expression of a basic theme in *FW*.[93] In *Love's Comedy* tea is spelt 'the'; and Joyce, who liked the play,[94] almost certainly noticed this. To guess that Ibsen's spelling of tea has contributed to the choice of the definite article as the final word of *FW* may not be too wide of the mark. In its primary function as an article it is the commonest (and in a way the least denotative and most comprehensive) word of the language; in its secondary sense of 'tea' it sums up the the essence, though not the whole, of life in Joyce's final work. And how like the author of *FW* to create a pun on a word as unpromising to a punster as 'the'.

Notes on Other Ibsen Plays

The notes are arranged in what seems to me the order of significance of the plays in *FW*.

Peer Gynt

Ibsen's hero is first found in *FW* four pages from the beginning; he appears in the picture of HCE snoring in the land-

---

[92] Similar extravaganzas are found in 242.12–16, 262.L2, and 114.29–31.
[93] In the general list of Ibsen allusions I have only included the word 'tea' when characters from *Love's Comedy* may be glimpsed in its immediate context.
[94] Cf. Ellmann, p. 79.

scape: 'peer yuthner in yondmist' (7.29–30). And his presence
is discreetly evoked in the word 'peer' throughout the book until
his last scene with Solvejg is remembered in Anna Livia's farewell monologue. The name functions as a *Leitmotiv*, turning
up in different passages, often in a form slightly different from
'Peer', stressing various aspects of Ibsen's hero.[95] But the motif
always alludes to HCE. Peer falls, tempted by young girls, and
is thus a suitable companion for the fallen HCE whom we meet
in Book I, Chapter 1. And when Joyce's protean innkeeper is
about to rise again at the beginning of I, 4 he prays 'on anxious
seat', 'kunt ye neat gift mey toe bout a peer of saft eyballds!'
(75.16–17). The first five words of this prayer suggest two possible readings in Norwegian, either 'Can you [not] marry me'
or 'can you [not] give me'. The latter reading becomes a cry for
two good eyes and echoes Peer's anxiety in the Hall of the Troll
King where he fights against the trolls who want to cast a lasting spell over his eyesight. Peer succeeds first against the trolls
('has a tussle with the trulls' (134.33) and then the boyg (which
we meet as book-keeper in *FW* – 'So help me boyg who keeps
the book!' (313.12–13)); and like HCE he is soon at large again.
Peer's own voice breaks through in the advertisement for a
manservant in I, 6: 'he is fatherlow soundigged inmoodmined
pershoon but aleconnerman, nay, *that* must he isn't?' (141.24–
–26). This is Joyce's version of Peer's words about God after
the ship blew up in Act IV of *Peer Gynt:*

Han er faderligt sindet imod min Person; –
men Økonom, – nej, det er han ikke!

Joyce sent Ibsen's two lines to Harriet Shaw Weaver with the
following request: 'I want to see as a test if you can read these
2 lines of Norwegian?' She could not; and he gave her two
translations in a later letter, first Archer's,

[95] In the list of Ibsen refs. I have not included all 'peers' in *FW*, only
those with additional links with Ibsen's hero in their immediate context.
Neither have I attempted to list 'pair', 'pere', or 'per' (though they do provide a faint reminder of *Peer Gynt*) except where their contexts seem to
warrant an allusion to the play.

– He (God) is fatherly towards me in person
But economical – that he is not!

and then his own,

– He feels like a father for yours truly P. G.
But a stickler for thrift – Holy Paul, that he isn't![96]

But he did not materially change the version he had included
in I, 6. Other considerations than the wish to be understood
governed his inclusion of material in *FW*. For without some
knowledge of Norwegian and of *Peer Gynt* in the original a
reader can scarcely grasp the extent to which the advertisement for a manservant is a description of HCE himself.

As the Norwegian Captain, HCE is again called Peer ('like
the pervious oelkenner' – 321.01) when he is allowed a peep at
the Irish girl he is about to marry, 'a peep at me mow for Peer
Pol' (330.05). Then 'peal [Peer] will shantey soloweys sang!'
(330.08). And as we follow everything in *FW* through a whole
cycle – 'birth, copulation, and death' – we see Peer in death,
too; he is 'recalled and scrapheaped by the Maker' (98.17) – the
fate the Buttonmoulder told Peer was in store for him.

HCE, the Manservant and the Norwegian Captain are at
times indistinguishable in the references to *Peer Gynt* that are
discussed above. The use of Ibsen's play may thus support Mr
Hart's guess that 'often . . . he [the Norwegian Captain] is an
incarnation of Earwicker's anti-self, the Manservant (identified with the Cad) who, like Shem, is always associated with
the Norwegian language.'[97] The Norwegian language is even
more closely associated with HCE himself, and Peer is never the
Manservant only; but in a book where all the main characters
seem to find polar opposites in other characters and where these
opposites merge, it is not surprising that the Norwegian Captain can remind us of HCE as well as of his anti-self and that

[96] *Letters*, pp. 252, 254.
[97] Clive Hart, *Structure and Motif in Finnegans Wake* (London: Faber
and Faber, 1962), p. 125.

Peer Gynt is woven into contexts in which the self and the anti-self appear together.

'Cheekspeer' (257.20) and 'Chickspeer' (145.24) may be Joyce's tribute to the Shakespearian versatility of Peer as well as to the eminence of his creator (with a grain of salt added in 'cheek' and 'chick'!). But the identification of HCE with Peer is not complete. Versatile, active, sinning, beaten, on their feet again, each given a loving wife, and each fascinated by younger women, Peer and HCE are nevertheless widely different. For although Peer's life has its brilliance and its poetry, it is a failure; he has never found his true self. HCE, on the other hand, is overwhelmingly true to himself; he manifests his manifold but integrated personality ubiquitously in *FW;* and his life is, for all its falls, a triumph. This contrast is not only accounted for by the fact that the material – in this case *Peer Gynt* – which Joyce forced into his book proved a bit intractable here and there. As we have seen, Joyce *wanted* to be original; and he probably tried to avoid nursing the feeling in his readers that any other literary creation was compatible with his. He built his Earwickers of people from fact and fiction, from centuries before Christ to the nineteen-thirties, but of no one that was or even would seem to be identical with the innkeeper or his wife and children. This is a main reason for the extensive use Joyce makes of Ibsen-characters like Peer or Masterbuilder Solness: he could find room for them in his scheme because they were both like and unlike the characters he was giving life to.

That we should see Solvejg merging with Anna Livia is no surprise once the part that Peer plays in the novel is understood. We have seen that the Norwegian Captain, alias HCE, calls his fiancée Solvejg; and Solvejg's own song brings a note of poetry to a number of passages in the book. Shaun tells his father that 'sollyeye airly blew ye' (129.14–15). This is a double reference, to Peer Gynt and to the Irish folksong 'Johnny I Hardly Knew Ye'. In the song and the play alike, a husband returns and is kindly received by a faithful wife, though he is greatly changed and much reduced. And when out in the wide world Peer did not hear her song, Solvejg sang all the same, as

Joyce reminds us: 'Says to youssilves (floweers have ears, hea-hear!) solowly' (337.25–26). There may be a reference to their final reunion, in which he clings to her and she sings, in 'he clasp and she and she seegn her tour d'adieu, Pervinca calling, Soloscar hears' (580. 17–18): and in the end Anna Livia for a moment sees herself as Solvejg who on Whitsun morning sees the Peer in her lap as a boy rather than as an old man:

> And can it be it's nnow fforvell? . . . I had better glances to peer to you through this baylight's growing. . . . Yes, you're changing, sonhusband, and you're turning . . . (626.33–627.02)

Mother Åse is also present at Finnegan's Wake. Merging with old Norse gods (Norw.: 'ås'), she is Issy's 'old nourse Asa' (279. F1); and when HCE calls his children in he does so 'At Asa's arthre' (246.07). But what her relation to the Earwicker family is, I do not know. She may be an Anna Livia of an earlier generation, or she may be Kate, the maid, who is also a widow.[98]

A Doll's House and The Wild Duck

A Doll's House in Norwegian is Et dukkehjem; and this gave Joyce one of the bilingual puns he was unable to resist. The word 'duck' was made to mean both doll, since the sound and spelling resemble the Norwegian word for doll, and duck; and 'duck' thus refers to both A Doll's House and The Wild Duck. The reference is sometimes ostensibly to one of them, sometimes to the other, but both plays are probably meant to be evoked each time. There are not many references to these two plays where this pun is absent; and there is often little else than the verbal fun to be gleaned from the contexts where we find the word-play on 'duck'. Joyce obviously found it so rich and entertaining in itself that he had little need for additional references to Ibsen in such passages.

The heroine of A Doll's House, Nora (the 'duck'), is glimpsed as Anna Livia who often flitters about in FW as a domestic

[98] Cf. A. Glasheen, A Second Census of Finnegans Wake (Evanston: Northwestern Univ. Press, 1963), p. 136.

fowl. She is probably the 'weibduck' (138.34) of the first of the twelve questions in I, 6 and the 'wiffey-ducky' (577.01) of III, 4. Her Christian name, as well as the title of the play, is hidden in 'Nova Norening . . . and if thee don't look homey, well, that Dook can eye Mae' (330.25–27). 'Dook can eye Mae' gives at least three readings in Norwegian: 'you can own me', 'the doll own[s] me', and 'you cannot'. Two of them bring in the idea of ownership, of the wife being the property of the husband or *vice-versa* – a thought that was repulsive to Ibsen as well as to Joyce. HCE confesses to his jurors that he introduced his 'best-preserved wholewife' to 'our fourposter . . . in our altogether cagehaused duckyheim' (533.04, 16–18); and both wives, Anna Livia and Nora, are allowed to escape in the end from homes which have been 'cagehouses' to them. But though we meet Nora as Anna Livia in HCE's own speech there is little in *FW* to indicate that the husbands merge. Helmer of *A Doll's House* is mentioned in 'her elmer's almsdish' (243.15), but I cannot see that he is HCE in that passage. One would rather think that a pillar of society like Helmer might have contributed to Joyce's picture of Shaun, but there seems to be nothing to indicate that, either.

When Anna Livia cries out, '*Vuggybarney, Wickerymandy! Hello, ducky, please don't die!*' (200.06–07) we can, without stretching the imagination unduly, see her placed in Nora's situation when Helmer was seriously ill and she had to take affairs in her own hands as if he were a *vuggebarn,* a child in the cradle. But an even closer parallel comes to light if we regard this as a facetious comment on *The Wild Duck,* where Gregers Werle, the arch-idealist, wants Hedvig to shoot the wild duck as a sacrifice to her father. Anna Livia speaks both for herself and her creator when she reacts against such barren and joyless idealism.

A laugh at the expense of the plot of *The Wild Duck* is also heard in a little jingle in a footnote in 'Lessons'[99] which says,

Braham Baruch
he married his cook

[99] The first to point this out was Mr Atherton. See *op. cit.,* p. 155.

to Massach McKraw
her uncle-in-law
who wedded his widow to Hjalmar Kjaer
who adapted his daughter to Braham the Bear.
(284.F4. Joyce prints it as prose.)

In the play Werle Sr. had a maid who was pregnant with his child married to Hjalmar Ekdal ('kjær' is Norwegian for 'dear'), who believes the little girl to be his own until the revelation towards the end of the play. Joyce's version is fantastic, but no less efficient as a parody for that reason. Another convenient location of the paternity of a child – in a play that like *The Wild Duck* has a pattern of family relations which easily lends itself to ridicule – is remembered in the same footnote in 'Lona the Konkubine', who is Lona Hessel of *Pillars of Society*. The Stephen of *A Portrait* and *Ulysses* was preoccupied with the problems of paternity spiritual and temporal; and Joyce has probably from his first Ibsen-enthusiasm noticed Ibsen's interest in the same complex of ideas. The 'Epilogue to Ibsen's "Ghosts"', which Joyce wrote while his work was in progress, has a couple of lines on it:

> Paternity, thy name is joy
> When the wise sire knows which is which.

Namely, which child is whose! The idea of paternity as something more complicated than one side in a simple husband-wife-child triangle and also as something different from biological procreation is less prominent in *FW* than in the two preceding novels. In *A Portrait* Stephen finally addresses Deadalus, and not his own father, with the words, 'Old father, old artificer, stand me now and ever in good stead.' In *Ulysses* the sonless Bloom becomes a father to Stephen, because of his fatherly concern for him, and on analogy with the *Odyssey*. But in these two novels the theme, prominent though it may be, is not directly related to Ibsen. It is only in Joyce's last work that it is decked out on a couple of occasions with material from the plays of the Norwegian.

Joyce honours the daughter in *The Wild Duck*, Hedvig Ekdal, and her fate by giving her a line in *FW:* 'and, elfshot,
headawag, with frayed nerves' (274.17–18). Her mother, Gina
Ekdal, is summed up in the word 'ginabawdy' (95.07). But
these are passing references to Ibsen's play; and I can find no
convincing evidence that the cast of *The Wild Duck* play
more active parts in *FW*, for instance by merging with main
characters.

There is, however, another theme from the play that is ger-
mane to Joyce's novel. Dr Relling says, 'Take the saving lie
from the average man and you take his happiness away, too',[100]
while Gregers Werle presses the truth, however unpalatable,
on his friend. With Captain Alving in 'Epilogue to Ibsen's
"Ghosts"' Joyce in *FW* is not quite sure – indeed not interested
in – 'which is which', what is truth and what is fiction. The
narrow concept of truth and idealism which Ibsen attacks in
Gregers Werle is transcended in Joyce's phantasmagoria, in
which 'the unfacts, did we possess them, are too imprecisely
few to warrant our certitude' (57.16–17).

When We Dead Awaken

In his article 'Ibsen and *Finnegans Wake*' Mr Carlson lists four
references to the Irene of *When We Dead Awaken*.[101] One of
these is primarily and almost exclusively an allusion to Iren-
aeus, the Church Father, and two are doubtful as references to
Ibsen; but on page 471 'Irine!' is one of the rainbow girls, and
this links her clearly with Ibsen's Irene, since she played the
temptress to Rubek, who preferred art to life. Rubek himself
appears as 'Roebuck' (70.12 and 142.12); and 'Rhoebok' (129.
23) is said to be a 'pigeonheim' – Norw. 'pike' or 'pige' ('girl')
and 'heim' (home') can be seen in the word – that HCE has
inhabited. At the trial in Book I, 4 a witness calls the prisoner 'The rudacist rotter in Roebuckdom' (90.26–27). I fail to
see how an awareness of Ibsen's play can enrich this passage,

---

[100] Una Ellis-Fermor's translation.
[101] *Comparative Literature*, Vol. XII, No. 2 (Spring 1960), p. 136.

nor can I find any evidence that Rubek's personality spreads to characters or incidents in the contexts of these references. But the 'Roebuck' pun itself makes sense if we take it to indicate the way in which Ibsen's tragic hero finds new life in *FW*. Joyce's early novels extol the isolated artist, but in *FW* artists and citizens are alike in sharing a crude vitality that Rubek denies himself in *When We Dead Awaken*. Therefore he is not only a sculptor, but also a roebuck in *FW*.

As early as in *Exiles* Joyce had pondered upon the question Ibsen asks in his last play: is a career devoted to art worth the sacrifices it involves? In Joyce's play Richard Rowan is given the choice between Bertha, who stands for earthly life and fertility, and Beatrice, who is cold but whose intellectual and artistic gifts could help Richard in his writing. The same problem is considered – and answered – in *FW*. As the answer is given in Norwegian (and in Ibsen's spelling) Joyce probably acknowledges an impetus from the Norwegian dramatist: 'Was liffe worth leaving? Nej!' (230.25). The river Liffey and Alp's years as a Dublin housewife are remembered in this sentence; but as I understand the passage in which we find it, the voice is also that of HCE himself, and 'liffe' means life. The irrepressible Issy parodies it in one of her footnotes in the textbook chapter, 'feeling dead in herself. Is love worse living?' (269.F1). A typical contrast between the old Ibsen and the elderly Joyce is revealed here. They are so often interested in the same problems, but their attitudes differ, sometimes entirely, sometimes in emphasis. Ibsen makes much of the question and little of the answer in his play, while in *FW* HCE confidently assures us that life is worth living and his daughter implies that love is not bad living at all.[102] None of the four main characters in *When We Dead Awaken* would deny this, but there is little confidence in their homage to life, by which they have all been trapped. Ulfhejm was deceived by his great love; Rubek and Irene were hopelessly entangled in a web of outward indifference and inward frustration; Mrs Rubek has looked for life but

[102] Cf. FW, 12.01–02, and J. S. Atherton, *op. cit.*, p. 157.

never found it. HCE's life does not lead him along the primrose path of dalliance either, but in him life asserts itself in a buoyancy that Ibsen may have looked for but could not find in his dramatic imagination in 1900.

The Lady from the Sea

The lady fram the sea in Ibsen's play is Ellida Wangel, who left the lighthouse in which she had grown up to move inland and marry a middle-aged doctor with two girls from a previous marriage. Her husband is remembered in the word 'wangles' as one of 'four middleaged widowers' (390.13–14),[103] another term for the four old men in FW. Dr Wangel is a very nice old man in The Lady from the Sea, but enough of an oracle and sufficiently thwarted in his sexual life to fit into the general characterization of the Four.

Ellida longs to go back to the sea and, on a deeper psychological level, to feel free from the ties of a marriage that she thinks circumstances have forced her into, but at the same time she loves Dr Wangel; she is indeed, as Joyce puts it, 'aequal to yoursell and wanigel to anglyother' (300.04–05). Things reach a crisis in the play when a man from the sea, a sailor who had once charmed Ellida into a brief, intense infatuation, returns after many years.[104] She is fascinated and frightened by his enigmatic eyes, which may be remembered in 'oyne of an oustman in skull of skand' (310.31 – 'øyne': Norwegian for 'eyes'). Mr Carlson is right, I think, in taking pp. 232–233 to be Joyce's version of what then happens in The Lady from the Sea:[105]

> For directly with his whoop, stop and an upalepsy didando a tishy, in appreciable less time than it takes a glaciator to submerger an Atlangthis, was he again, agob, before the trembly ones, . . . gotten orlop in a simplasailormade and shaking the storm out of his hiccups. (232.30–35)

[103] Another of the 'four middleaged widowers' is 'sangles' whom I take to be Pastor Sang of Bj. Bjørnson's Over Ævne I.
[104] Cf. p. 56.
[105] Cf. Carlson, op. cit., p. 138.

He is guessing at hers for all he is worse, the seagoer. Hark to his wily geeses goosling by, and playfair, lady! And note that they who will for exile say can for dog while them that won't leave ingle end says now for know. (233.11–14)

And he did a get, their anayance, and slink his hook away, aleguere come alaguerre, like chimista inchamisas, whom the harricana hurries . . . (233.29–31)

This account can be taken to follow Ibsen's play to the end, where the sailor slinks away and Ellida in full freedom chooses Dr Wangel.[106] In this reading the sailor would be Shem who in vain tries to win Issy in 'The Mime'. But as a sailor, this character cannot easily be dissociated from the Norwegian Captain, who is a manifestation of HCE. This ambiguity is reflected in 'And he did a get, their anayance, and slink his hook away'. If taken to refer to Shem, this line says that he saw that he annoyed them, and retreated. If about HCE, the first part of the sentence suggests that he gets her (their Anna/Issy), and the second can be read as a description of the end of the sexual act. This ambiguity is, of course, in tune with the rest of *FW*, in which sons and daughter merge with their parents. Even the Norwegian Captain, humpbacked hero like Humphrey C. Earwicker, reminds one not only of the father; he seems at times more like the manservant; and as one of two suitors and a traveller, he resembles Shem. The identification of the sailor with both HCE and Shem explains why Dr Wangel is one of the Four: the sailor (Shem) becomes the husband and father (HCE), and Dr Wangel must join the shadowy band of old men who are spectators and no longer actors at life's feast and wake.

Eventually, the heroine of *FW* does leave for the sea; and the departure is seen in terms of *The Lady from the Sea*, to which Joyce now gives an ending that tastes less of placid domesticity than Ibsen's. The washerwomen in I, 8 seem to have a presentiment of what is to happen and implore her, 'Missus,

[106] This was a situation that had interested Joyce earlier, too. Cf. my discussion of *Exiles*.

be good and don't fol in the say!' (208.30–31). The sailor in the play is red-haired; and confronted with this fiery stranger, Ellida-Alp leaves her home, first in Issy's footnote version: 'Frech devil in red hairing! So that's why you ran away to sea, Mrs Lappy' (268.F6), then at the end of *FW* when she sees him as her mad, strange father. Since Ellida got a number of letters from her sailor, the title of the play becomes 'fresk letties from the say' (540.23). This correspondence is perhaps remembered on the last page of *FW*, too. The first letter the sailor sent her from the sea came from Arkhangel'sk, which Ibsen spells 'Ark-angel':

> If I seen him bearing down on me now under whitespread wings like he'd come from Arkangels, I sink I'd die down over his feet, humbly dumbly, only to washup. (628.09–11)

There is an obvious pun on Arch-angel (and perhaps one on the Ark) which can account for the inclusion of the word; but Joyce's spelling as well as the situation allows us to guess that Ibsen's lady again enriches the portrait of her Joycean sister.

An Enemy of the People

There are few obvious references to *An Enemy of the People (En folkefiende)* in *FW*. About a page before his long list of Ibsen-plays HCE refers to himself as an 'enemy, among these plotlets' (539.23–24), and three pages later he declares that 'I demosthrenated my folkfiendship, enmy pupuls . . .' (542.18). Ibsen's title is ironic, for Dr Stockmann, who is called an enemy of the people, is really a man who wants to give society sound foundations. Joyce retains the irony and lets HCE say that he is an enemy of the people with pride and in the assurance that his very individuality is a better contribution to society than pusillanimous acquiescence. There is another point, too, in Ibsen's play that enabled Joyce to incorporate Dr Stockmann in his Dublin innkeeper: just as Dr Stockmann was not subdued when the authorities tried to force him into silence, HCE, alias Tim Finnegan, rises from his bier against the wish of the people at the wake who desperately try to hold him down.

Since Dublin's motto, *Obedienta civium urbis felicitas,* is quoted at the end of – almost as part of – the list of Ibsen plays on p. 540, I think Mr Atherton is right in assuming that this is

> Another *leit-motiv* which Joyce connects with Ibsen ... Ibsen believed in the exact opposite of this [Dublin's motto]; but nearly quotes it in *An Enemy of the People* when the mayor of the town, Peter Stockman, says to his brother, 'The individual ought undoubtedly to acquiesce in the subordinating himself to the community – or, to speak more accurately – to the authorities who have the care of the community's welfare.'[107]

The main reason for Joyce's interest in the motto[108] derives from Vico's theory of the development of languages, which the Neapolitan philosopher saw as one of three stages: first gestures, then 'heraldic' speech, and at last the languages of the earth as we know them. The second stage remains vague in Vico (or at least to me), but Joyce revived it in *FW* in references to heraldry and related disciplines. But this does not, of course, rule out the assumption that *An Enemy of the People* contributed to the prominent place Dublin's heraldic motto got in the book. Indeed, 'Peter's burgess' (277.10), which follows one of the Joycean versions of the motto, is a reference to Peter Stockmann, Magistrate and Chief Constable of Ibsen's little township.[109]

Pillars of Society

The only appearance of the Norwegian title of this play, *Samfundets støtter,* is found in I, 4 ('The Lion'), 'the sibspeeches of all mankind have foliated (earth seizing them!) from the root of some funner's stotter' (96.30–31). In *FW* speech, as well as all other aspects of civilization, comes from a funny man that stutters.[110] Because HCE's stuttering reveals guilt, we are stead-

---

[107] Atherton, *op. cit.,* p. 154.
[108] *Obedientia civium urbis felicitas* appears at least eleven times in *FW:* 23.12–14, 76.08–09, 140.06–07, 266.01–02, 277.07–08, 347.35, 358.08–09, 371. 22, 494.21–22, 540.25–26, and 610.07–08.
[109] Another indication that the motto is associated with Ibsen can be found on p. 371.22,28.
[110] Cf. Atherton, *op. cit.,* p. 31.

ily reminded of the fall that lies at the very beginning of *FW*'s world. But HCE rises again and again to become a true pillar of society. This development is illustrated by the fortunes of the protagonist of *Pillars of Society*. Consul Bernick has also fallen, has suffered under his guilt, and finally rises above it.

Ibsen's title is only partly ironic, for Consul Bernick deserves that epithet in the end when he has confessed his sins and offers his services to his fellow citizens. This does not prevent Joyce, however, from giving it a twist. He calls the play 'pullars off societies' (540.24–25), probably in remembrance of the many times Ibsen, Samson-like, pulled the pillars away from under a society that was rotten or hardened.

There is a reference to Lona Hessel, a lady the young Joyce expressed his admiration of,[111] in 284.F4, but the more meaningful allusion in this footnote is to *The Wild Duck*.

The Warrior's Barrow

In *FW* the giant's grave, or mound, hides HCE interred in the landscape; the grave has peaks or upright stones at feet, middle, and head – the initial letter of his family name turned back and down. As inhabitant of this tomb, HCE is thought of as a Viking or more generally as a warrior from early Irish history.

As one of Ibsen's early plays has the title *Kjæmpehøien* (the closest translation is *The Giant's Mound* though the most common is Archer's *The Warrior's Barrow*) and is set at the foot of a mound, Joyce may well want to evoke it some of the times he mentions this scenic manifestation of HCE. It is unlikely, though not impossible, that Joyce should have read this insignificant little play; but the title could in itself serve his purpose of enriching the tomb with memories of Ibsen's vikings. Indeed, in 'Here is viceking's graab' (18.13) both 'graab' (Norw. 'grav' ('tomb')) and Jute's reaction in the next line, 'Hwaad!' (Norw. 'Hvad' ('what')) are close to Norwegian spelling and may be meant as pointers to the Norwegian dramatist.

---

[111] *Critical Writings*, p. 46.

The general list gives other instances where the mound is specially reminiscent of *The Warrior's Barrow*.

Brand

In the majority of the instances where the word 'brand' is found in *FW* it is simply the English word and carries with it only a very faint reminder of Ibsen's play. But Ibsen's moral giant, who is portrayed as a son and a husband and thinks he is sent by God to the little fjord community where he is vicar, appears in 'our goodsend Brandonius, *filius* of a Cara, spouse to Fynloguc' (327.02–03); and the play is remembered in 'a brand rehearsal' (617.16). In these two allusions Brand is HCE, but as far as I can see the Norwegian pastor does not contribute more than his name to the Irish publican on these occasions.

In Ibsen's production *Brand* and *Peer Gynt* are companion plays, both concerned with the moral flaws Ibsen had detected in his countrymen. Once, they are found together in *FW*, too: 'a peer of trouders under the pattern of a cassack ... the mouthbrand from his firepool' (311.28–31). There is more stress in *FW* on the sexual aspects of life, glimpsed, I think, in 'a peer of trouders', than on ideas preached from pulpits ('the pattern of a cassack'). The 'all or nothing' call of the clergyman in a narrow Norwegian fjord is foreign to HCE, whose appetite for life is too gargantuan for him to understand Brand's (and Kierkegaard's) moral slogan.

Little Eyolf

I can find only two allusions to this play. Little Eyolf himself is remembered in 'abbles for Eyolf' (201.33–34), and the awe-inspiring Rat-wife may be hidden in 'old Roastin the Bowl Ratskillers' (231.33). But as Joyce was particularly impressed by *Little Eyolf* when he wrote *FW* – he praised the play as one of Ibsen's masterpieces to James Stephens in 1936[112] – I suppose

---

[112] See Ellmann, pp. 709–710.

it may have found its way into other passages in the novel where it lies undetected by the present writer.

Hedda Gabler

See general list (373.22, 540.24, and 601.26–27). In the last of these allusions Hedda is one of the rainbow-girls, a suitable role for a tempting, though cold woman.

Allusions to *Catilina* (307.L), *John Gabriel Borkman* (85.13 and 578.11, 30–31), *Emperor and Galilean* (540.23), *The Warriors (Vikings) at Helgeland* (257.34, 388.19–20, and 596.07, 15) and to 'On the Fells' (579.08) are quoted in the general list.

General Comments

FW constitutes a repository for a great deal of what Joyce himself retained from his experience of life and literature; and, being the result of more than fifteen years of dedicated work, it reflects not only ephemeral, but also relatively constant aspects of his mind and thought. Thus it provides, among other things, an authentic, if incomplete, catalogue of Joyce's literary interests; for it can be assumed that the greater the number of references to any one author in *FW*, the more prominent is that writer's place in Joyce's consciousness. Consequently, the fact that Ibsen is a persistent presence in *FW* has a direct bearing on the question of his importance to Joyce's earlier work; while at the same time, of course, it is the Ibsen influence already apparent in those earlier works that does most to stimulate the search for Ibsen in *FW* – there is a constant and fruitful interplay here.

Ibsen's presence in *FW* should, however, be considered in the perspective created by all the other allusions in the book. Without the cumulative force of these thousands of allusions to the facts and fiction that are our cultural heritage, the book would not be able to impress itself on the reader as an encyclopaedic and all-encompassing artifact. Although an Ibsen character is once hailed 'Amid the soleness', the Norwegian dramatist is never given a one-man show in the book. Ibsen's primary role in it is no different from Shakespeare's, or Wellington's, or Noah's: he is present with his characters at an enormous rally where sheer mass counts for more than individuals. It must therefore be made clear that the great number of references to Ibsen which I have discussed should not be taken as an indication that Ibsen towers head and shoulders over other writers as a literary source for *FW*, nor that he is indispensable in all the contexts where he appears. Next to Shakespeare, to whom Mr M. J. C. Hodgart has found nearly 300 allusions,[113] he is the most important dramatist at the wake;[114] but it would not surprise me if lists of allusions to a dozen historical, literary, and mythical figures were found to run to a similar or even greater number of items.

It is against this background that the function of the allusions to Ibsen must be considered. As the discussion of individual references in the earlier parts of this chapter has shown, most of them contribute to the texture and structure of *FW* in one of three ways. (1) There is the material, chiefly from *The Masterbuilder* and *Ghosts*, that has gone into the making of the supporting girders of this monumental novel. Our notions of HCE as a builder and creator, and of the pattern of family relations in which everything repeats itself in the next generation, would not have had the form and emphasis which they actually possess if Joyce had not known these plays. (2) A significant number of allusions to Ibsen form short verbal units that recur with varying degrees of frequency. These *Leitmotivs* have been discussed earlier; the most important of those that derive from Ibsen is the 'bygmester' motif; less prominent, but quite frequent, are the variations on 'peer' and 'tea'. (3) Finally, a character or a title of a play may be evoked for a moment in a given passage, never again to return to the surface of the book. Such allusions are often clearly and obviously related to the main trends in the passages where they occur, but not always.

---

[113] See 'Shakespeare and *Finnegans Wake*', *The Cambridge Journal*, Vol. 6 (Sept., 1953), p. 735.
[114] Cf. Atherton, *op. cit.*, p. 151.

Sometimes their relevance to their immediate context is tenuous or even imperceptible or non-existent.

Against the mass of references of which *FW* is made up the allusions in this last category seem insignificant, and of no importance at all when they cannot be seen as organic parts of their contexts. It is tempting to dismiss them as so much bric-a-brac that Joyce found intrinsically interesting, but which he was unable to fuse with his other material in *FW*. This temptation may arise from the assumption that *FW* is, or should be, a post-Jamesian novel with a plot and a point of view that strictly unify and pattern everything in the book. But this ideal does not obtain in *FW* studies (if it was found to obtain, the book could be shown to be an indisputable failure, and there would be little need for further time and energy spent on it). Any discussion of *FW* that wants to proceed beyond a summary dismissal must accept it as a novel that is different from the well-made novels of Henry James. As I see the book, it is an attempt to write a novel about a whole world – replete with human beings, giants, gods, history, geography, sciences, languages, and religions. This is in itself no insuperable obstruction to a presentation at once all-encompassing and structurally unified. Mediaeval and Renaissance writers could find room for the whole universe in their works; this was made possible by their belief in the ordered nature of Creation and by the availability of symbols – spatial, numerical and other – that could represent the cosmos. It could be argued that 'If the world is God's poem, the converse can also be true – a poem can constitute a world by virtue of its proportions.'[115] Joyce too wants to compress 'Allspace in a Notshall' (*FW* 455.29), and he makes important structural use of ancient symbols like the circle and the square, as well as of symbolic numbers, to give shape and meaning to his book. Resent researchers, Mr Clive Hart in particular, have shown how extensive and intricate is Joyce's use of these ordering symbols. No one, however, has thought of *FW* as a book in which everything can be, and will

[115] M.-S. Røstvig, in 'Renaissance Numerology: Acrostics or Criticism?', *Essays in Criticism*, Vol. 16, No. 1 (Jan. 1966), p. 7.

be, placed in a proper perspective by such symbolic patterns. And rightly, I think. There is in *FW* a considerable residue, a continuous litter, that no neat symbolic order can tidy up. For Joyce is here, as in his earlier work, a realist in the sense that his material is an everyday world, not a highly stylized human and moral landscape. The world as presented in *FW* is at once a cosmos and a chaos. And the chaos is as essential a part of the whole as the order.

This left Joyce, it seems to me, with an insoluble problem: how could he give a comprehensive account of a chaos that would not yield to any formulas? *FW* defiantly attempts the impossible: to list the items of which chaos consists. It is only at times that the list gives an illusion of totality, and therefore the book does not completely realize itself. But the attempt provides an interesting justification of the inclusion of the bric-a-brac that will not fit any patterns in *FW;* and it provides a wide frame in which the passing allusions to Ibsen can be seen to work. Moreover, Joyce's attempt gives to each individual allusion an autonomy that is normally lost when material from another writer is used in a more traditional work of art, in which all component parts will be modified by (and themselves modify) a stricter over-all design.

This forces an interesting problem on critics of *FW*. Since normally we relate details in a work to some unifying pattern that decides the function and makes clear the meaning of each detail, we dismiss as faults those which we cannot link to the whole in any satisfactory way. In the present study I have used this traditional method, and asked, as regards the allusions to Ibsen: in what way do they fit into greater units and finally into patterns that I see as central to the whole book? And because *FW* for all its strangeness has much of the framework of a traditional novel this approach is justifiable. In the last instance it is probably also the only sympathetic and rational approach the human mind is capable of: we place our impressions of life and literature in what for us are meaningful sets of correlatives. But this method must not be applied so rigidly or mechanically to *FW* that we dismiss the chaotic and mystifying as nonsensical without giving any further attention to it. Let me illustrate this by an example. Most of the references to *The Wild Duck* fit into major themes and stories in *FW*, but two allusions, to Hedvig (274.17–18) and to Gina (95.07), seem unrelated to these organizing forces. That there can be a relation, which I have been unable to see, is a possibility that must be kept in mind; but if the premise that they are unrelated is granted, there are two possibilities. We can either find them completely nonsensical in the contexts where they appear, or we can modify our habitual expectations and see them as representing that part of the world which does not yield to any all-inclusive system, i.e. as items in the chaos which *FW* does not attempt to impose order upon. This view allows these allusions, and a multitude of similar references, to refer to all the associations that the words can trigger, and not only to a set of thoughts relevant to a particular theme. This makes *FW* a book more profuse in human material than a traditional novel; and criticism is extant which demonstrates that it can, as a result, encourage the kind of almost unlimited inventiveness in the reading that serves only to distort the work as a whole. However, though the richness may be confusing, it is not in principle absurd. For even the chaos must, and can, in the last instance, be seen as related to something – to a fictional world that is chaotic and cosmic at the same time. In this world chaos and order are juxtaposed, and the juxtaposition provides a perspective in which both make sense.

Joyce's refusal to make his world neater is understandable. A vision of a confusing world leads to the writing of a book which embodies and reflects the confusion. Joyce is not unique in his attempt; the same *Zeitgeist* moves behind the items of chaos incorporated in *FW* and behind the disjointed fragments that the 'I' of *The Waste Land* has shored against his ruins. The chaos of *FW* is, however, far more chaotic than that of *The Waste Land*. A reason for this, and perhaps a justification, can be found in Joyce's 'cultic use of fiction', to use Smidt's term.[116]

[116] See *James Joyce and the Cultic Use of Fiction* (Oslo Univ. Press, 1959).

The Waste Land is an exposition of a world that is chaotic, but it does, as Eliot said of the function of art, impose 'a credible order upon ordinary reality, and thereby [elicits] some perception of an order *in* reality.'[117] As I have shown, there is indeed *some* order to be perceived in *FW*, but the book is also purposely mystifying. Just as HCE becomes a rival to God, so the world of the book becomes a pendant to creation and the book itself a holy book; and, as such, it needs the impenetrable as an ingredient. That Joyce does not *want* to give an understandable account of everything in *FW* is obvious from the development of some of the allusions in 'Work in Progress'.

Thus, 'somefunner's stotter' (British Museum Add. Ms. 47472, p. 285) becomes 'some funner's stotter' (*FW* 96.31), and is immediately less easily recognizable to a reader who knows that the Norwegian title of Ibsen's play is *Samfundets støtter*. That 'duckhouse' (*FW* 395.29) is *Et Dukkehjem* is more apparent from the earliest version where Joyce wrote the word with a capital 'D'; and it is easier to see that '*Natten den Sorte*' is a quotation from the poem 'Borte!' than to grasp the allusion in the final '*Nattenden Sorte*' (*FW* 608.29). A general trend in the writing becomes apparent: the original meaning – in this case allusions to Ibsen – has often been obscured in the attempt to add further connotations to it.[118] When Joyce quotes Ibsen in the original (and even distorts the original almost beyond recognition) he is not put off by the fact that the allusion will be grasped only by a reader with a very special background. On the contrary, Ibsen helps Joyce to make *FW* 'wilfully obscure'.[119]

Through the earlier chapters of this study we have traced Joyce's use of fictional point of view. With Stephen of *A Portrait*, and like the Ibsen he had praised in his early enthusiasm for drama, Joyce wanted to be 'like the God of the creation . . . within or behind or beyond or above his handiwork,

[117] T. S. Eliot, in *Poetry and Drama* (Harvard University Press, 1951), pp. 43–44.
[118] Cf. A. Walton Litz, *The Art of James Joyce* (London, Oxford Univ. Press. 1961), p. 114.
[119] Glasheen, *op. cit.*, p. xvii.

invisible, refined out of existence...'.[120] But in one respect
Ulysses and *Finnegans Wake* are more personal than the earlier work (with the possible exception of *Stephen Hero*): Joyce
crowded them with an immense mass of material that came
directly from his own experience and which is not as immediately relevant to a central theme as the personal material in *A
Portrait*. Neither book is about Dublin in general, nor an attempt to give a general survey of Ireland's capital; they are both
descriptions of *Joyce's* Dublin, and the inclusion of a certain
amount of material in both books seems to have been due almost
exclusively to the fact that it was part of the Dublin gossip
Joyce had amassed in his fine memory. *FW* is, of course, more
idiosyncratic than *Ulysses*. In at least one respect the seeming
universality of its frame of references is indeed only seeming;
what the book is a nearly complete record of is Joyce's own
mind, not a whole world. As a counterbalance to this excessively personal aspect, the point of view is so involved that it might
refine a host of authors out of existence. The author's simple
'I' is never heard, nor are characters and incidents described as
by an omniscient author in a straightforward narrative. The
subtle point of view in the early chapters of *Ulysses* where
Joyce speaks now through his characters, now by their side, is
as blunt as any outright first-person narrative compared to the
multitude of voices and view-points contained in a single passage in *FW*. A member of the Earwicker family is not allowed
to speak alone for long. Through his or her voice break those of
other Earwickers – or of minor characters. Where things are
revealed about the characters in *FW* the author's voice is hidden behind an impenetrable facade of rumours and evidence
from a plethora of different sources. The intricacy of this complex of points of view adds to – and is itself increased by – the
general obscurity of the book. In this way Joyce remains true
to the letter of Stephen's proclamation of artistic intention: he
is indeed 'within or behind or beyond or above his handiwork';
and a trait in Joyce's work that was inspired by Ibsen is thus
still visible.

[120] *A Portrait*, p. 215.

The preceding pages demonstrate, I hope, that, though *FW* is an obscure book and in parts incomprehensible, the obscurity is clearly related to the standard of integrity that Joyce set himself: life should not be made simpler than it is. But to say this should not be to obscure the fact that there is also much in *FW* that is immediately understandable and enjoyable. A great many of the allusions to Ibsen are clear and simple and make good sense in their contexts as soon as they are noticed; and many of the characters from Ibsen's dramatic world are made to play their parts in the Earwicker family with ease, as the following chart can show us.[121] The chart also testifies to the fact that *FW* can (and should?) be read primarily as a novel about a father, a mother, and three children. Such a reading, which I have attempted, sometimes to the exclusion of more esoteric aspects, seems to me to encompass much in the book that other readings exclude, and to be by far the most entertaining approach.

Ibsen characters in the Earwicker family:

	HCE	ALP	SHAUN	SHEM	ISSY
The Master-builder	Halvard Solness	Aline	Rag-nar		Hilde Wangel
Love's Comedy			Lind	Falk	
Peer Gynt	Peer Gynt	Solvejg			
Ghosts	Captain Alving Osvald			Osvald	Regine
A Doll's House		Nora			
An Enemy of the People	Dr Stock-mann				
Rosmersholm	Rosmer?		Mrs Rosmer		Rebekka West

[121] I have taken the idea of such a chart from Adaline Glasheen, *op. cit.*, pp. lx–lxvi. An analogous, less elaborate chart is found in Kristian Smidt, *op. cit.*, p. 86.

	HCE	ALP	SHAUN	SHEM	ISSY
The Lady from the Sea	The Sailor	Ellida Wangel		The Sailor	Ellida Wangel
Pillars of Society	Consul Bernick				
Brand	Brand				
The Pretenders			Haakon	Earl Skule	
Hedda Gabler					Hedda Gabler
John Gabriel Borkman	Bork- man				

A List of Ibsen Allusions in *FW*

The list should be used in conjunction with the earlier parts of this chapter, where most of the entries are discussed in the sub-chapters to which they belong:

references to Ibsen's name and his poems are analysed in 'Ibsen – Obscene and Creative',

references to *The Masterbuilder* in 'Bygmester Finnegan',

references to *Rosmersholm, The Pretenders, The League of Youth, When We Dead Awaken,* and *Ghosts* in 'Joyce's Revenants',

references to *Love's Comedy* in 'Tea, *Love's Comedy,* and the Last Word in *Finnegans Wake*',

references to Ibsen's other plays, plus a body of references to *When We Dead Awaken,* in 'Notes on Other Ibsen Plays'.

The list includes a number of references that are not discussed in the text, as I have no significant comments to make on their function. Doubtful identifications are preceded by a question-mark; reasons for the inclusion of some of these are indicated if they have not been discussed earlier.

Identifications made in similar lists already in print are acknowledged by the following abbreviations:

Atherton – J. S. Atherton, *The Books at the Wake* (London: Faber and Faber, 1959).

Carlson – Marvin Carlson, 'Henrik Ibsen and *Finnegans Wake*', *Comparative Literature*, Vol. 12, No. 2 (Spring 1960), pp. 133–141. Since Mr Carlson's *list* includes references to *titles* of plays only, I acknowledge references made in the text of his article, too.

Christiani – D. B. Christiani, *Scandinavian Elements of* Finnegans Wake (Evanston, Ill.: Northwestern Univ. Press, 1965).

In each case I give the name of the author in whose list the identification was first made. Needless to say, references to Ibsen have been discussed, though not listed, in works by other Joyceans. Footnotes in the earlier parts of this chapter acknowledge my indebtedness to these.

4.18–19	Bygmester Finnegan, of the Stuttering Hand, freemen's maurer	*The Masterbuilder* (*Bygmester Solness*). Atherton, p. 257.
4.35–36	a waalworth of a skyerscape of most eyeful hoyth entowerly	?*The Masterbuilder*, who was a great builder of towers.
6.08–11	His howd feeled heavy, his hoddit did shake . . . Mastabatoom, mastabadtomm	*The Masterbuilder*, who, with Tim Finnegan of the ballad, fell down.
7.29–30	peer yuthner	*Peer Gynt.*
12.01–02	lifework leaving	*When We Dead Awaken.* A *Leitmotiv* connected with the play.
17.22–23	his Inn the Byggning to whose Finishthere Punet	?*The Masterbuilder*. 'Bygning' is Norw. for 'building'. Perhaps a reference to the fall (and the sex life) of Bygmester Solness.
18.13	Mutt: – Here is viceking's graab.	?*The Warrior's Barrow* (*Kjæmpehøien*). Atherton p. 258.
19.04	ragnar rocks	*The Masterbuilder*, in which Ragnar Brovik represents the younger generation. Carlson, p. 133.

23.19	Norronesen or Irenean	?*When We Dead Awaken (Når vi døde vågner)*. Irene is a main character. Carlson, p. 136.
24.14	my deading is a? Wake?	*When We Dead Awaken.* A *Leitmotiv* connected with the play.
28.26–27	*Les Loves of Selskar et Pervenche,* freely adapted to *The Novvergin's Viv.*	?*Peer Gynt.* Two Norw. words 'elsker' ('loves') and 'viv' ('wife'), and 'Per-' and his Norwegian wife, Solvejg, make this a probable all. to *Peer Gynt.*
37.35	littlebilker	*The Masterbuilder (Bygmester Solness).*
38.32 & 39.05	Mère Aloyse . . . peer	*Peer Gynt.* Mother Åse is a main character.
40.08–10	(the 'girls' he would keep calling them for the collarette and skirt, the sunbonnet and carnation) . . . fossil-	?*The Masterbuilder.* The skirt, collar, and bonnet are found in the stage-direction introducing Hilde Wangel into the play. Another young woman in the play is Kaja Fossli; an anagram of her family name may be found in 'fossil'.
49.17, 28–29	doomster . . . a Northwegian and his mate of the Sheawolving class	Ibsen the author of 'Et vers' (see pp. 139–140), and George Bernard Shaw.
51.13	ghoatstory	?*Ghosts.*
53.08–09	Christianier . . . sage	Ibsen lived in Christiania (later spelt Kristiania, now Oslo) in his first years as a dramatist and returned there as an old man. It was to that city Joyce sent his letter to Ibsen.
56.16–19	the ghost of resignation . . . a young man's drown o'er the fate of his waters may gloat, similar in origin and akkurat in effective to a beam of sunshine upon a coffin plate.	*Ghosts (Gengangere).*

56.20	Inn the days of the Bygning	?*The Masterbuilder (Bygmester Solness)*. 'Bygning' is Norw. for 'building'.
57.13–14	the Barrow for an People, one Jotnursfjaell	*The Warrior's Barrow (Kjæmpehøien)*. 'Jotnursfjaell' means 'The Giants' Mountain'.
57.24–28	a flashback in which he sits sated, gowndabout, in clericalease habit, watching bland sol slithe dodgesomely into the nethermore, a globule of maugdleness about to corrugitate his mild dewed cheek	*Ghosts (Gengangere)*.
58.16–17	Oho, oho, Mester Begge, you're about to be bagged in the bog again. Bugge.	*The Masterbuilder (Bygmester Solness)*. Atherton, p. 257.
62.03, 08	baggermalster . . . bilder	*The Masterbuilder*. Atherton p. 257.
63.13	Archer	?William Archer, who translated and campaigned for Ibsen.
68.33	obseen	?Ibsen. Christiani, p. 106.
69.06	Gyant	?*Peer Gynt*.
70.12–13	roebucks raugh at pinnacle's peak	?*When We Dead Awaken (Når vi døde vägner)*. Professor Rubek.
75.16–17	(kunt ye neat gift mey toe bout a peer saft eyballds!)	*Peer Gynt*. Atherton, p. 257.
77.03	our misterbilder, Castlevillainous	*The Masterbuilder (Bygmester Solness)*. Atherton, p. 257.
77.07	thorpeto	'Til min Ven Revolutions-Taleren!' Christiani, p. 109.
85.11–12	alpenstuck in his redhand	?*The Masterbuilder*, in which Hilde Wangel is first seen with one in hand.
85.13–14	(beware to baulk a man at his will!)	*John Gabriel Borkman*. Borkman's will is baulked, and the results shown in the play.

85.15–17	Butt's, most easterly (but all goes west!) of black-pool bridges, as a public protest and naturlikevice, . . . for the wrathbereaved ringdove.	?*Rosmersholm.* 'Naturligvis' is Norw. for 'of course'.
90.26–27	The rudacist rotter in Roebuckdom.	?*When We Dead Awaken* (*Når vi døde vågner*). Professor Rubek.
92.25–26	a lovelooking leapgirl, all all alonely, Gentia Gemma of the Makegiddy-culling Reeks	?*The Masterbuilder* (*Bygmester Solness*). Hilde Wangel.
95.07	ginabawdy	*The Wild Duck* (*Vildanden*). Gina Ekdal is Werle's former mistress.
96.31	some funner's stotter	*Pillars of Society* (*Samfundets støtter*). Atherton, p. 258.
98.16–17	he saw the family saggarth, resigned, put off his remainders, was recalled and scrapheaped by the Maker.	*Peer Gynt.* Christiani, p. 113.
98.18–19	An infamous private ail-ment (vulgovarioveneral) had claimed endright, closed his vicious circle, snap.	?*Ghosts (Gengangere).*
100.30	his dode canal sammen-livers	?*When We Dead Awaken* (*Når vi døde vågner*). A word from the title of the play and 'sammen' ('together') and 'lever' ('lives') are present here.
111.20–21	(the overcautelousness of the masterbilker here, as usual, signing the page away)	*The Masterbuilder* (*Bygmester Solness*). Atherton, p. 257.
117.32	Huhu	?*Peer Gynt.* Huhu is one of the inmates of the madhouse.
124.20	some peerer or peeress	*Peer Gynt.* Carlson, p. 140.

126.10–11	What secondtonone myther rector and maximost bridgesmaker was the first to rise taller	The Masterbuilder (Bygmester Solness). Perhaps also an allusion to Maximos, the mystic, who tries to bridge the gap between Christianity and paganism in Emperor and Galilean (Kejser og Galilæer) Carlson, p. 136.
126.15	chainganger's	Ghosts (Gengangere). Atherton, p. 257.
129.14–15	when sollyeye airly blew ye	Peer Gynt, of which 'Solvejg's Song' is an important part.
129.23	Rhocbok	?When We Dead Awaken (Når vi døde vågner). Professor Rubek. Carlson, p. 136.
131.6, 13–14, 17	learned how to fall; ... put a matchhead on an aspenstalk and set the living a fire; ... god at the top of the staircase ...	The Masterbuilder (Bygmester Solness).
133.36	kongsemma	The Pretenders (Kongs-emnerne). Atherton, p. 257
134.33	has a tussle with the trulls	Ibsen in 'Et vers' ('A Verse'), Christiani, p. 121.
136.07–08 11–12	go away, we are deluded, come back, we are disghosted ... he has founded a house, Uru, ... to which he has assigned its fate	?Ghosts (Gengangere).
138.32–33	woollem the farsed, hahnreich the althe, charge the sackend	English kings, but also three playwrights: William Shakespeare, Henrik Ibsen, and Gerhart Hauptmann.
138.34	weibduck	?The Wild Duck (Vildanden) and A Doll's House (Et dukkehjem).
139.19	'twould grig	Edvard Grieg, who wrote the music for Peer Gynt. Christiani, p. 122.
141.3, 5	ducking ... Shalldoll	?The Wild Duck (Vildanden) and A Doll's House (Et dukkehjem).

141.24–26	he is fatherlow soundigged inmoodmined pershoon but aleconnerman, nay, *that* must he isn't?	*Peer Gynt.* A quotation from Act IV.
142.12	Roebuck's	?*When We Dead Awaken (Når vi døde vågner).* Professor Rubek.
143.03	panorama	?*A Doll's House (Et dukkehjem).* An anagram of Nora? Cf. *A Wake Newslitter* (Newcastle, New South Wales) No. 1 (March 1962), p. 6.
143.14	redissolusingness	?*The Masterbuilder (Bygmester Solness).*
145.24	Chickspeer's	?*Peer Gynt*
147.12	Hilda	*The Masterbuilder. (Bygmester Solness).* Hilde Wangel is sometimes called Hilda in English translations.
152.26	masterplasters	*The Masterbuilder (Bygmester Solness).*
154.23	Let Pauline be Irene.	?*When We Dead Awaken (Når vi døde vågner).* Irene. Carlson, p. 136.
159.25–26	my vaultybrain ... I am a ... deserving case by genius.	'Et vers' ('A Verse'). Christiani, p. 125.
167.18–19	Topsman to your Tarpeia! This thing, Mister Abby, is nefand.	*The Masterbuilder (Bygmester Solness).*
169.04	Ragonar Blaubarb	*The Masterbuilder (Bygmester Solness).* Ragnar Brovik, the representative of a new generation, is prob. one of the Ragnars alluded to. Carlson, p. 133.
170.18	when wee deader walkner	*When We Dead Awaken (Når vi døde vågner).* Atherton, p. 258.
170.26–27	he preferred Gibsen's teatime salmon tinned	Ibsen. Atherton, p. 257.

173.26	his rotten little ghost	? *Ghosts (Gengangere)*.
175.16	*Not yet his Arcobaleine forespoken Peacepeace upon Oath;*	? *The Masterbuilder (Bygmester Solness)*. Aline is Solness's wife.
185.30–31	obscene matter not protected by copriright in the United Stars	Ibsen. See pp. 136–146.
191.34–36	our visionbuilders, Baaboo, the bourgeoismeister, who thought to touch both himmels at the punt of his risen stiffstaff	*The Masterbuilder (Bygmester Solness)*. Carlson, pp. 134, 141.
197.13–14, 20	For mine ether duck I thee drake. And by my wildgaze I thee gander . . . doll	*A Doll's House (Et dukkehjem)* and *The Wild Duck (Vildanden)*.
199.04–05	holding doomsdag over hunselv	'Et vers' ('A Verse'). A quotation from the last two lines. Atherton, p. 258.
199.06–07	droming on loft till the sight of the sternes	? 'Margrethe's Cradlesong' from *The Pretenders (Kongs-emnerne)*.
199.08–09	to peer was Parish worth thette mess	*Peer Gynt.* The passage is rich in Ibsen-allusions; and Peer is seen merging with Henry IV of France. Christiani, p. 131.
200.06–07	*Vuggybarney, Wickerymandy! Hello, ducky, please don't die!*	*The Wild Duck (Vildanden)* and *A Doll's House (Et dukkehjem)*.
200.09, 12	Madame Delba to Romeoreszk? . . . sangs from over holmen	*Rosmersholm*. 'Sang' is Norw. for 'song'.
201.33–34	the cane for Kund and abbles for Eyolf	*Little Eyolf (Lille Eyolf)*. Atherton, p. 257.
203.01–05	before she ever dreamt she'd lave Kilbride and go foaming under Horsepass bridge, with the great southerwestern . . . robecca or worse	*Rosmersholm*. Rebekka West.

208.30–31	Missus, be good and don't fol in the say!	? *The Lady from the Sea (Fruen fra havet)*. Carlson, p. 138.
219.08	ghosters	*Ghosts (Gengangere)*. This passage is about a play or a mime. Carlson, p. 140.
221.23–24	Rocknarrag	*The Masterbuilder (Bygmester Solness)*. An anagram of Ragnar (Brovik) and Ragnarrock. Carlson, p. 133.
222.08–09 11–12	O, Mester Sogermon . . . Till the summit scenes of climbacks catastrophear	*The Masterbuilder (Bygmester Solness)*. 'Til' is Norwegian for 'to'.
224.22–23	The youngly . . . frilles-in-pleyurs . . . if in florileague	*The League of Youth (De unges Forbund)*.
226.28	Andecoy	? *The Wild Duck (Vildanden)*.
230.12	teto-dous as a wagoner	*When We Dead Awaken (Når vi døde vågner)*. 'Tod' is German for 'death'.
230.25	Was liffe worth leaving? Nej!	*When We Dead Awaken.* Cf. discussion p. 175.
231.33	the Bowl Ratskillers	? *Little Eyolf (Lille Eyolf)*. The Rat-wife.
232.32–35	he again, agob, before the trembly ones, a spark's gap off, doubledasguesched, gotten orlop in a simpla-sailormade and shaking the storm out of his hiccups.	*The Lady from the Sea (Fruen fra havet)*. Carlson, p. 138.
233.11–14	He is guessing at hers for all he is worse, the seagoer. . . . playfair, lady! And note that they who will for exile say can for dog while them that won't leave ingle end says now for know.	*The Lady from the Sea (Fruen fra havet)*. Carlson, p. 138.
233.12	wily geeses	*The Wild Duck (Vildanden)*. Atherton, p. 258.

242.31–33	allinall ... she not swop her eckcot hjem for Howarden's Castle, Englandwales.	*The Masterbuilder (Bygmester Solness)*. Aline's own home – Norw. 'eget hjem' – burns down and she does not like the new house Solness builds.
243.15	her elmer's almsdish	*A Doll's House (Et dukkehjem)*. Cf. 'hjem' in the preceding entry. Helmer is Nora's husband.
246.07	At Asa's arthre	*Peer Gynt.* Mother Åse. Atherton, p. 258.
252.15	crown pretenders	*The Pretenders (Kongs-emnerne)*. Atherton, p. 257.
252.16	obscindgemeinded	Ibsen.
254.25–28	we are recurrently meeting em ... in various phases of scripture as in various poses of sepulture	? *When We Dead Awaken (Når vi døde vågner)*, in which so much of the dialogue is about a sculpture. Carlson, p. 136.
254.32–33	when his magot's up he's the best berrathon sanger in all the aisles of Skaldignavia.	? Ibsen himself or *The Master-builder.* Bygmester Solness built churches and Hilde heard him sing on top of the spire. 'Sanger' is Norw. for 'singer'. Carlson, p. 134.
257.20	Cheekspeer	? *Peer Gynt.*
257.34	Gunnar's	? *The Warriors at Helgeland (Hærmænderne på Helgeland)*. Cf. line 36 in which Snorre is mentioned.
263.18–19	Saaleddies er it in this warken werden, mine boerne, and it vild need ...	? *The Wild Duck (Vildanden)* may be found in 'vild need'. 'Således er det i denne vakre verden, mine barn' (in modern Norwegian spelling) means 'It is like that in this beautiful world, my children'; it sounds like a quotation, but I have not been able to trace its origin. Atherton, p. 258.
268.F6	French devil in red hairing! So that's why you ran away to sea, Mrs Lappy.	? *The Lady from the Sea (Fruen fra havet)* in which the sailor is red-haired and 'frekk', which is Norwegian for 'forward, saucy'.

268.F7	A washable lovable float-able doll	? *A Doll's House (Et dukkehjem)*.
269.F1	With her poodle feinting to be let off and feeling dead in herself. Is love worse living?	? *When We Dead Awaken (Når vi døde vågner)*. Cf. 230.33 and discussion p. 175.
274.08–09, 11, F1	daring Dunderhead to shiver his timbers and . . . ministerbuilding . . . Go up quick, stay so long, some down slow!	*The Masterbuilder (Bygmester Solness)*. Carlson, p. 141.
274.17–18	and, elfshot, headawag, with frayed nerves	*The Wild Duck (Vildanden)*. Hedvig Ekdal.
277.07–10	To obedient of civicity in urbanious at felicity . . . Peter's burgess	*An Enemy of the People (En folke-fiende)*. Peter Stockmann.
279.F1	grig	? Edvard Grieg, who composed the music for *Peer Gynt*.
279.F1	Nature tells everybody about but I learned all the runes of the gamest game ever from my old nourse Asa.	*Peer Gynt*. Mother Åse. Atherton, p. 258.
283.19	a league of archers	? *The League of Youth (De unges Forbund)* and William Archer. Carlson, pp. 139–140.
283.F2	Gamester Damester	? *The Masterbuilder (Bygmester Solness)*, the hero of which is indeed a master of dames.
284.F4	Braham Baruch he married his cook to Massach McKraw her uncle-in-law who wedded his widow to Hjalmar Kjaer who adapted his daughter to Braham the Bear.	*The Wild Duck. (Vildanden)*. Hjalmar Ekdal.
284.F4	H for Lona the Konkubine	*Pillars of Society (Samfundets støtter)*. Lona Hessel.

291.F4	Mester Bootenfly	*The Masterbuilder (Bygmester Solness).*
294.F1	dolls' home	*A Doll's House (Et dukkehjem).* The closest translation is 'A doll's home'. Atherton, p. 257.
296.07	monsterbilker	*The Masterbuilder (Bygmester Solness).* Atherton, p. 257.
300.04–05	aequal to yoursell and wanigel to anglyother	*The Lady from the Sea (Fruen fra havet).* Ellida and Dr Wangel. Carlson, p. 138.
302.24	Orbison	? Ibsen.
307.L	*Catilina*	*Catilina.* Atherton, p. 257.
308.01 02	Gobble Anne: tea's set	? *Love's Comedy (Kjærlighedens komedie).* Anna.
309.13	mysterbolder	*The Masterbuilder (Bygmester Solness).* Carlson, p. 141.
310.17	the Ligue of Yahooth o.s.v.	*The League of Youth (De unges Forbund).* 'o.s.v.' is Norwegian for 'and so on'. Atherton, p. 257.
310.30	oyne of an oustman in skull of skand	*The Lady from the Sea (Fruen fra havet),* in which the sailor's eyes are often mentioned. 'Øyne' is Norw. for 'eyes'. Cf. p. 56.
311.29	peer	*Peer Gynt.* Cf. next item. Atherton, p. 257.
311.31	brand	*Brand.* Cf. preceding item and discussion of *Brand.*
313.12–13	So help me boyg who keeps the book!	*Peer Gynt.* The Boyg. Atherton, p. 258.
321.01	like the pervious oelkenner	*Peer Gynt.* Cf. 141.24–26.
323.01	wanderducken	*The Wild Duck (Vildanden).*
323.35–36	ghustorily spocking, gen and gang	*Ghosts (Gengangere).* Atherton p. 257.
323.36	like the dud spuk	?*When We Dead Awaken (Når vi døde vågner).*

324.27	the allexpected depression over Schiumdinebbia	? Ibsen, whose plays are often said to be depressing. Cf. next item.
324.27–28	a bygger muster of veirying precipitation	*The Masterbuilder* (*Bygmester Solness*). Atherton, p. 257.
325.16	gosse	? Sir Edmund Gosse was one of Ibsen's advocates in England. ('Gosse' is Swedish for 'boy'.)
326.10	aase	? *Peer Gynt*. Mother Åse. Atherton, p. 258.
327.02–03	our goodsend Brandonius, *filius* of a Cara, spouse to Fynlogue	*Brand*.
328.10–11	prodestind arson, . . . the volumed smoke	? *The Masterbuilder* (*Bygmester Solness*). Solness feels guilty for the burning down of his wife's home.
329.06	the good lifebark Ulivengrene of Onslought	? *Pillars of Society* (*Samfundets støtter*). A ship that is important to the plot is called 'Palmetræet' ('The Palmtree'). 'Olivengrene' is Norw. for 'olive branches'. 'Onslought' may hide Oslo.
329.25	Ghoststown	*Ghosts* (*Gengangere*).
330.05	Peer	*Peer Gynt*.
330.08	peal vill shantey soloweys sang!	*Peer Gynt*, 'Solvejg's Song'. Atherton, p. 258.
330.25–27	Nova Norening . . . and if thee don't look homey, well, that Dook can eye Mae	*A Doll's House* (*Et Dukkehjem*).
331.05–09	there's a windtreetop whipples the damp off the mourning. . . . And the lunger it takes the swooner they tumble two. He knows he's just thrilling and she's sure she'd squeam. The threelegged man and the tulippied dewydress.	?*The Masterbuilder* (*Bygmester Solness*). Ragnar's comment on the song Hilde hears, and the fall. Carlson, p. 135.

331.31–32	To the laetification of disgeneration by neu- humorisation of our kristianiasation.	Ibsen.
332.18	Kaemper Daemper	? *The Warrior's Barrow* (*Kjæmpehøien*).
337.18–19	Then inmaggin a stotterer. Suppoutre him to been one biggermaster Omnibil.	*The Masterbuilder* (*Bygmester Solness*). Atherton, p. 257.
337.25–26	Says to youssilves (floweers have ears, heahear!) solowly . . .	*Peer Gynt*. Solvejg, who sang her song alone.
343.10–11	Orops and Aasas were chooldrengs and micramacrees!	*Peer Gynt*. Mother Åse, and per- haps a rough anagram of 'Peer'. 'Dreng' is Norw. for 'boy' and/or 'servant'.
347.07–08	moist moonful datc man aver held dimsdzey death with	'Et Vers' ('A Verse'). A reference to the last two lines.
356.36– 357.01,–03	a master of vignettiennes . . .arsoncheep	? *The Masterbuilder* (*Bygmester Solness*). Cf. Stanislaus Joyce, *My Brother's Keeper*, pp. 98–99.
358.18	the harpermaster	*The Masterbuilder* (*Bygmester Solness*).
359.26	Goes Tory	? *Ghosts* (*Gengangere*).
361.25	budkley mister	*The Masterbuilder* (*Bygmester Solness*).
364.28–29	They seeker for vannflaum all worldins merkins. I'll eager make lyst turpidump undher arkens.	'Til min Ven Revolutions- Taleren!' A quotation from the concluding couplet. Christiani, p. 180.
365.06	for groont a peer	*Peer Gynt*.
369.10	Gazey Peer	*Peer Gynt*.
371.03, 07–08	swinglyswanglers . . . Like wather parted from the say	? *The Lady from the Sea* (*Fruen fra havet*). Wangel.

371.28	You here nort farwellens rouster? Ashiffle ashuffle the wayve they.	'Borte!' ('Gone!') A quotation from the first stanza.
373.22	Rina	? *Hedda Gabler.* Rina Tesman.
373.27	That was when he had dizzy spells.	*The Masterbuilder (Bygmester Solness).*
374.15	duckbboard pointing to peace at home	*A Doll's House (Et dukkehjem).*
374.36– 375.01	How you fell from story to story like a sagasand to lie.	? *The Masterbuilder (Bygmester Solness).*
377.26	our myterbilder his fullen aslip	*The Masterbuilder (Bygmester Solness).* Atherton, p. 257.
377.36– 378.02	Isn't it great he is swaying above us for his good and ours. Fly your balloons, dannies and dennises! He's doorknobs dead.	*The Masterbuilder (Bygmester Solness),* from the dialogue in the last scene.
378.24–25	Shaw and Shea are lorning obsen	Ibsen. Atherton, p. 257.
378.28	gayleague	? *The League of Youth (De unges Forbund).*
379.17–18	he sthings like a rheinbok. One bed night he had the delysiums that they were all queens mobbing him.	*Peer Gynt.* Peer's tale about his ride on a reindeer; and the scene in the Hall of the Mountain King.
383.22	Downbellow Kaempersally	? *The Warrior's Barrow (Kjæmpehøien).* Atherton, p. 258.
388.19–20	from Hedalgoland, round about the freebutter year of Notre Dame 1132 P.P.O.	*The Vikings at Helgeland (Hærmændene paa Helgeland).* Christiani, p. 185.
389.23	his peer of quinnyfears	? *Peer Gynt.* Peer is afraid of the saintly Solvejg as well as of the Troll King's daughter. 'Kvinne' is Norw. for 'woman'. Atherton, p. 257.
390.03	Gosterstown	? *Ghosts (Gengangere).*

390.13–14	four middleaged widowers, ... wangles	The Lady from the Sea (Fruen fra havet). Dr Wangel.
393.08	Bargomuster Bart	? The Masterbuilder (Bygmester Solness).
395.07	their pair of green eyes and peering in	? Peer Gynt.
395.29	duckhouse, the vivid girl	A Doll's House (Et dukkehjem). Atherton, p. 257.
406.28	Houseanna! Tea is the Highest! For auld lang Ayternitay!	? Love's Comedy (Kjærlighedens komedie). Anna Halm.
420.23	Norse Richmound	? The Warrior's Barrow (Kjæmpehøien).
424.22	rackinarockar!	? The Masterbuilder (Bygmester Solness). Ragnar Brovik.
425.24	Outragedy of poetscalds! Acomedy of letters!	? Love's Comedy (Kjærlighedens Komedie).
440.03–04	William Archer's a rompan good cathalogue	William Archer, the translator of Ibsen's plays. Carlson, p. 139.
444.34–35	You was wiffriends? Hay, dot's a doll yarn! ... I'll homeseek	A Doll's House (Et dukkehjem). Carlson, p. 140.
445.31	the rattle of doppeldoor-knockers	? The Masterbuilder (Bygmester Solness), in which the young come knocking on the door.
471.01	Irine!	? When We Dead Awaken (Når vi døde vågner). Carlson, p. 136.
471.08–10	when next to nobody expected, their star and gartergazer at the summit of his climax, he toppled	The Masterbuilder (Bygmester Solness).
487.29–30	gangin I am. Gangang is Mine and I will return.	Ghosts (Gengangere).
488.07, 15	Ibn Sen ... itsen	Ibsen.

493.30	On the vignetto is a ragingoos	? *The Masterbuilder* (*Bygmester Solness*). Cf. 356.36.
493.36–494.01	What a surpraise, dear Mr Preacher, I to hear from your strawnummical modesty!	*Love's Comedy* (*Kjærlighedens komedie*). Pastor Strawman. Carlson, p. 137.
497.13–14	from Vico, Mespil Rock and ...	? Ibsen. An anagram.
506.02, 05	the climber clob aloft ... Muster of the hoose	*The Masterbuilder* (*Bygmester Solness*). Carlson, pp. 134–135.
510.27–28	the depredations of Scandalknivery	Ibsen, a Scandinavian, whose plays were denounced as scandalous depredations. Cf. 324.27.
530.02	fallensickners	*The Masterbuilder* (*Bygmester Solness*). Cf. 530.32 ff.
530.23–24	– *Day shirker four vanfloats he verdants market. High liquor made lust torpid dough hunt her orchid.*	'Til min Ven Revolutions-Taleren!' Cf. 364.28–29.
530.31–35	Norganson? And it's we's to pray for Bigmesser's conversions? Call Kitty the Beads, the Mandame of Tipknock Castle! ... He's cookinghagar that rost her prayer to him upon the top of the stairs. She's deep, that one.	*The Masterbuilder* (*Bygmester Solness*). Atherton, p. 257.
532.04, 18–20	Arise, sir ghostus! ... On my verawife I never was nor can afford to be guilty of crim crig con of malfeasance trespass against parson with the person of a youthful gigirl frifrif friend	*Ghosts* (*Gengangere*).
533.18	cagehaused duckyheim	*A Doll's House* (*Et dukkehjem*) and *The Wild Duck* (*Vildanden*). 'Heim' is modern Norwegian for 'home'. Atherton, p. 257.

535.16–17	Man sicker at I ere bluffet konservative?	'Til min Ven Revolutions-Taleren!' A quotation from the first line. Christiani, p. 207.
535.17–18	Such ratshause bugsmess	The Masterbuilder (Bygmester Solness).
535.19	Ibscenest nansence!	Ibsen. Atherton, p. 257.
535.19	Noksagt!	The League of Youth (De unges Forbund). Daniel Hejre's catchword.
535.19	Per	Peer Gynt.
536.12–13	Guestermed with the nobelities, to die bronxitic in achershous!	? 'Paa Akershus.' Cf. discussion above, p. 145.
539.04–05	on my honour of a Nearwicked	Ibsen. HCE identifies himself with a Norwegian poet, Ibsen, while discussing Dante, Goethe, and Shakespeare.
539.23–24	encmy, among these plotlets	An Enemy of the People (En folkefiende).
540.22–23	peers and glnts	Peer Gynt. Atherton, p. 258.
540.23	quaysirs and galleyliers	Emperor and Galilean (Kejser og Galilæer). Atherton, p. 257.
540.23	fresk letties from the say	The Lady from the Sea (Fruen fra havet), 'fresk' may be a phonetical representation of Norw. 'frisk' ('fresh' or 'well'). Atherton, p. 257.
540.24	stale headygabblers	Hedda Gabler. Atherton, p. 257.
540.24	gaingangers	Ghosts (Gengangere). Atherton, p. 257.
540.24	dudder wagoners	When We Dead Awaken (Når vi døde vågner). Atherton, p. 258.
540.24–25	pullars off societies	Pillars of Society (Samfundets støtter). Atherton, p. 258.
540.25	pushers on rothmere's homes	Rosmersholm. Carlson, p. 141.

540.25–26	Obeyance from the townsmen spills felixity by the toun.	*An Enemy of the People (En folkefiende).*
540.26–27	Our bourse and politicoecomedy	*? Love's Comedy (Kjærlighedens komedie)* and/or *The League of Youth (De unges Forbund).* Atherton, p. 257.
542.18	I demosthrenated my folksfiendship, enmy pupuls	*En Enemy of the People (En folkefiende).* Atherton, p. 257.
545.03–06	an illfamed lodginghouse, more respectable than some, teawidow pension but held to purchase, ... head of domestic economy never menioned ... reputed to procure	*? Love's Comedy (Kjærlighedens komedie).*
560.18	Nogen, of imperial measure, is begraved beneadher.	*? The Warrior's Barrow (Kjæmpehøien).* 'Nogen' is 19th century Norwegian for 'somebody'; 'begravet' is 'buried'.
560.29–30	As keymaster fits the lock it weds so this bally builder to his streamline secret.	*? The Masterbuilder (Bygmester Solness).*
565.13–14 22–23	What boyazhness! Sole shadow shows. ... grossman's bigness	*The Masterbuilder (Bygmester Solness).*
568.17, 26, 29	boorgomaister ... An allness eversides! ... By the splendour of Sole!	*The Masterbuilder (Bygmester Solness).* Carlson, p. 141.
568. 35–36	(his scaffold is there set up, as to edify, by Rex Ingram, pageantmaster)	*? The Masterbuilder (Bygmester Solness).*
572.02–03	When the youngdammers will be soon heartpocking on their betters' doornoggers	*The Masterbuilder (Bygmester Solness),* in which youths (Norw.: 'ungdommer') come knocking on the door.
576.18	boomooster giant builder	*The Masterbuilder (Bygmester Solness).* Carlson, p. 141.

576.28	Big Maester Finnykin	*The Masterbuilder (Bygmester Solness)*. Atherton, p. 257.
577.01, 16	wiffeyducky ... screendoll Vedette	*A Doll's House (Et dukkehjem)*. Atherton, p. 257.
578.11, 30–31	Norkmann ... The solvent man in his upper gambeson	? *John Gabriel Borkman*.
579.08	Bolt the grinden	? 'På Vidderne'. The word 'grinden' ('the gate') has probably come to Joyce from this poem. Christiani, p. 219.
580.17–18	he clasp and she and she seegn her tour d'adieu, Pervinca calling, Soloscar hears.	? *Peer Gynt*. Peer and Solvejg in Act V.
587.02	wind thin mong them treen	*The Masterbuilder (Bygmester Solness)*. Ragnar Brovik's comment in the final scene.
587.32–33	Mister Beardell, an accompliced burgomaster	*The Masterbuilder (Bygmester Solness)*.
594.01–02	Scatter brand to the reneweller of the sky, thou who agnitest!	? *Brand*. Brand and Agnes. Carlson, p. 140.
594.26	ghostly gossips	? *Ghosts (Gengangere)*. Carlson, p. 140.
595.33	Thus faraclacks the the friarbird. Listening, Syd!	'The Eider Duck' ('Ederfuglen'). A reference to the last line of the poem. Christiani, pp. 222–223.
596.07–08, 15	warmen and sogns til Banba ... Gunnar, of The Gunnings	? *The Vikings at Helgeland (Hærmændene på Helgeland)*. Gunnar is one of the main characters. 'Til' is Norw. for 'to'.
601.26–27	S. Heddadin Drade's	*Hedda Gabler*.
602.34–35	a passable compatriate proparly of the Grimstad galleon...	Ibsen, who wrote *Catilina* in Grimstad. Christiani, p. 226.
606.16–17, 18, 23	in a purvious century ... trolly ways ... Ah, fairypair!	? *Peer Gynt*.

607.28, 30–31	Solsking . . . Boergemester 'Dyk' ffogg of Isoles, now Eisold	*The Masterbuilder (Bygmester Solness).* Atherton, p. 257.
608.18	the voice of Alina gladdens the cocklyhearted dream-erish	? *The Masterbuilder (Bygmester Solness).* Aline Solness.
608.29	*Nattenden Sorte*	'Borte!' ('Gone!'). A quotation from the last stanza.
613.32–33	toilermaster. You yet must get up to kill (nonparti-cular).	*The Masterbuilder (Bygmester Solness).*
615.03	Giacinta, Pervenche	? *Peer Gynt.*
617.16	a brand rehearsal	*Brand.* Atherton, p. 257.
618.33–34	a Nollwelshian which has been oxbelled out of crispianity	? Ibsen.
622.25	the Wald Unicorns Master, Bugley Captain	? *The Masterbuilder (Bygmester Solness).*
623.18–19	Plain fancies. It's in the castles air.	? *The Masterbuilder (Bygmester Solness).* Solness promises Hilde a castle in the air. Carlson, p. 135.
624.10	how Jove and the peers talk	*Peer Gynt.* Carlson, p. 135.
624.10–12	Amid the soleness. Tilltop, bigmaster! Scale the sum-mit! You're not so giddy any more.	*The Masterbuilder (Bygmester Solness).* Atherton, p. 257.
626.34– 627.02	I had better glances to peer to you through this bay-light's growing. . . . Yes, you're changing, sonhus-band, and you're turning . . .	*Peer Gynt.*
628.10	like he'd come from Arkangels	? *The Lady from the Sea (Fruen fra havet).* The sailor sent his first message from Arkhangel'sk.
628.16	the	? *Love's Comedy (Kjærlighedens komedie).* Ibsen's spelling of 'tea'. See discussion, p. 167.

VIII

INDEBTEDNESS AND
ORIGINALITY

At the very beginning of his career Joyce had presented himself
unreservedly as Ibsen's disciple, regarding himself, he said, as a
minister of the gospel he had found in the plays of the Norwegian dramatist. But when he left Ireland, his situation changed, and so, too, did his attitude to his immediate surroundings.
In a home of his own and with a growing family, his position
was no longer analogous to that of Falk in *Love's Comedy*.
The moral example that Ibsen's heroes provided was something
Joyce was in desperate need of in Ireland, but in Trieste and
Pola it lost some of its relevance. As we have seen, his comments
on Ibsen from his early years on the Continent indicate that he
is no longer the deferential admirer. Though he may not, in fact,
have succeeded in freeing himself from the enthusiasm of his
'teens quite as completely as he thought or wished, he set about
giving himself and others the impression that he had done so.
He began to see faults in Ibsen and mentioned him with a critical detachment that is not found in his essays before 1903.[1] In
later life, Joyce's praise of Ibsen as a playwright again becomes more lavish, but it is no longer a praise of him as *the*
Master. And it may be noted, too, that this praise of Ibsen comes
at a time when Joyce's own originality as a novelist is firmly
established.

Any description of an author's mind rather than his work –
and in particular any account of his motives – can, of course,
never be more than tentative. Yet it seems to me that a pattern
is discernible behind Joyce's comments, or lack of comments,
on Ibsen and certain other literary figures; and it seems worth

[1] See Chapter III.

while attempting to work out that pattern. At the very least it is one which takes account of – and sometimes seems to account for – a good many established facts.

Joyce does acknowledge some literary debts readily – and indeed with some *bravura*. It is interesting to note, however, that the authors whom he thus acknowledges are so widely different from him in most respects that no one would ever suppose their influence to be something that was not completely under Joyce's own control. He pointed to Édouard Dujardin's *Les Lauriers sont coupés*, for instance, as the source of the interior monologue. But nobody knew of Dujardin except as a minor symbolist poet; he was clearly not a writer whose reputation could overshadow Joyce's; and, despite the device of the interior monologue, which Dujardin had certainly made use of many years before Joyce, the differences between *Les Lauriers sont coupés* and *Ulysses* are enormous. Moreover, the stream of consciousness method is only one among many novel stylistic devices in *Ulysses*. In short, Joyce's claim to originality was in no danger here. Similarly, his strenuous denials of any debt to Freud[2] may also show him consciously or unconsciously on his guard; for Freud's importance is in fact so pervasive that no one living and writing after him can really escape his ideas. Joyce could well have felt that here was a congenial spirit, but to have admitted this would have been to admit that a number of psychological insights and new methods of communication in fiction were not quite so fully his own as he liked to believe, and liked others to believe. The professed enthusiasm for Giambattista Vico can be interpreted in the same way: a debt to a relatively obscure philosopher like Vico would not rob Joyce of much credit for the structure and themes of *Finnegans Wake*. Not, of course, that Joyce by this time had any reason to be circumspect – his readers were impressed by his originality, if sometimes by nothing else! But the need for a reputation for independence had by now – as I see it – become an integral part of Joyce's mental make-up. Thus, he never mentioned the

[2] See Ellmann, p. 538 and *passim*.

indebtedness of *Finnegans Wake* to Ezra Pound's concept of imagism,[3] or the striking similarity between the juxtaposition of seemingly discordant and unconnected fragments in *The Waste Land* and the apparently irreconcilable elements in portmanteau words or whole sentences in *Finnegans Wake*.

This instinct, assuming I have described it correctly, is not, I think, a mere concern with reputation. As well as to be *known* as an original author, Joyce wanted to *be* truly original in his books. He broke away from his childhood home, his church, and Irish literary circles, indeed everything except a family of his own, in which dependence could make sense as a virtue; and he made independence a final value. It became his programme and it defind his role as an artist.

Independence in a human being is always a relative concept, as Joyce must have known well enough; and originality, too, can only be seen for what it is within some context or frame of reference: which is to say that it, too, can never be an absolute. We must consider therefore what we mean by originality in literature, and to what extent it really is a virtue in a work of art. And does the stage of composition at which a book is influenced by other books make any difference to the literary quality – and the originality – of the finished work? An analysis of Joyce's work can, I think, suggest a way in which a discussion of literary influences can throw light on the nature of originality in fiction.

T. S. Eliot defines originality as either genuine or spurious; genuine originality is a further development of tradition, spurious originality is either 'the imitation of development' or 'the imitation of some Idea of originality'.[4] Joyce's early production can provide neat examples of both the spurious and the genuine – the spurious in *Stephen Hero*, the genuine in *Dubliners*, and both sorts of originality together in *A Portrait*. The style and structure of *Stephen Hero* are lacking in true originality for the

[3] See A. Walton Litz, *The Art of James Joyce* (London: Oxford Univ. Press, 1961), pp. 53–62.

[4] 'Introduction: 1928' in Ezra Pound, *Selected Poems* (London: Faber and Faber, 1948), p. 10.

very reason that Joyce was dazzled by – and imitated – the novels of Flaubert and the dramas of Ibsen. But when he turned to the *genre* of the short story, and so could not imitate his masters as closely as in a novel, he produced his first successful book, *Dubliners*. In terms of genuine originality, as in most other respects, *A Portrait* is a tremendous advance on *Stephen Hero*. The novel has a style and a form which is Joyce's own; its presentation of the development of Stephen in dramatic 'acts' owes something to drama yet leaves no taste of undigested Ibsenism. The theme of the book, on the other hand, reveals one element of indebtedness which limits rather than enriches Joyce's treatment of his material. We have seen that though the theme of the artist-versus-the-world has its roots in Joyce's own early life, it had been nourished by Joyce's discovery of similar, but not identical, conflicts in Ibsen's plays. In 1914 Joyce was still limited by the personal emotions which these conflicts had stirred in him; and he therefore gives us a version of the theme which is too obviously an *apologia pro vita sua,* and smacks too much of a superficial, but enthusiastic, reading of Ibsen. Even in the early *Love's Comedy* Ibsen plays more subtly on the predicament of the youthful artist than does Joyce in *A Portrait.* Joyce's personal involvement becomes a blindfold; he can see only a limited number of the emotional and intellectual consequences of his hero's situation; and for this reason he is not able to make a really profitable use of Ibsen in his portrayal of Stephen. The book becomes an imitation of his own personal development and of Ibsen – with insufficient grasp of both. It is a tribute to Joyce's growing mastery of style and form that in spite of these limitations *A Portrait* remains a fine novel. A third work, the play *Exiles,* was needed to convince Joyce that the artist as a young man could no longer serve as an embodiment of more than a fraction of his understanding of life.

Ulysses contains much more than the basic theme and situation that Joyce had used in both autobiographies, in *Dubliners* and in *Exiles;* it is far richer in human significance than anything Joyce had written before. Stephen and his old problems are here once more, but they are found in a different world from that of the earlier books – a world which they enrich and by which they are enriched. Each trait from the earlier books that is retained in *Ulysses* is woven into a more comprehensive pattern. *Ulysses* is such a vast storehouse of human experience that it has been seen (I follow S. L. Goldberg's summary of interpretations) as 'a naturalistic Irish comedy', a book expressing 'complete, cosmic indifference to all moral values', the expression of 'mystical, esoteric or metaphysical belief', 'a pessimistic rejection of modern life', and as 'an optimistic acceptance of life as it is'. And, as Mr Goldberg observes, 'each of them seems . . . true but limited.'[5] These interpretations are not as mutually exclusive as they may seem; in fact *Ulysses* can encompass them all, and do so without leaving any feeling of vagueness in the reader. This astounding coherence is not only the result of the consistent psychological verisimilitude in or behind the many styles of the book, of the many interwoven verbal motifs, or of the apparatus of Homeric and other correspondences; it is a result of a moral vision which is at once complex and whole.

The excellence of *Ulysses* raises an important question concerning any literary influences that we may find in it. If the book is a coherent and organic whole, then all the raw materials that have gone into the making of it have been fused into something new, and the ideas and features that Joyce took over from earlier writers have gone through the same process and acquired a function, and largely a meaning, that they never had before. Stephen is again an illustrative example. In *Ulysses* he is much the same young man that we met in the autobiographical novels, though he suffers now from the agenbite of inwit – the price he had to pay for his independence. But this Stephen, made of traits that we remember from Ibsen, is now placed in a new world. And it is the relief which Bloom, Mulligan, and the other characters gives to the portrait of the young artist that provides it with its full meaning. In one way literary influence loses in importance and interest: Joyce is so completely in com-

---

[5] *The Classical Temper* (London: Chatto and Windus, 1961), pp. 20–21.

mand of his fictional world that no one previous author or book or enthusiasm is allowed more than the precise part it must play according to the strict rules inherent in the artifact in which they are found. *Ulysses* can serve as an illustration of T. S. Eliot's theory that the poet cannot 'form himself wholly on one or two private admirations, nor can he form himself wholly upon one preferred period.'[6] Joyce does not do so in *Ulysses;* the past as we experience it in that book is the whole of Europe's past (and that of other continents as seen from the point of view of a European) – not in a large lump, not indiscriminately ubiquitous, but made part of a pattern which the book itself provides. This pattern makes the human experience – past and present – recorded in *Ulysses* at once well-known and novel. And it is this structuring of human experience which makes the book unique, and which is what we grope for in any analysis that we hope to make relevant and meaningful.

Thus *Ulysses* cannot properly be regarded as the sum total of the literary tradition behind it. It builds on this tradition, but is something different from it. There is, it seems, in the creation of a great art an essential novelty which limits the uses of a study of literary influence. We have seen in Chapter VI that there are a number of parallels between Peer Gynt's and Bloom's homecomings, and we assume that Joyce had Ibsen in mind when he wrote 'Eumaeus' and 'Ithaca'. But we cannot conclude that *Peer Gynt* exerted any decisive influence on these chapters in *Ulysses;* for if the book is an integrated work of art, each component part depends on the rest in content, form, and function; each episode is necessitated, in outline and detail, by the other chapters.

Ulysses it not faultless. But it shares with other great novels the capacity to live down its flaws. As we read on we forget the tenuous connection between the styles and the content of 'Oxen of the Sun'. The flaws are not many, and I cannot find any connection between any of them and the features in the book behind which we can glimpse Ibsen. If he could be discovered

---

[6] 'Tradition and the Individual Talent', *Selected Essays* (London: Faber and Faber, 1934), p. 16.

in passages that are not quite convincingly made part of the rest of the book, a case could have been made for Ibsen influence of a more direct kind than is actually found. Such a simple and direct influence from the Norwegian dramatist can be seen at work in *Exiles,* which is not a success. In characterization, dialogue, and themes Joyce imitated Ibsen; and this is an imitation which does not fuse the elements from *When We Dead Awaken* and *The Lady From the Sea* into a new unity which is strong enough to make them seem inevitable. In such a case a study of literary indebtedness can be very useful in showing at what point and in what respects the writer lost control of his design and virtually left his work in the hands of his predecessors.

Finnegans Wake is in a category by itself. Obviously, everything that has gone into the making of it, from literature and life, has been placed in a context which is completely new. When Ibsen's lines from 'To My Friend the Revolutionary Orator' were needed, they were incorporated in this form:

> – *Day shirker four vanfloats he verdants market.*
> *High liquor made lust torpid dough hunt her orchid.*
> (*Finnegans Wake,* p. 530. See also my
> discussion in the previous chapter.)

One can scarcely argue that these lines have not been adapted to the exigencies of Joyce's passage; indeed, it takes some time before the original lines are recognized behind the version in which they are quoted in *Finnegans Wake.* This book, which is so rich in literary allusions, rarely makes one without distorting the reference by various additions to it. But in another sense *Finnegans Wake* is as imitative as ever *Exiles* was. It is an attempt to create the all-inclusive artifact, a book whose world is as complete and varied and rich as that of Creation itself. There are signs of order and system in this world, but it is also chaotic. But how could Joyce represent in *Finnegans Wake* that which could not be contained in neat symbols and symbolic structures because it lacked order and could not be systematized? The only possible method, and the one that Joyce adopted, was to refer to the individual things that chaos consisted of.[7] Since the rivers of the world could not be seen as instances of a Platonic idea of a river (though the Liffey could serve as a rough symbol for them all) Joyce had to name them, as he tries to do in 'Anna Livia Plurabelle', to ensure the all-comprehensive nature of his book. Similarly with the inclusion of Ibsen's plays. There was a place for them in the cycles that Joyce discerned in his world and in a number of recurrent themes, but they could not quite be contained in any circle or set of themes. Ibsen's plays had to be present in *Finnegans Wake* as something unique; and Joyce consequently gives us a list of them:

> For peers and gints, quaysirs and galleyliers, fresk letties from the say and stale headygabblers, gaingangers and dudder wagoners, pullars off societies and pushers on rothmere's homes.
> (*Finnegans Wake*, p. 540)

It is very difficult, probably impossible, to fit all these items naturally into the narrative and thematic context in which they appear in *Finnegans Wake*. They stand for things which cannot be reduced to any order which the story or structure of *Finnegans Wake* might impose on them. If the book is to be about everything, each thing must be allowed to appear as it 'really' is, not as it would be in a book which rigidly imposed its own meaning and form on it. (Not that Joyce gives us Ibsen's Norwegian titles in their correct forms; he puns and comments on them: Hedda Gabler is 'stale' and 'heady'. But the list of plays has not been streamlined to suit one particular purpose or one interpretation that the context might have forced on it in a more traditional novel.)

It is easier to see why Joyce wanted to write such a book than with what artistic success he solved the problems that it involved. It requires no stretching of the imagination to suppose that it became natural for the writer who had dismissed the divine Creator to think of the artist as the maker of all things,[8]

---

[7] Cf. pp. 185–186.

[8] See Smidt, *James Joyce and the Cultic Use of Fiction* (Oslo: Oslo Univ. Press, 1959), p. 66.

and to entertain the hope that it should be possible for a writer
to create a fictional world which in size and complexity could
rival the external. But this very purpose seems to be incompatible with the nature of art, which is to single out from what is
or may seem chaotic something which is made meaningful just
because of the precision and conciseness, the focussing, of its
emotional and intellectual appeal.

In theory Joyce attempted the impossible; but *Finnegans
Wake* does impose some sort of order on its chaos; it is, for all
its extremity, a compromise. This compromise, by which material is included, partly because it serves only the basic principle of all-inclusiveness, partly because it serves characterization, story, themes, and symbols as in a more conventional
novel, will perhaps never be aesthetically satisfactory. All the
rivers of the world are *not* mentioned in 'Anna Livia Plurabelle', but nor are all of the 200 or more that Joyce included
needed to create the mood that the author wanted. However,
much explanatory work and much general discussion of the
book are needed before one can come to anything like a final
verdict on the success or failure of Joyce's experiment. What is
relevant to this discussion of literary influence is that, in one
very special sence, *Finnegans Wake* makes indiscriminate use
of Ibsen. At times the dramatist and his work appear in it without having been through a fusion of the kind that changed the
meaning of everything that went into *Ulysses*.

These considerations may seem to leave little room for a
study of literary influences; the better the work, the greater the
inner necessity which governs the inclusion of material and the
more completely changed the nature and purpose of elements
from earlier writers. This is, I think, a point of view which is
nearly always relevant in comparative literature, and which is
some times disregarded with the disturbing result that authors
are 'hustled into mutuality'[9] with insufficient regard for their
uniqueness. But it practically never rules out the possibility of

---

[9] See e.g. Ruth Mateer, 'Improbable Metamorphosis', a review of M.
Spilka, *Dickens and Kafka, A Mutual Interpretation* in *Essays in Criticism*,
Vol. 15, No. 2 (April 1965), p. 229.

a discussion of influence. For there is, in the life of a writer and in the genesis of a work, a preparatory stage at which a *Weltanschauung* and basic principles about literary art are sought for and adopted. At this stage there is no conflict between the use of earlier writers and the inner 'laws' of a finished work, for this is the time when these 'laws' are being conceived. There may also be intermediate stages in the development of a work of art at which new finds in earlier writers can be incorporated without any damage to the coherence and unity of the finished product. But the strict demands of what is there already will grow; and when the work is actually being written, there will in most cases be very few opportunities for such inclusions.

At the early stages of its history the most truly original masterpiece is indebted to its predecessors. As T. S. Eliot reminds us in 'Tradition and the Individual Talent', no poem, no novel, is created in a vacuum, but with an awareness on the part of the author of the pastness *and* contemporaneity of tradition. At this preparatory stage in the history of Joyce's novels, when the author consciously or unconsciously took stock of his material and his intention, there was a manifold benefit to be had from Ibsen.

Some of these benefits were impulses of a relatively simple kind. When Joyce became an exile from home, church, and country, he could find strength in Ibsen's own example, and in the heroes of some of Ibsen's early plays. Ibsen's spirit, says *A Portrait*, was one of 'wayward boyish beauty'; but it is equally significant that even at this early stage in Joyce's career Ibsen's creative energy and perseverance are acknowledged: the 'keen wind' of Ibsen's spirit met Stephen 'as he went by Baird's stonecutting works'. This association of Ibsen with a stonecutting works may have come to Joyce from the poem 'Bergmanden' ('The Miner'), in which Ibsen sees himself as hammering his way down to a deep ore; in any case, it reveals Joyce's awareness of the hardships of a career devoted to art. The seven years spent on *Ulysses* and the fifteen on *Finnegans Wake* testify to the same undaunted perseverance in Joyce as he had noticed in Ibsen.

The aloofness that Joyce admired in Ibsen's career and in his attitude to his characters became an ideal for the Irishman. In Ibsen he found the 'classical' temper,[10] which, as S. L. Goldberg has shown, becomes a central concept in Joyce's art and an aspect of the moral vision inherent in the art. Joyce's attempt to approach a classical temper can be seen in the development that transforms the romantic enthusiasm for the artist into a more complex view of artists and citizens, and it is parelleled by the growing subtlety in Joyce's use of fictional point of view that I have traced in the earlier chapters of this study.

A third of these early and profound influences is the realism that Joyce found and admired in Ibsen: 'Life we must accept as we see it before our eyes, men and women as we meet them in the real world, not as we apprehend them in the world of faery.'[11] The last sub-clause reveals Joyce's awareness of the other course he could have taken – that which led into Irish mysticism. W. B. Yeats and A. E., poets that Joyce respected, must by their example have attracted him. Realism was not a popular programme in Ireland in 1900; and without Ibsen's example Joyce would probably not have taken it up at all. But he did; and 'life – real life' is the material that the early novels and *Ulysses* are made of. What is not so obvious is the realism of *Finnegans Wake*. This night-piece with its private language and its hallucinatory scenes may seem like a product of the romantic imagination; it can, however, be regarded as realism taken to extremes. Flaubert never tried to find room for more than a representative slice of life in his art; Joyce's last book attempts to include all life between its covers. In principle, it is more realistic than the most faithful presentation of selected parts of life can be, for it *is* the world and the universe. As a realistic novel it faces the artistic problems of extreme realism: how can a picture of life that is not (read: is not meant to be) modified by any interpretation put on it by the author give us an experience that is different from what life around us can provide? It is taken for granted nowadays that the school of

[10] See *Critical Writings*, p. 100.
[11] *Ibid.*, p. 45.

realists give a special interpretation of life in their books, but this wisdom after the event does not affect the principal question: when, or if, it is possible to write a novel that is completely faithful to all human experience of all aspects of life, will not that book lack the structuring of experience and the ordering of a multifarious world that we look for in novels and find in those that we call successful works of art? This can serve, I think, as one way of defining the failure of *FW* to appeal to a great many readers. Its successful reception with others may, conversely, be due to the fact that Joyce did not write a completely realistic book. He did impose his own interpretation and form on the world he describes, thereby restricting the 'realism' and making room for 'art' in the traditional sense of the word. In any case, the applicability of such considerations indicates that *FW* can be looked upon as a product of a realistic view of literature. That Joyce was aware of this, and that he regarded his approach as a heritage from Ibsen, can be seen in *FW* itself, where the word 'poetographies' (242.19) is one way of describing what *FW* does, while at the same time it is an echo of Ibsen's words when he turned away from his early romanticism. He would become a photographer, he told Bjørnstjerne Bjørnson in a letter.[12]

In one respect, in the attempt to recreate a whole world in *FW,* Joyce takes his realism to extremes which Ibsen never approached. In another respect both authors are cautious: neither Ibsen nor Joyce is a naturalist in the sense that their books illustrate an absolute determinism. A number of reasons can be suggested for Joyce's avoidance of this extreme: his Roman Catholic background, his wish to imitate Ibsen's aloofness, and in particular the view of the role of the author that he develops partly on the basis of Ibsen's example. The author shall be 'like the God of the creation', hidden in his work. No patterning must be introduced 'ex machina'; the structuring of human experience in a novel must emerge from character and action; and

---

[12] See *Hundreårsutgaven*, Vol. XVI, p. 199. Cf. D. B. Christiani, *Scandinavian Elements of* Finnegans Wake (Evanston: Northwestern Univ. Press, 1965), p. 141.

the people and the incidents that fill the novel must be of a sort that we recognize from our own daily experience. To present only those aspects of life that seemed to deny moral values and moral incentive, would imply drastic limitations on that 'real life' on which the novelist should work.

Realism is the firm basis of Joyce's art and of nearly all Ibsen's plays after *Peer Gynt;* but it is, of course, no formula that explains everything. Joyce and Ibsen can both be seen as influenced also by the Byronic individualism of *Childe Harold* and *Don Juan:* the exceptional individual is the hero, and he is a man in conflict with his society. In *Stephen Hero* and *A Portrait* Joyce writes, in a realistic manner, about life as he had experienced it and seen it in his immediate surroundings; but suggested for Joyce's avoidance of this extreme: his Roman the interpretation of it that Stephen represents is romantic. In these early novels the young hero is described with little irony. He is right nearly all the time, and his view of life is pressed on the reader. This view is one in which the sensitive and ambitious artist is alienated from his surroundings. The alienation is definite; for family, groups of friends, class, and nation are all the enemies of the hero. In order to realize himself he must imitate Byron's heroes and become an exile.

Joyce's choice of this theme cannot be assigned to one particular literary source. The most forceful suggestions must have come from his own Dublin life, in which there were so many incidents that naturally could be interpreted in the light of the romantic conception of the life of the artist. As I have suggested earlier, I am not convinced by the critics who have seen Ibsen as the motive force behind Joyce's behaviour as a son, a Roman Catholic, and an Irishman. Attitudes to family, country, and creed seem to me to be such integral parts of the personality that they are not often changed decisively by books read in the late 'teens, unless, of course, such books stir what is already there. There was confirmation and a clearer articulation of these attitudes to be found in Ibsen, but not influence of the radical kind that the Norwegian exerted on Joyce's conception of artistic ways and means. At a later stage, when he actually started the work on his autobiographical novels, Joyce had to be convinced that the predicament of the artist could be made the theme of a book; and on this point help could be found in Ibsen – and in authors of the Romantic Period.

It is interesting to note that an impulse from English Romanticism reached Joyce by way of Scandinavia. Ibsen's friend, the Danish critic Georg Brandes, devoted the fourth volume of his *Hovedstrømninger* to the Romantic Period in England; and he gave most space and most praise to Byron, heading three of the chapters on the poet, characteristically, 'The Individual Passion', 'The Immersion of the I in Itself', and 'The Revolutionary Spirit'. *Catilina*, which Joyce reviewed in 1903, offers abundant evidence of this romantic heritage in Ibsen.[13] As in *Catilina*, the focus of interest in *Brand* and *Peer Gynt* is the exceptional individual; in the latter work the hero tours the world much as do Childe Harold and Don Juan. Peer Gynt is unheroic in his cowardice and carelessness; but he is like Brand, Harold, and Juan in that he is at odds with his society, and is more sensitive and has greater visions than the common men around him.

It is tempting to see the relationship between Joyce and Ibsen solely in terms of the romantic revolt of the individual against its surroundings. Hugh Kenner assigns Stephen's 'arrogant gestures' to Brand;[14] and the notion that *Exiles* is Joyce's definite farewell to Ibsen is built on the idea that the individual in revolt was the only theme to be found in Ibsen: when Joyce made Bloom the central character of *Ulysses* he left Ibsen behind.[15] But such a conclusion is built on an oversimplified view of Joyce's development as well as of Ibsen's attitude to the exceptional individual. We need only consider the fact that Stephen is still present in *Ulysses* – and in himself not greatly changed from *A Portrait* – and that Shem in *Finnegans Wake* is a near

[13] Cf. Halvdan Koht, *Henrik Ibsen. Eit diktarliv*, Vol. I (Oslo: Aschehoug, 1928), p. 53.
[14] See 'Joyce and Ibsen's Naturalism', *Sewanee Review*, Vol. 59 (1951), p. 89.
[15] See e.g. A. Walton Litz, *The Art of James Joyce* (London: Oxford Univ. Press, 1961), p. 4.

relative of his, to see how faithful Joyce is to the character and the theme of the young artist. The interpretation offered changes; but the man and the problem are still there. What is more important is that Joyce did not see only 'the arid "revolt" of Ibsen, whose gestures are still frozen in the mould of denial.'[16] Ibsen had other values to offer Joyce than those of the iconoclast. Indeed, there is in Ibsen a similar ambiguity in the attitude to the young artist as in the older Joyce. The development in the two writers makes up no exact parallel, but the resemblances are interesting because they reveal a broadening of artistic sympathy and an adjustment of moral values in both. This is accompanied by a richer irony in the character-portrayal, a richness that is made possible by a more inclusive, but still coherent moral awareness in both authors.

In *Love's Comedy* Falk embodies a view of life almost identical with the one Stephen represents in *A Portrait,* but even in this early play Ibsen places his hero in a position which is more clearly ironic than Stephen's. There is no great change to be seen in this aspect of Ibsen's *heroes:* Brand, Peer Gynt, Mrs Alving and Professor Rubek are all exceptional individuals who possess a grandeur that makes them heroic. And at the same time they are presented in an ironic situation: life offers them a combined peripety and recognition in which they see the futility of their past lives. But the characters to whom these heroes and heroines are contrasted are not all unsympathetic and false. In *Love's Comedy* the wholesale merchant, Guldstad, is right in saying that the prosaic necessities of life will prove stronger than the claims of art; and he attains a certain dignity at the end, though he is at the same time, with all the other tea-drinking ladies and gentlemen of the play, something of a caricature. Run-of-the-mill people in *Brand* and *Peer Gynt* are presented with greater asperity. The inhabitants of Brand's narrow valley are mean or insane; and the guests at Hægstad are ridiculous in their boorishness. But with Ibsen's turn to realism come a number of subsidiary characters who stand in

---

[16] S. L. Goldberg's description of Hugh Kenner's interpretation. See *The Classical Temper* (London: Chatto and Windus, 1961), p. 105.

15

contrast to the hero, but are without the unpleasant traits that
we find in the 'ordinary' people in the earlier plays. Being a
member of society and being committed to that society is no
longer a moral fault; and many of the small men and women
in Ibsen's later plays have a nobility of mind that makes them
heroic against another scale of values than that which makes
the hero an Aristotelian protagonist. Mrs Linde, Gina and
Hedvig, Dr Wangel, Miss Tesman, and even Mrs Rubek in
Ibsen's last play belong to this group. Their blend of humanity
and social acquiescence is perhaps more immediately palatable
than Leopold Bloom's, but they embody similar values, values
that neither Ibsen nor Joyce recognized in some of their early
works.

The corresponding development in Joyce entailed the introduction of a new hero, radically different from the young artist
that goes into exile. Gabriel Conroy in 'The Dead', Leopold
Bloom, and HCE have no counterpart in *Stephen Hero* or *A
Portrait*; indeed, they are quite unthinkable there.

The new hero can be seen as a late result of the enthusiasm
for the commonplace which Ibsen inspired in Joyce. '. . . out of
the dreary sameness of existence, a measure of dramatic life
may be drawn. Even the most commonplace . . . may play a
part in a great drama.'[17] For Joyce to write only about Stephen
when he no longer thought of himself as a young artist in a
clean-cut opposition to his surroundings would have been to
describe a 'world of faery', and not what he saw before his eyes.
It does not make sense to say that 'With all their complexity
and freshness of technique, *Ulysses* and *Finnegans Wake* are
but new visions of the world described in *Dubliners, Stephen
Hero* and *A Portrait*.' Admittedly, and this must be what Dr
Litz primarily has in mind, we admire and are struck by 'Joyce's
tenacious hold on the concrete elements of his early experience';[18] but *Ulysses* and *Finnegans Wake* offer, beside their
new techniques, an interpretation of life which is so radically
different from that of *A Portrait* that the world in which it is

[17] *Critical Writings*, p. 45.
[18] A. Walton Litz, *op. cit.*, pp. 121–122.

embedded becomes different. Joyce's early life in Dublin gives him the concrete elements for the setting and for a great many minor characters in *Ulysses* and *Finnegans Wake;* but if one wants to trace the central preoccupations illustrated in the heroes of *Ulysses* and *Finnegans Wake* to any biographical source, it must be to Joyce's life as husband and father – and artist; in other words, to a set of practical and moral problems that he did not encounter in Ireland. Joyce's last novels give us main characters who are husbands and fathers like millions of other men; and these common men are now shown to be sympathetic towards the artist and even themselves artistic in their own way. They are not heroic in the traditional sense: there is something ludicrous in their shortcomings. In spite of his visions and the poetry of his thoughts – and his kindness – Bloom is thoroughly common; and he is lazy and inadequate as a breadwinner and a husband. HCE seems fonder of talking than of acting. But from the portrayal of these men emerges a moral vision of mankind which is more comprehensive and more representative than the Aristotelian view of the hero as someone of higher birth and of finer moral qualities than his fellow men. There is room for both artist and common man in Joyce's new vision; the antagonism in the early novels has mellowed and now creates a perspective that enables us to see both Stephen and Bloom as common and vulgar human beings, though with a capacity for poetry and generosity. The old values that the young artist embodied are not discarded, they have become parts of a more inclusive *Weltanschauung* that gives a balanced account of both artist and citizen.

There is a common ground here, on which the interests of Ibsen and Joyce meet. I do not want to make a case for any direct influence from Ibsen on Joyce's growing sympathy for the common man. It is probably related to the demand which Joyce found in Ibsen's plays that real life should be used as subject-matter; but the basic sympathies in a work of art are too intimately related to the whole fictional world in which they are found – and to the whole personality of the writer – to be the result of a particular literary influence. And even though

Joyce and Ibsen are interested in the same problems, the 'answers' that they suggest are different. Joyce finds that he can combine what were incompatible ways of life in his early fiction in his later heroes. This does not make Bloom or HCE into moral paragons; there is always something petty and trivial about them, but their lives are not tragic or worthless. *Ulysses* ends on 'yes', *Finnegans Wake* on 'the', which is more noncommittal, but still no negation. In most of his plays Ibsen found that he could not combine the exceptional, heroic individual and the common man in one character. The hero remains heroic, in the traditional sense of the word, and ends tragically. But a Miss Tesman and a Mrs Rubek remind us that the values represented by the tragic hero or heroine are not the only ones. Indeed, just as Stephen was taken down from the pedestal, Ibsen's later heroes and heroines, Hedda, Borkman, and Rubek, are sent through an ordeal that leaves us in doubt about their moral status. All the values that they think they represent are shown to be fragile or even illusory in the isolation in which the hero acts and thinks. A Bloom never appears in Ibsen, but the ground is prepared for him.

In the last instance there is no one formula by which the relationship between the works of Joyce and Ibsen can be summed up. Ibsen taught Joyce to be faithful to what he saw before his eyes; and this faithfulness led to the creation of a fictional world in *Ulysses* that is not simplified – or falsified – to fit a preconceived maxim about life or art. Ibsen's plays go beyond the slogans he was sometimes so fond of; Joyce's mature novels elude the brief summing-up. Their intellectual, emotional, and moral challenge cannot be separated from the fiction by which it is created, for, as Joyce said in an early tribute to Ibsen, it is 'a principle of all patient and perfect art which bids [the writer] express his fable in terms of his characters.'

APPENDIX

Norwegian words in the 'Norwegian Captain'
by
B. J. Tysdahl and Clive Hart[1]

The following list of Norwegian words[2] from the 'Norwegian Captain' episode in *Finnegans Wake* is a combined effort, though it owes its final form to Mr Tysdahl. Mr Hart drew up an original list, which was then corrected and enlarged by Mr Tysdahl.

Modern Norwegian spelling is used, but we have indicated the instances in which an earlier spelling would be more revealing. The choice of modern spelling is practical but quite arbitrary, since this must be the only form of Norwegian that Joyce did not know. It was established by an official reform in 1938, but the changes were not radical, being for the most part an attempt to make the spelling more phonetic. In grammar, idiom, and vocabulary, the changes from Ibsen's day to 1938 are not great. Norwegian remains essentially the same language during this period (although there were spelling reforms in 1907 and 1917 also).

Words have been included in the list according to the following principles:

[1] My thanks are due to Mr Clive Hart, as co-author of this list and as co-editor of *A Wake Newslitter* in which it first appeared, for permission reprint it here. B.J.T.

[2] Most of the Scandinavian words woven into *FW* can be both Danish and Norwegian. The two languages are so similar in grammar, idiom, vocabulary, and spelling that it often takes a context to tell which language one is reading. For this reason we might have called the list one of 'Dano-Norwegian' words. However, we follow Joyce's usual practice in calling the Scandinavian language that he knew Norwegian. He taught himself this language in Dublin to be able to read Ibsen in the original, and in Paris in the nineteen-twenties he studied under a number of Norwegian teachers. That Joyce's intimary with Norwegian was great is also indicated by the fact that he makes frequent use in *FW* of words that are exclusively Norwegian, and even of words from *landsmål*, an official form of Norwegian which is closer to Old Norse and less like Danish. B.J.T.

(1) when the Norw. element in them is easily recognizable and clear beyond doubt (usually because Norw. spelling and the Norw. syntactical function of the word are intact);

(2) when a word or part of a word that may be Norw. adds significantly to the meaning of its context when so read.

In respect of Point (2), consider a word like 'Sheeroskouro' (317. 33). One can, without being too fanciful, find at least fourteen Norw. words in it: ski, i, er, ro, ros, os, sko, skur, skor, ku, kor, kur, ur, uro – all of them common words that Joyce certainly knew. But 'Sheeroskouro' (and with it an enormous number of words in *FW*) read thus would make sense only on that hypothetical ultimate plane where everything (and nothing) makes sense. These readings have therefore been omitted; their inclusion would be no help to *FW* studies.

Some Swedish words are translated where they occur. The transliterations 'ä' and 'aa' have had to be used in place of their Norw. equivalents.

Page 311
05 le (laugh)
    luffe (flipper)
    öre (ear; the coin)
06 hor (whoredom, adultery)
    töyle (rein; most common
        as a verb)
08 hale (to pull; tail)
10 propp (stopper)
11 bar (naked, bare)
16 dubbe (to bob up and down)
17 sval (cool)
    svale (to cool)
    baas (stall)
19 trygg (safe)
21 sagt (said)
    hus (house)
22 hvor (where)
23 sut (care)
24 taleren (the speaker)
    töyle (to rein)
    laase opp (to unlock)
25 kant (edge, border)

27 fakke (catch, nab)
    make (spouse)
29 Peer (boy's name)
    patter (nipples)
    patte (to suck)
    kassa (the money-box;
        the cashier's desk or
        office)
31 brann (fire)
    begge (both)
    tape (lose)
32 baste (bind)
    padden (the toad)
33 tog (train)
    tog (19th cent.: took)
    leve (live)
    butikk (shop)
34 tull (nonsense)
    sult (hunger)
    barter (moustaches)
    lik (like; corpse)
    parter (parts)

Page 312
01 lugg (hair of the head)
   lugge (to lug by the hair)
   stolpe (post, mast)
   bak (behind, back; bottom)
02 svarte (answered; Sw.
   svarade)
   som (as, like)
   blaafisk (bluefish)
   skolen (the school; though
   not in the tense of 'shoal')
03 lykke (happiness, fortune)
   hud (skin)
   jord (earth)
   ikke (not)
   vin (wine)
05 vaas (nonsense)
   anker (anchor)
   Norge (Norway)
06 seilende (sailing)
07 tom (empty)
   fat (vat, tray)
   fram (forward; by context,
   Nansen's 'Fram')
   fra (from)
08 til (to)
   hor (whoredom, adultery)
   venstre (left)
09 fare (danger; to travel)
10 tid (time)
11 vär (weather, rain)
12 bukket (the bow: bowed)
   bukk (he-goat)
16 nett (nice, neat)
   nettopp (just so; just now)
17 regner (rains; reckons)
18 ramp (ruffian, hooligan)
19 et (a)
   godt (good)
   haap (hope)
20 tripper (trips)
   mette (satisfied; to satisfy;
   to still hunger)
25 rar (queer, strange)

rarere (queerer, stranger)
27 piler (arrows)
31 maa (must)
   maake (gull; to shovel
   away)
   grop (cavity)
   rope (to cry out)
32 annendags (of the second
   day)
35 skinner (rails (n.); shines
   (v.))

Page 313
02 hope (to heap)
03 innhold (contents)
   inneholder (contains)
   oppholder (supports;
   detains)
   opphold (sojourn)
04 fort (quickly)
05 hus (house)
   hose (stocking)
   gode (good)
   skip (ship)
08 blankett (form)
10 saa (so)
11 saga
   sag (a saw)
   sage (to saw)
13 böyg (ogre, monster)
14 hvorefter (whereafter)
   hest (horse)
15 baare (bier)
   regne (to rain; to reckon)
   jarl (earl)
   rogn (fish-spawn)
   Irland (Ireland)
16 penge (coin)
   penger (money)
   pike (girl)
   pigg (spike)
17 liv (life)
18 sot (soot)
   vokse (grow)

21 vel (well)
ut (out)
22 pike (girl; Sw. piga)
pigg (spike)
24 brok (trousers)
kopp (cup)
token (Sw. the fool)
tok (took)
en (one)
25 nummer (number)
26 meg (me; old-fashioned
spelling: mej)
deg (you; earlier spelling:
dig)
30 stiv (stiff)
pengepung (purse)
innhold (contents)
finnen (the Finn)
31 bratt (steep)
34 ? tövär (thaw-weather)
35 hodet (the head)
pokal (cup)
pukkel (hump, hunch)
lide (suffer)
liten (little; earlier spelling:
liden)
36 gammel (old)

Page 314
02 olding (old man)
05 -un's kiddy might be
Sw. önskade (wished)
15 legen (the doctor)
leken (the game, the play;
earlier sp.: legen)
mor (mother)
tar (takes)
20 trave (trot)
ulv (wolf)
23 dram
24 selv (self)
selve (adj.: very)
26 lus (louse)
29 due (dove)

30 döpe (baptise)
31 ungkar (bachelor)
32 ?jutul (giant)
pukkel (hump, hunch)
tvile (to doubt)
33 lapp (patch, piece)
lappe (to patch)
34 ros (praise)
35 skule (to scowl)
skole (school)
36 natt (night)

Page 315
06 maatte (must, had to)
token (Sw.: the fool)
07 rap (belch)
09 efter (after)
lag (company, party)
10 bra (well)
hoste (to cough)
12 rolle (role)
13 si (say)
sant (neut. of 'sann', true)
samt (together with; and
also)
14 skipper (skipper)
16 puffe (thrust)
19 takk (thank you, thanks)
20 kul (bump, hump)
21 sa (said; earlier sp.: sagde)
bosted (domicile)
22 hive (to heave, to throw)
noksagt (enough said)
sekund (second (n.))
23 straks (straightaway)
Öresund
öre (ear)
snareste (quickest)
veg, vei (road)
24 hore (prostitute)
höre (hear)
lugg (hair of the head)
li (slope)

25 til (to)
   to (two)
26 vagge (to rock, to waddle)
   vugge (cradle)
   tagg (spike)
   tak (roof; earlier sp.: tag)
28 fanden (the devil)
   ulker, sjöulker (old salts)
   monne (might; avail)
29 ennu (yet, still)
30 strandvei (seaside road)
   fond (fund)
   sut (care)
   pen (handsome, pretty)
   ?fremmed (foreign;
      foreigner)
31 fordi (because)
   lengsel (yearning,
      longing)
   ?langsciling (long-
      distance sailing)
   tolk (interpreter)
   holt (grove)
32 tyve (twenty)
   og (and)
   hug (mind)
   fjorten (fourteen)
   kablen (the cable)
   skjelving (a tremble)
   uppe (up; above)
33 koble (to couple)
34 skipperen (the skipper)
   kommet (come, p.p.; earlier
      form: kommen)
   butikk (shop)
   pukkel (hump, hunch)
35 paa (on; pron. approx.
      'paw')
   rav (amber)
   rave (to totter)
   telle (to count)
   love (to promise; to praise)
36 kikke (to peep)
   kikker (one who peeps)

Page 316
01 Pukkelsen ('Humpson')
   tiltalt (charged, accosted,
      addressed)
02 pröve (try)
05 tysk (German)
   hanrei (cuckold)
   summe seg (to compose
      one's mind)
07 mor (mother)
   mer (more)
08 hefte (notebook; booklet;
      delay)
   Gammel-Erik (the devil)
09 brev (letter)
12 ben (leg; bone)
   bent (adv.: straight)
   skjäre (magpie; to cut)
13 kinkig (awkward)
   borg (castle)
14 overleve (survive, outlive)
17 dom (judgment)
   dommer (judge)
   tid (time)
   peis (chimney-place)
   pike (girl)
18 sess (seat)
19 bölge (wave, billow)
   lokker (allures, entices;
      curls)
20 ran (assault)
21 mor (mother)
22 gang (occasion, time;
      corridor)
   holmgang (single combat)
24 faa (few)
27 bli (smiling; become)
   Leif
28 brast (burst, (past t.))
   furte (sulk)
30 stripe (stripe)
31 ild (fire)
   felle (trap; to fell)
32 anlegg (gift (for), knack;

engineering project)
lek (play, game; earlier sp.:
   leg)
33 heim (home; pron. approx.
   'hame')
   sa (said; earlier sp.: sagde)
36 sa (said)
   til (to)
   dobbelt (double)

Page 317
01 sting (stich; sting)
   sa, sagde (said)
   t.d. (= til dömes; New
     Norw. (*Landsmaal*): for
     instance)
04 sa, sagde (said)
07 tolk (interpreter)
   sil (sieve)
   tanker (thoughts; tanks)
   tolder (customs officer)
09 stall (stables)
   fram (forward (adv.))
10 ekspedere (to serve, to des-
   patch)
11 fester (feasts; fastens)
12 disk (counter)
   öst (east)
   ost (cheese; pl.: oster)
   östers (oyster)
   svanger (pregnant)
13 sann, sand (true; sand)
14 ven (pretty)
   venn (friend)
   fin (fine; delicate)
15 ekspedere (to serve, to des-
   patch)
15–16 sulten (hungry; the
   hunger)
16 oppvarte (wait upon)
   ham (him)
18 mer (more)
   syk (sick)
20 fare (danger; to travel)

24 dum (silly)
   munn (mouth)
26 mistenke (to suspect)
27 taler (speaks; speaker;
   speeches)
28 mand, mann (man)
29 skaar (shards)
31 latterlig (ridiculous)
34 mennesker (people)
   haar (hair)
35 pike (girl)

Page 318
04 aner (forefathers)
10 stilling (position)
   kursus (course)
13 fast (firmly, tightly)
14 han in hende (han = he;
   i hende = in hand; henne
   = her; so perhaps 'hand
   in hand he will grow in
   her' – cf. 'handmarriage',
   masturbation, pregnancy,
   etc.)
   grov (coarse; rude)
15 Aten (Athens)
19 min (mine)
20 saape (soap)
22 gammel (old)
27 löpe (to run)
29 mörk (dark)
   mörke (darkness)
30 miste (lose)
31 kold (cold)
   brun (brown)
   koldbrann (gangrene)
   natt (night)
   ild (fire)
   eldste (oldest)
33 ulv (wolf)
35 glide (slip, glide)

Page 319
06 dommer (judgments; judge
   (n.))

svir (drunkenness; sears,
    smarts)
06–7 hester (horses)
07 gnier (miser)
    gni (to rub)
08 taler (speaks; speaker)
09 tap (loss)
12 flue (fly)
15 plump (coarse)
    plumpe ut (blurt out)
16–17 damper (steamship)
18 draape (drop)
20 gubbe (old man)
21 fatter (the 'governor,' the
    'old man')
    bukse (trousers)
    seiler (sailor)
    seil (sail)
    hora (the whore)
23 sa, sagde (said)
    Pukkelsen ('Humpson')
27 ström (stream)
    Olaf
28 at väre (to be)
    si (say; earlier sp.: sige)
    sige (settle, sag)
29 murer (mason)
30 sa, sagde (said)
34 mot (against; courage)
36 dempe (soften, damp
    down)

Page 320
01 hop (crowd)
    haap (hope)
    döpe (baptise)
    sa, sagde (said)
    and (duck)
    aand (spirit)
    ende (end)
    ender (ducks; ends)
    endre (to alter)
    dyp (deep)

02 haape (to hope)
    döper (baptises; baptist)
    sa, sagde (said)
03 innunder (beneath)
04 skredder (tailor)
05 bud (order, commandment;
    messenger)
    innhold (contents)
    inneholder (contains)
    sa, sagde (said)
06 sa, sagde (said)
08 flikke (to patch)
    vid (wide)
    hvit (white)
    ask (ash-tree)
    aske (ashes)
    sa, sagde (said)
    bag (behind; back, bottom)
09 ham (skin; him)
    toller (customs officer,
    publican)
    tåler (bears, stands)
    sa, sagde (said)
    frokost (breakfast)
    kost (victuals)
10 bange (afraid)
    flis (splinter)
11 sa, sagde (said)
    uthus (shed, outhouse)
    hus (house)
12 sa, sagde (said)
13 munn (mouth; earlier sp.:
    mund)
    Erik
    skald
14 gitter (railing, trellis,
    lattice, grate; valve-grid)
    hemme (restrain)
16 fisk (fish)
19 skjorte (shirt)
20 fjell (mountain)
22 lund (grove)
    rund (round)
    tur (tour)

bag (back)
til (to)
tretti (thirty)
hore (whore)
öre (ear; the coin)
uke (week)
23 pesende (panting)
25 ild (fire)
26 gammel (old)
irer (Irishman)
vakker (pretty)
27 vinke (beckon)
far (father)
fare (to travel)
28 Blaaland ('Blueland' – old
Norse name for Africa)
29 bake (bake)
baken (the bottom)
30 skaper (creator)
skipper (skipper)

Page 321
01 ölkjenner (aleconner)
04 stift (pin, tack; bishopric)
08 Thule
barn (children; earlier
form: börn)
11 galler (Gaul)
12 gal (wrong; mad)
haven (the garden)
havn (harbour)
14 nordmann (Norwegian)
15 bolle (bowl)
17 funn (discovery, find)
flamme (flame)
24 blanding (mixture)
blande (mix)
rum (room)
25–26 pattedyr (mammal)
28 dronning (queen)
31 foss (waterfall)
32 pike (girl)
34 naken (naked)

Page 322
01 lo (laughed)
03 kone (wife)
08 ta paa (take on, touch)
av (off; earlier sp.: af)
12 klok (wise)
16 Haakon
20 spark (kick; to kick)
21 tasse (toddle)
25 feller (fells)
32 Nilsen (Sc. fam. name)
33 konge (king)

Page 323
01 bomull (cotton-wool)
vandre (wander)
dukken (the doll)
04 blö (bleed)
Blodöks (Erik Blodöks,
Norw. king; 'Bloodaxe')
05 krype (creep)
lenge (long)
06 landsmaal (New Norw.,
one of the two official
forms of Norw.)
09 sludder (nonsense)
13 var (was, were)
gaas (goose)
14 sal (saddle; hall)
sale (to saddle)
16 pukkel (hump, hunch)
20 Island (Iceland)
innabords (on board)
21 dunder (noise, thunder)
22 foran (before)
23 tale (speech)
hull (hole)
bak (behind, bottom)
28 tummelumsk (bewildered,
dizzy)
i natt (tonight)
31 troll
32 ?Boraas (in Sweden)
34 rambukk (battering ram)

bukk (he-goat)
36 spök (joke)
spökelse (ghost)
gjenganger (revenant)
död (dead)

Page 324
01 troll
varig (lasting, wearing
well)
03 ond (evil)
ernäre (nourish, support)
svelt (hunger)
05 bulk (dent)
06 rede (nest)
07 gardin (curtain)
08 murer (mason)
09 mer (more)
13 lumpent pakk (scurvy mob)
bund (bottom)
overrasket (surprised)
14 sot (soot)
sott (plague)
oppsitter (freeholder)
17 skaal!
skaalde (scald)
19 perse (squeeze)
Persen (N. fam. name)
20 hoved- (head-, in com-
pounds)
politi (police)
mester (master)
21 fire (four)
eller (or)
ellers (otherwise)
kallen (the old man)
kalle (to call)
24 velter (overturns)
25 nord (north)
27 bygge (build)
byge (shower)
27–8 byggmester (master-
builder)
28 vär (weather, buck)

Harald
faa (few)
29 kokken (the cook)
hoven (swollen)
hoven (the hoof)
Kjöbenhavn
ekstra (extra)
30 Middelhavet (the
Mediterranean)
33 mandig (manly)
mandag (Monday)

Page 325
01 greve (count)
grov (rude; coarse)
06 dyr (dear, expensive;
animal)
by (town)
07 padde (toad)
10 torsdag (Thursday)
11 ja (yes)
16 taler (speaks; speaker;
specches)
gosse (Sw.: boy)
17 hun (she)
hora (the whore)
18 tale (speak; speech)
skatt (treasure; tax)
20 betvinge (conquer,
suppress)
21 make (spouse)
fisk (fish)
flesk (pork)
22 mand (man)
munn, mund (mouth)
26 svale (swallow)
far (father)
31 hval (whale)
32 lus (louse)
konge (king)

Page 326
01 tabell (table)
taler (speaks; speaker;

speeches)
taaler (stands, bears)
03 padde (toad)
05 heil! (Old Norse greeting:
hail!)
07 Oscar, Erik
08 farfar (paternal grandfather)
först (first)
gjeld (debts)
10 Aase
11–12 pukkelen (the hump)
12 Helsinki
13 dannet (well behaved,
cultivated)
16 aske, oske (ashes)
säl (blessed, happy)
17 god kveld (good evening)
en skur (a shower)
18 hälsosam (Sw.: healthy)
19 seil (sail)
21 Nansen
alltid (always)
halte (limp; hauled)
22 overtro (superstition)
hvorfor (why)
pokker (a mild oath)
23 mand, mann (man)
stor (big; pl.: store)
hullsalig (graceful; ful-
some)
24 daad (deed)
döpe (baptise)
gudfar, gudfader (god-
father)
25 djevlen (the devil)
domkirke (cathedral)
26 aa, herre (O sir, O lord)
Peder
Paulsen
29 skole (school)
30–31 Leif Erikson
32 sopper (mushrooms)
33 dottren (Sw.: the daughter)

34 dyp, dyb (deep)
skodden (the fog)
35 lukke (to shut)
lykke (happiness)
36 sort (black)

Page 327
01 smukk (pretty)
forlöper (precursor)
02 brand (fire)
05 stor (big)
07 foster (foetus)
09 fare (to travel; danger)
10 saft (juice)
13 lus (louse)
19 fort (quickly)
20 sommervär (summer
weather)
kald (cold)
22 titte (peep)
drömmer (dreams;
dreamer)
23 flyvende (flying)
27 röver (robber, scamp; robs)
28 gift (married; poison)
30 susen (rustle, whispering)
Norge (Norway)
borg (castle)
31 timer (hours)
32 lover (laws; promises (v.))
34 'aasbukividdy' – aas (mountain ridge); buk (belly); i
(in); vidde (vast expanse,
moor)
36 Hugin
Munin

Page 328
02 brun (brown)
lun (snug, cosy)
06 lovsang (song of praise)
13 skip (ship)
16 olding (old man)
elde (antiquity)

eld, ild (fire)
17 liv (life)
19 fyr (fellow, chap; fire;
   light)
   fyrstikk (match)
   först (first)
   hull (hole)
22 hagen (the garden)
   brott (surf)
24 spille (to play)
25 seng (bed)
   eng (lea, pasture)
26 gutt (boy)
   mann (man)
33 overse (overlook)
35 röd (red)

Page 329
03 bud (messenger; order,
   commandment)
06 olivengrönn (olive)
   Oslo
07 fosterfar (foster-father)
08 grav (grave, trench, etc.)
09 grov (coarse; rude)
   anker (anchor)
10 nappe (snatch)
12 skip, skib (ship)
14 fin (fine)
   gal (mad)
17 bölge (wave, billow)
20 ryss (Sw.: Russian)
24 mor (mother)
   mann (man)
27 dum (silly)
28 reir (nest, eyrie)

Page 330
01 svenn, svend (apprentice)
02 spark (kick)
03 spark (kick)
05 Peer
07 Ja, vi elsker dette landet/
   Med de tusen hjem (Yes,

we love this country with
its thousand homes – the
first and fourth lines of
Norway's national
anthem, by Björnstjerne
Björnson)
08 pil (arrow)
   ?Peer
   vil (will)
   Solvejgs sang (Solvejg's
   Song, from *Peer Gynt*)
09 tyr (bull)
   hane (cock)
   tyrann (tyrant)
   laks (salmon)
10 leder (leader; leads)
12 leken, legen (the play)
   lekende, legende (playing)
   legende (legend)
18 sinn (mind)
19 rope (cry out)
20 rape (to belch)
21 holder (holds)
24 holme (islet)
   fjord
25 Nora
   forening (union, society)
26 du (you)
   kan (can)
27 meg (me; pron. approx,
   'mae')
33 kilder (sources, fountain-
   heads)
   mase (insist, nag)
   uhindret (unhindered)
34 barn (child, children)
   dansk (Danish)
   danske (Dane)
36 mor, moder (mother)

Page 331
01 sky (cloud)
06 lunger (lungs)
11 polka

12 bar (naked)
   barnet (the child)
14 Balder
   sol (sun)
15 og saa videre (and so on)
   seks (six)
   aand (spirit)
   ondt (evil)
16 kropper (bodies)
   maake (gull)
17 gribb (vulture)
18 karl (fellow, chap)
20 munden (the mouth)
   viken (the creek)
   Viken (Old Norse name for
     the Oslo Fjord)
21 vidde (moor, vast expanse)
   tuft (foundations of a
     house)
   foss (waterfall)
   fjell (mountains)
   haug (knoll)
   sjö (sea)
   lund (grove)
22 gard (farm)
   dal (valley)
24 dukke (doll, to duck)
25 farmor (paternal grand-
     mother)
   kar (man, chap)
   lik (like; corpse)
   Eva (Eve)
26 sommer (summer)
   viv (poetical for wife)
   bil (automobile, car)
27 gasje (salary)
   lavvanne (low water; ebb)
   vade (wade)
   vaade (danger)
28 leg, lek (play)

   tvilet (doubted)
32 Kristiania
   begjärlig (desirous)
36 Bornholm

Page 332
01 Snipp, snapp, snute. Naa er
   historien ute (formula
   with which fairy-tales
   are ended)
02 trapp (steps; staircase)
   treskoene (the clogs)
   skonner (schooner)
04 han igjen (he again)
   hun igjen (she again)
05 inni (inside)
07 parre (copulate)
10 tolk (interpreter)
11 daap (baptism)
12 tog (train)
   tok (took)
   to gutter (two boys)
14 gaas (goose)
15 gribb (vulture)
16 lik en and (like a duck)
18 kjemper (giants; fights;
     Sw.: kämper)
   demper (subdues)
19 ribben (rib-bone)
20 grunde (to muse, to ponder)
   mann, mand (man)
   haar (hair)
   haard (hard)
   här (army)
22 blaabär (bilberries)
   ledig (vacant)
28 synd (sin)
   sinn (mind)
   bilde, billede (picture)

BIBLIOGRAPHY

James Joyce

Chamber Music. London: Jonathan Cape, 1927.
The Critical Writings of James Joyce, ed. E. Mason and R. Ellmann. London: Faber and Faber, 1959.
'Daniel Defoe', ed. Joseph Prescott, *Buffalo Studies,* Vol. 1, No. 1 (December 1964), pp. 1–27.
Dubliners. London: Jonathan Cape, 1950.
Epiphanies. Buffalo: Lockwood Memorial Library, 1956.
The Essential James Joyce, ed. Harry Levin. London: Jonathan Cape, 1948.
Exiles. London: Jonathan Cape, 1952.
Finnegans Wake. London: Faber and Faber, 1950.
A First-Draft Version of Finnegans Wake, ed. David Hayman. Austin: University of Texas Press, 1963.
Letters of James Joyce, ed. Stuart Gilbert. London: Faber and Faber, 1957.
Pomes Penyeach. Paris: Shakespeare and Company, 1927.
'A Portrait of the Artist', *The Yale Review,* Vol. 49, No. 3 (March 1960), pp. 360–366.
A Portrait of the Artist as a Young Man. New York: The Viking Press, 1964.
Scribbledehobble: The Ur-Workbook for Finnegans Wake, ed. Thomas E. Connolly. Evanston: Northwestern University Press, 1961.
Stephen Hero, ed. Theodore Spencer. New York: New Directions, 1955.
Ulysses. New York: The Modern Library (Random House), 1934.
'Work in Progress'. For details of publication see Alan Parker. *James Joyce: A Bibliography of His Writings, Critical Material and Miscellanea* (Boston: F. W. Faxon, 1948), pp. 109–115, and John J. Slocum and Herbert Cahoon, *A Bibliography of James Joyce [1882–1941]* (New Haven: Yale University Press, 1953), pp. 99–104.

Manuscript material.
    (a)British Museum Additional MSS 47471–47488. Manuscripts for 'Work in Progress' and *Finnegans Wake.*
    (b) The Cornell Joyce Collection, items 15–17. Unpublished epiphanies.

(c) The Cornell Joyce Collection, item 25. An alphabetical
notebook with a short note on 'Ibsen (Henrik)'.
(d) The Lockwood Memorial Library, University of Buffalo.
A large notebook, published as *Scribbledehobble:
The Ur-Workbook for Finnegans Wake* (see above).

Henrik Ibsen

In Norwegian:
Letters to William Archer. British Museum Add. Ms. 45292,
    pp. 234–258.
Samlede verker. 21 vols. Oslo: Gyldendal, 1928–1957.
    (The centenary edition.)

In translation:
The Collected Works of Henrik Ibsen. London: Heinemann, 1908.
A Doll's House and Two Other Plays, tr. R. Farquharson Sharp.
    London: J. M. Dent, 1910.
Henrik Ibsen's Prose Dramas, ed. William Archer. London:
    Walter Scott, 1890–91.
Lyrical Poems, selected and tr. by R. A. Streatfeild. London:
    Elkin Matthews, 1902.
Lyrics and Poems from Ibsen, tr. F. E. Garrett. London:
    J. M. Dent, 1912.
The Master Builder and Other Plays, tr. Una Ellis-Fermor.
    London: Penguin, 1958.
Peer Gynt. A Dramatic Poem, tr. William and Charles Archer.
    London: Walter Scott, 1892.
Peer Gynt. A Dramatic Poem, tr. R. Farquharson Sharp. London:
    J. M. Dent, 1927.
Peer Gynt, tr. Michael Meyer. London: Hart-Davis, 1963.
Peer Gynt. A Dramatic Poem, tr. Rolf Fjelde. New York: The New
    American Library, 1964.
The Prose Dramas of Henrik Ibsen, ed. William Archer. London:
    Walter Scott, 1900–1901.
Three Plays, tr. Una Ellis- Fermor. London: Penguin, 1950.

Secondary sources

Adams, Robert M. 'Light on Joyce's *Exiles?* A New Ms, a Curious
    Analogue, and Some Speculations', *Studies in Bigliography,*
    XVII (1964), pp. 83–105.
—   *Surface and Symbol: The Consistency of James Joyce's* Ulysses.
    New York: Oxford University Press, 1962.

Archer, Charles. *William Archer: Life, Work and Friendships.*
London: Allen and Unwin, 1931.

Archer, William. 'Introduction' in Henrik Ibsen, *An Enemy of the People.* London: Walter Scott, 1901.

Archer, William and Charles Archer. 'Introduction' in Henrik Ibsen, *Peer Gynt.* London: Walter Scott, 1892.

Atherton, James S. *The Books at the Wake: A Study of Literary Allusions in James Joyce's* Finnegans Wake. London: Faber and Faber, 1959.

— 'A Few More Books at the Wake', *James Joyce Quarterly,* Vol. 2, No. 3 (Spring 1965), pp. 142–149.

— 'Introduction' in James Joyce, *A Portrait of the Artist as a Young Man.* London: Heinemann, 1964.

— 'Islam and the *Qur-an* in James Joyce's *Finnegans Wake*', *Litera,* Vol. 1 (1954), pp. 68–71.

Baker, James R. 'Ibsen, Joyce and the Living Dead: A Study of Dubliners', *A James Joyce Miscellany: Third Series,* ed. M. Magalaner. Carbondale: Southern Illinois University Press, 1962.

Bates, Ronald. 'The Correspondence of Birds to Things of the Intellect', *James Joyce Quarterly,* Vol. 11, No. 4 (Summer 1965), pp. 281–290.

Beckett, Samuel *et al. Our Exagmination Round His Factification for Incamination of Work in Progress.* London: Faber and Faber, n.d..

Beebe, Maurice. *Ivory Towers and Sacred Founts: The Artist as Hero in Fiction from Goethe to Joyce.* New York: New York University Press, 1964.

Benstock, Bernard, *Joyce-again's Wake: An Analysis of* Finnegans Wake. Seattle: University of Washington Press, 1965.

— 'Joyce's *Finnegans Wake,* Book II, Chapter II, Footnotes', *The Explicator,* Vol. 20, No. 4 (December 1961).

— 'Persian in *Finnegans Wake*', *Philological Quarterly,* Vol. 44, No. 1 (January 1965), pp. 100–109.

Bergwitz, Joh. K. *Henrik Ibsen i sin avstamning. Norsk eller fremmed?* Kristiania and Copenhagen: Gyldendal, 1916.

Berry, Thomas, C. P. *The Historical Theory of Giambattista Vico.* Washington DC: The Catholic University of America Press, 1949.

Boldereff, Frances M. *Reading* Finnegans Wake. Woodward: Classic Nonfiction Library, 1959.

Bonheim, Helmut. *Joyce's Benefictions.* Berkeley: University of California Press, 1964.

Brandes, Georg. *Hovedströmninger i det 19de Aarhundredes*

Litteratur: Naturalismen i England. Byron og hans Gruppe.
Copenhagen: Gyldendal, 1875.

Burgess, Anthony. *Here Comes Everybody: An Introduction to James Joyce for the Ordinary Reader.* London: Faber and Faber, 1965.

Campbell, Joseph and Henry Morton Robinson. *A Skeleton Key to Finnegans Wake.* London: Faber and Faber, 1947.

Carlson, Marvin. 'Henrik Ibsen and *Finnegans Wake'*, *Comparative Literature,* Vol. 12, No. 2 (Spring 1960), pp. 133–141.

Christiani, Dounia Bunis. *Scandinavian Elements of* Finnegans Wake. Evanston: Northwestern University Press, 1965.

Coffmann, Stanley K., Jr. *Imagism: A Chapter for the History of Modern Poetry.* Norman: University of Oklahoma Press, 1951

Colum, Mary and Padraic. *Our Friend James Joyce.* London: Victor Gollancz, 1959.

Colum, Padraic. 'Ibsen in Irish Writing', *Irish Writing,* No. 7 (February 1949), pp. 66–70.

— 'Working with Joyce', *The Irish Times,* October 5, 1956, p. 5, and October 6, 1956, p. 7.

Connolly, Thomas E. *The Personal Library of James Joyce: A Descriptive Bibliography.* New York: University of Buffalo, 1956.

Cope, Jackson E. 'The Rhythmic Gesture: Image and Aesthetic in Joyce's "Ulysses"', *ELH,* Vol. 29, No. 1 (March 1962), pp. 67–89.

Croce, Benedetto. *The Philosophy of Giambattista Vico,* tr. R. G. Collingwood. London: Howard Latimer, 1913.

Decker, C. R. 'Ibsen's Literary Reputation and Victorian Taste', *Studies in Philology,* Vol. 32, No. 4 (October 1935), pp. 632–645.

— *The Victorian Conscience.* New York: Twayne Publishers, 1952.

Deming, Robert H. *A Bibliography of James Joyce Studies.* Kansas: University of Kansas Press, 1964.

Douglass, James W. 'James Joyce's *Exiles:* A Portrait of the Artist', *Renascence,* Vol. 15, No. 2 (Winter 1963), pp. 82–87.

Ellis-Fermor, Una. *The Irish Dramatic Movement.* London: Methuen, 1954.

Eliot, T. S. 'Introduction: 1928' in Ezra Pound, *Selected Poems,* London: Faber and Faber, 1948, pp. 7–21.

— 'Tradition and the Individual Talent', *Selected Essays,* London: Faber and Faber, 1934, pp. 13–22.

— 'Ulysses, Order and Myth', *The Dial,* Vol. 75 (November 1923), pp. 480–483.

Ellmann, Richard. *James Joyce.* New York: Oxford University Press, 1959.

— 'Joyce: A Postal Inquiry', *The New York Review of Books,*
Vol. 7, No. 3 (September 8, 1966), pp. 24–28.
— 'The Limits of Joyce's Naturalism', *Sewanee Review,*
Vol. 63, No. 4 (Autumn 1955), pp. 567–575.
— '*Ulysses* and the Odyssey', *English Studies,* Vol. 43, No. 5
(October 1962), pp. 423–426.
— *Yeats: The Man and the Masks.* London: Macmillan, 1949.
Empson, William. 'The Theme of Ulysses', *A James Joyce
Miscellany: Third Series,* Carbondale: Southern Illinois
University Press, 1962, pp. 127–154.
Farrell, James T. 'Exiles and Ibsen', *James Joyce: Two Decades of
Criticism,* ed. S. Givens, New York: Vanguard, 1948.
pp. 95–131.
Fay, Gerard. *The Abbey Theatre: Cradle of Genius.* London:
Hollis and Carter, 1958.
Fergusson, Francis. *'Exiles* and Ibsen's Work', *Hound and Horn,*
Vol. 5, No. 3 (April–June, 1932), pp. 345–353.
— *The Idea of a Theater.* New York: Doubleday, 1953.
— 'Joyce's *Exiles', The Human Image in Dramatic Literature,*
New York: Doubleday, 1957, pp. 72–84.
Fisher, Marvin, 'James Joyce's "Ecce Puer"', *The University of
Kansas City Review,* Vol. 25, No. 4 (Summer 1959), pp. 265–271.
Forster, E. M. 'Ibsen the Romantic', *Ahinger Harvest,* London:
Edward Arnold, 1940, pp. 81–86.
The Fortnightly Review. Vols. 67–68. New Series.
January–December 1900.
Franc, Miriam. *Ibsen in England.* Boston: Four Seas Company, 1919.
Friedman, Melvin. *Stream of Consciousness: A Study in Literary
Method.* New Haven: Yale University Press, 1955.
Ghiselin, Brewster. 'The Unity of Joyce's "Dubliners"', *Accent,* Vol.
16, Nos. 2–3 (Spring and Summer 1956), pp. 75–88, 196–213.
Gilbert, Stuart. *James Joyce's Ulysses.* London:
Faber and Faber, 1952.
Goldberg, S. L. *The Classical Temper: A Study of James Joyce's
Ulysses.* London: Chatto and Windus, 1961.
— *Joyce.* London: Oliver and Boyd, 1962.
— 'Joyce and the Artist's Fingernails', *A Review of English
Literature,* Vol. 2, No. 2 (April 1961), pp. 59–73.
Goldman, Arnold. *The Joyce Paradox: Form and Freedom in His
Fiction.* London: Routledge and Kegan Paul, 1966.
Gorman, Herbert. *James Joyce: A Definitive Biography.* London:
John Lane, 1949.
Greene, Graham. *The Lost Childhood and Other Essays.* London:
Eyre and Spottiswoode, 1951.

Haakonsen, Daniel. *Henrik Ibsens realisme*. Oslo: Aschehoug, 1957.

Halper, Nathan. 'James Joyce and Rebecca West', *Partisan Review*, Vol. 16, No. 7 (July 1949), pp. 761–763.

Hardy, Barbara. 'Form as End and Means in "Ulysses"', *Orbis Litterarum*, Vol. 19, No. 4 (1964), pp. 194–200.

Hart, Clive. *A Concordance to* Finnegans Wake. Minneapolis: University of Minnesota Press, 1963.

— *Structure and Motif in Finnegans Wake*. London: Faber and Faber, 1962.

Hayman, David. 'Introduction' and 'Draft Catalogue' in James Joyce, *A First-Draft Version of* Finnegans Wake. Austin: University of Texas Press, 1963.

— '*A Portrait of the Artist as a Young Man* and *L'Education Sentimentale:* The Structural Affinities', *Orbis Litterarum*, Vol. 19, No. 4 (1964), pp. 161–175.

Hendry, Irene. 'Joyce's Epiphanies', *Sewanee Review*, Vol. 54, No. 3 (July 1946), pp. 449–467.

Herford, C. H. 'A Scene from Ibsen's "Love's Comedy"', *The Fortnightly Review*, Vol. 67 (February 1, 1900) pp. 191–199.

Hodgart, M. J. C. 'Shakespeare and *Finnegans Wake*', *The Cambridge Journal*, Vol. 6 (September 1953), pp. 735–752.

— 'Work in Progress', *The Cambridge Journal*, Vol. 6 (October 1952), pp. 23–39.

Hoffman, Frederick J. '"The Seim Anew": Flux and Family in *Finnegans Wake*', in *Twelve and a Tilly: Essays on the Occasion of the 25th Anniversary of Finnegans Wake*, ed. J. P. Dalton and Clive Hart, Evanston: Northwestern University Press, 1965, pp. 16–25.

Hough, Graham. *Image and Experience: Studies in a Literary Revolution*. London: Duckworth, 1960.

Hulme, T. E. *Speculations: Essays on Humanism and the Philosophy of Art*, ed. Herbert Read. London: Routledge and Kegan Paul, 1954.

Hutchins, Patricia. *James Joyce's World*. London: Methuen, 1957.

— *James Joyce's Dublin*. London: The Grey Walls Press, 1950.

Ibsen, Bergliot. *The Three Ibsens*. London: Hutchinson, 1951.

Jackson, Holbrook. *The Eighteen Nineties*. London: Jonathan Cape, 1931.

Jones, William Powell. *James Joyce and the Common Reader*. Norman: University of Oklahoma Press, 1955.

Joyce, Stanislaus. *The Dublin Diary of Stanislaus Joyce*, ed. George Harris Healey. London: Faber and Faber, 1962.

— *My Brother's Keeper*. London: Faber and Faber, 1958.

Kain, Richard M. *Fabulous Voyager: James Joyce's* Ulysses.
Chicago: The University of Chicago Press, 1947.
Kain, Richard M. and Robert E. Scholes. 'The First Version of Joyce's
"Portrait"', *The Yale Review,* Vol. 44, No. 3 (March 1960),
pp. 355–369.
Kenner, Hugh. *Dublin's Joyce.* London: Chatto and Windus,
1955.
— *Flaubert, Joyce and Beckett: The Stoic Comedians.*
London: W. H. Allen, 1964.
— 'Joyce and Ibsen's Naturalism', *Sewanee Review,* Vol. 59,
No. 1 (Winter 1951), pp. 75–96.
— 'Joyce's *Ulysses:* Homer and Hamlet', *Essays in Criticism,*
Vol. 2, No. 1 (1952), pp. 85–104.
Kohl, Halvdan. *Henrik Ibsen, Fit diktarliv.* 2 vols. Oslo:
Aschehoug, 1928–29.
Levin, Harry. *James Joyce: A Critical Introduction.* London:
Faber and Faber, 1944.
Levin, Richard and Charles Shattuck. 'First Flight to Ithaca – A New
Reading of Joyce's *Dubliners*', *Accent,* Vol. 4, No. 2
(Winter 1944), pp. 75–99.
Litz, A. Walton. *The Art of James Joyce: Method and Design*
in Ulysses *and* Finnegans Wake. London: Oxford
University Press, 1961.
— 'Uses of the *Finnegans Wake* Manuscripts', in *Twelve and*
a Tilly: Essays on the Occasion of the 25th Anniversary of
Finnegans Wake, ed. J. P. Dalton and Clive Hart, Evanston:
Northwestern University Press, 1965, pp. 99–106.
Lynch, Hannah. '"Fécondité" *versus* the "Kreutzer Sonata"', *The*
Fortnightly Review, Vol. 67 (January 1, 1900), pp. 69–78.
Macleod, Vivienne K. 'The Influence of Ibsen on Joyce', *PMLA,*
Vol. 60, No. 3 (September 1945), pp. 879–898.
Magalaner, Marvin. *Time of Apprenticeship: The Fiction of Young*
James Joyce. London: Abelard-Schuman, 1959.
Magalaner, Marvin and R. M. Kain. *Joyce: The Man, the Work, the*
Reputation. New York: New York University Press, 1956.
Mateer, Ruth. 'Improbable Metamorphosis', *Essays in Criticism,*
Vol. 15, No. 2 (April 65), pp. 224–229.
Mjöberg, Jöran. 'James Joyce – Henrik Ibsens arvtagare', *Samtiden*
(Oslo), Vol. 69, No. 6 (1960), pp. 324–331.
Moore, George. 'A Preface to "The Bending of the Bough"', *The*
Fortnightly Review, Vol. 67 (February 1, 1900), pp. 317–324.
Morse, J. Mitchell. *The Sympathetic Alien: James Joyce and*
Catholicism. London: Peter Owen, 1959.
Northam, J. R. *Ibsen's Dramatic Method.* London:

Faber and Faber, 1953.
— 'The Substance of Ibsen's Idealism', in *Contemporary Approaches to Ibsen,* ed. Daniel Haakonsen, Oslo: Oslo University Press, 1966, pp. 9–20.
Parker, Alan. *James Joyce: A Bibliography of His Writings, Critical Material and Miscellanea.* Boston: The F. W. Faxon Company, 1948.
Peter, A. *Dublin Fragments.* Dublin: Hodges, Figges and Co, 1925.
Praz, Mario. *The Romantic Agony.* London: Oxford University Press, 1951.
Robinson, Lennox. *Ireland's Abbey Theatre: A History 1899–1951.* London: Sidgwick and Jackson, 1951.
Röstvig, Maren-Sofie. 'The Hidden Sense', in *The Hidden Sense and Other Essays,* Oslo: Oslo University Press, 1963, pp. 1–112.
— 'Renaissance Numerology: Acrostics or Criticism?', *Essays in Criticism,* Vol. 16, No. 1 (January 1966), pp. 6–21.
Scholes, Robert E. 'The Broadsides of James Joyce', in *A James Joyce Miscellany: Third Series,* ed M. Magalaner, Carbondale: Southern Illinois Univ. Press, 1962, pp. 8–18.
— *The Cornell Joyce Collection: A Catalogue.* Ithaca: Cornell University Press, 1961.
— 'Joyce and the Epiphany: The Key to the Labyrinth?' *Sewanee Review,* Vol. 72, No. 1 (Winter 1964), pp. 65–77.
Scholes, R. and R. M. Kain (eds.). *The Workshop of Daedalus: James Joyce and the Raw Materials for* A Portrait of the Artist as a Young Man. Evanston: Northwestern University Press, 1965.
Schutte, William M. *Joyce and Shakespeare: A Study in the Meaning of 'Ulysses'.* New Haven: Yale Studies in English, Vol. 134, 1957.
Sharp, William. 'The Dramas of Gabriele D'Annunzio', *The Fortnightly Review,* Vol. 68 (September 1, 1900), pp. 391–409.
Shaw, George Bernard. *The Quintessence of Ibsenism.* London: Walter Scott, 1891.
— *The Quintessence of Ibsenism: Now Completed to the Death of Ibsen.* London: Constable, 1922.
Slocum, John J. and Herbert Cahoon. *A Bibliography of James Joyce [1882–1941].* New Haven: Yale University Press, 1953.
Smidt, Kristian. *James Joyce and the Cultic Use of Fiction.* Oslo: Oslo University Press, 1959.
— 'Joyce and Norway', *English Studies,* Vol. 41, No. 5 (October 1960), pp. 318–321.
— 'Joyce's Norwegian Teachers', *English Studies,* Vol. 44, No. 2 (April 1963), pp. 121–122.
Spencer, John. 'A Note on the "Steady Monologuy of the Interiors"',

A Review of English Literature, Vol. 6, No. 2
(April 1965), pp. 32–41.

Stewart, J. I. M. *James Joyce.* London: Longmans, 1957.

Strong, L. A. G. *The Sacred River: An Approach to James Joyce.*
London: Methuen, 1949.

Symons, Arthur. *The Symbolist Movement in Literature.* London:
Constable, 1908.

Tillotson, Kathleen. *The Tale and the Teller.* London:
Hart-Davis, 1959.

Tindall, William York. 'James Joyce and the Hermetic Tradition',
Journal of the History of Ideas, Vol. 15, No. 1
(January 1954), pp. 23–39.

— *James Joyce: His Way of Interpreting the Modern World.*
London: Charles Scribner's Sons, 1950.

— *A Reader's Guide to James Joyce.* London:
Thames and Hudson, 1963.

Tysdahl, B. J. 'Ibsen-brev i Britisk Museums Archer-samling',
Edda (Oslo), Vol. 53, No. 4 (1966), pp. 246–259.

Vico, Giambattista (Giovanni Battista). *The New Science of
Giambattista Vico,* tr. from the third ed. (1744) by Thomas
Goddard Bergin and Max Harold Fisch. Ithaca: Cornell
University Press, 1948.

A Wake Newslitter. Nos. 1–18 (1962–63) and New Series,
Vols. 1–3 (1964–66).

Wildi, Max. 'James Joyce and Arthur Symonds', *Orbis Litterarum,*
Vol. 19, No. 4 (1964), pp. 187–193.

Wilson, Edmund. 'The Dream of H. C. Earwicker', in *The Wound
and the Bow: Seven Studies in Literature,* London:
W. H. Allen, 1952, pp. 218–243.

Yeats, W. B. *A Vision.* London: Macmillan, 1962.

The Yellow Book, Vol. 5 (1895).

Zucker, A. E. *Ibsen: The Master Builder.* London: Thornton
Butterworth, 1930.

INDEX

Names and Titles

Ibsen's plays are listed here under their English titles. Characters in the works of Joyce and Ibsen are not included; the only exception is Stephen Daedalus (Dedalus).